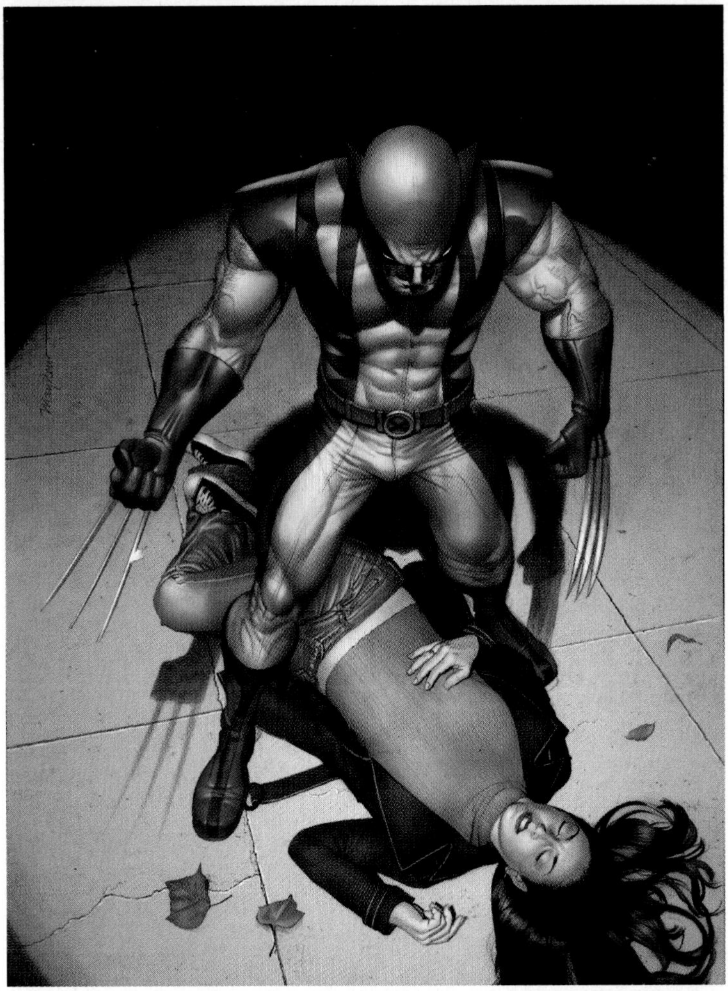

July issue of *The Pulse*

Ben Urich, Staff Writer

Jessica Jones, a former costumed super hero, is now the owner and sole employee of Alias Investigations--a small private investigative firm.

Jessica is pregnant with the baby of her boyfriend Luke Cage, hero-for-hire. She is in the second trimester.

Jessica has taken a job with The Daily Bugle as a super-hero analyst. Publisher J. Jonah Jameson has teamed her up with award-winning reporter Ben Urich to help him paint a fair and balanced picture of the world of super heroes.

Luke Cage has recently joined the New Avengers.

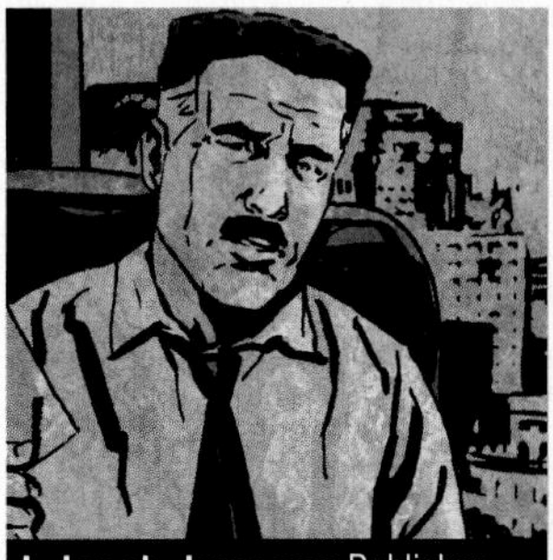

J. Jonah Jameson Publisher

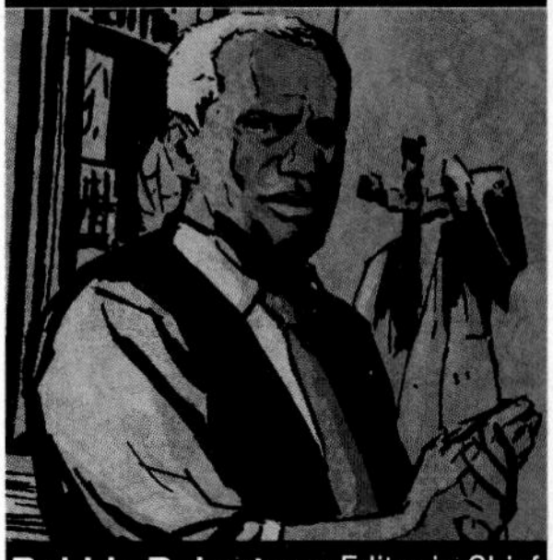

Robbie Robertson Editor in Chief

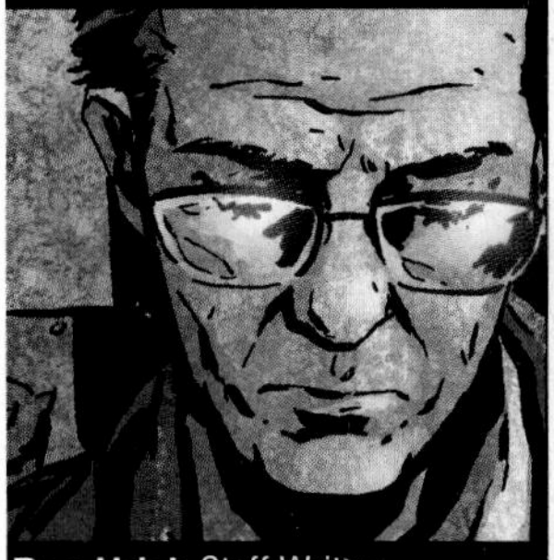

Ben Urich Staff Writer

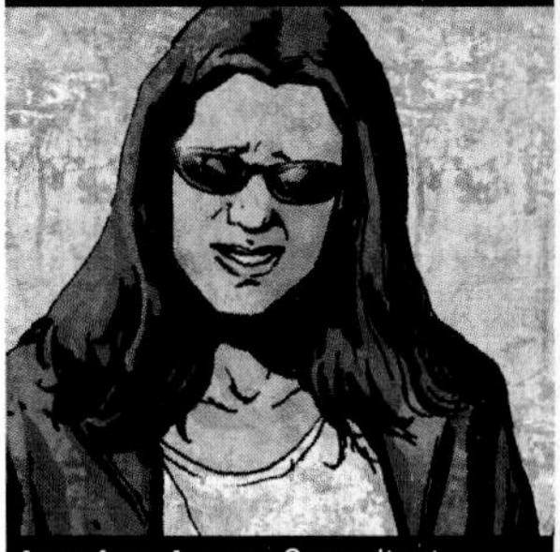

Jessica Jones Consultant

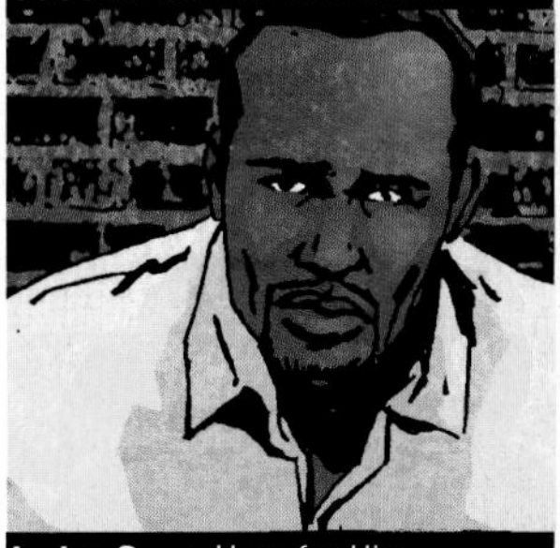

Luke Cage Hero for Hire

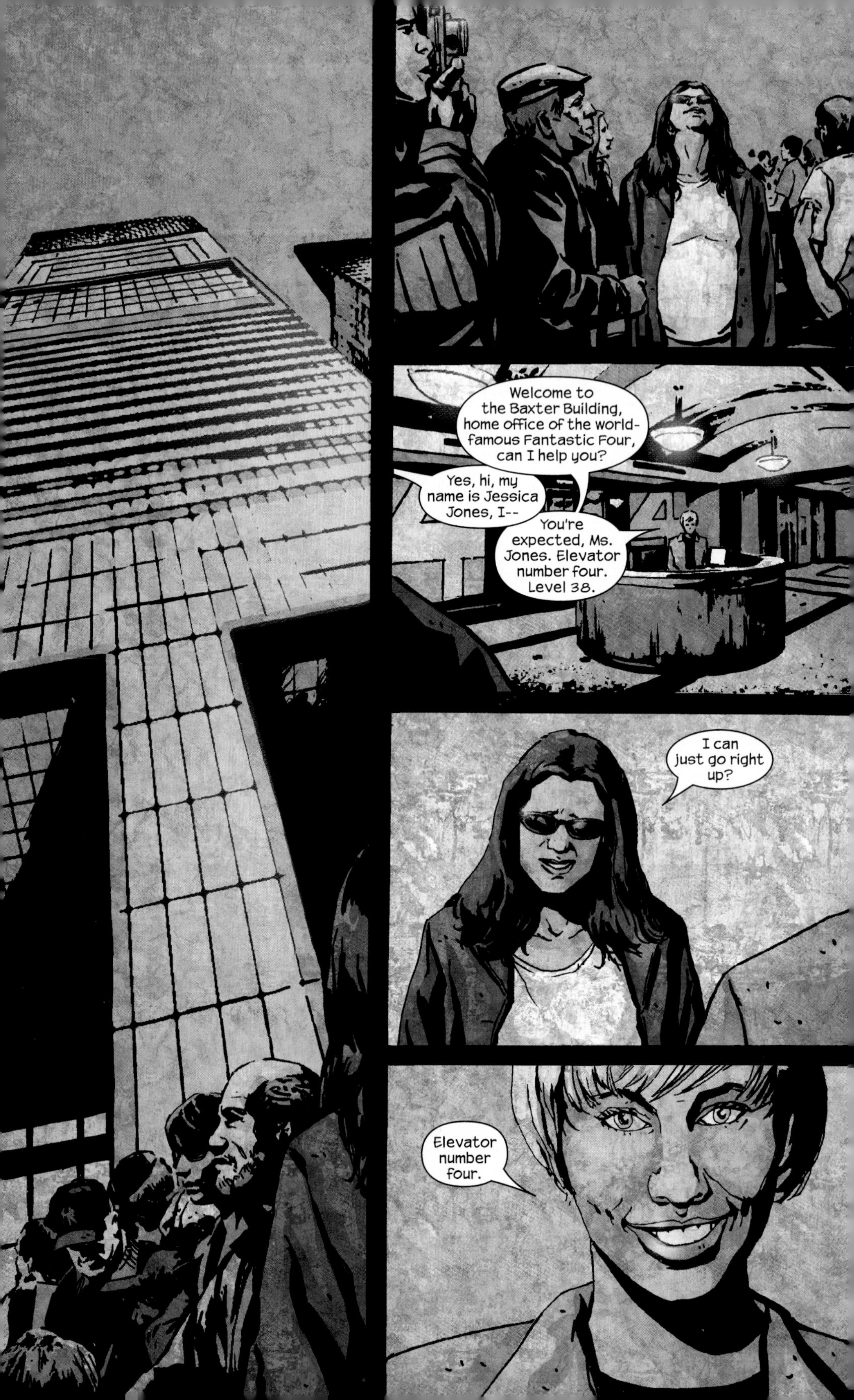
Welcome to the Baxter Building, home office of the world-famous Fantastic Four, can I help you?
Yes, hi, my name is Jessica Jones, I--
You're expected, Ms. Jones. Elevator number four. Level 38.
I can just go right up?
Elevator number four.

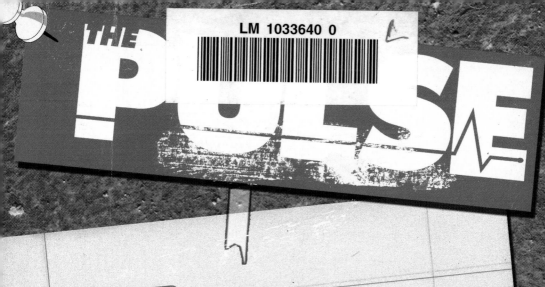

FEAR

Writer: Brian Michael Bendis

Artist: Michael Gaydos

Colorist: Matt Hollingsworth

Letterer: Virtual Calligraphy's Cory Petit

Cover Art: Mike Mayhew with Avalon's Andy Troy

Assistant Editors: Aubrey Sitterson & Molly Lazer

Editor: Andy Schmidt

New Avengers Annual #1

Writer: Brian Michael Bendis

Penciler: Olivier Coipel

Inkers: Drew Geraci, Drew Hennessy, Livesay, Rick Magyar, Danny Miki, Mark Morales, Mike Perkins & Tim Townsend

Colorists: June Chung, Richard Isanove & Jose Villarrubia

Letterer: Comicraft's Albert Deschesne

Assistant Editors: Aubrey Sitterson & Molly Lazer

Asscoiate Ediror: Andy Schmidt

Editor: Tom Brevoort

The Pulse created by Brian Michael Bendis

Collection Editor:
Jennifer Grünwald
Assistant Editor:
Michael Short
Associate Editor:
Mark D. Beazley
**Senior Editor,
Special Projects:**
Jeff Youngquist

Vice President of Sales:
David Gabriel
Production:
Jerron Quality Color
Vice President of Creative:
Tom Marvelli

Editor in Chief: Joe Quesada
Publisher: Dan Buckley

LM 1033640 0

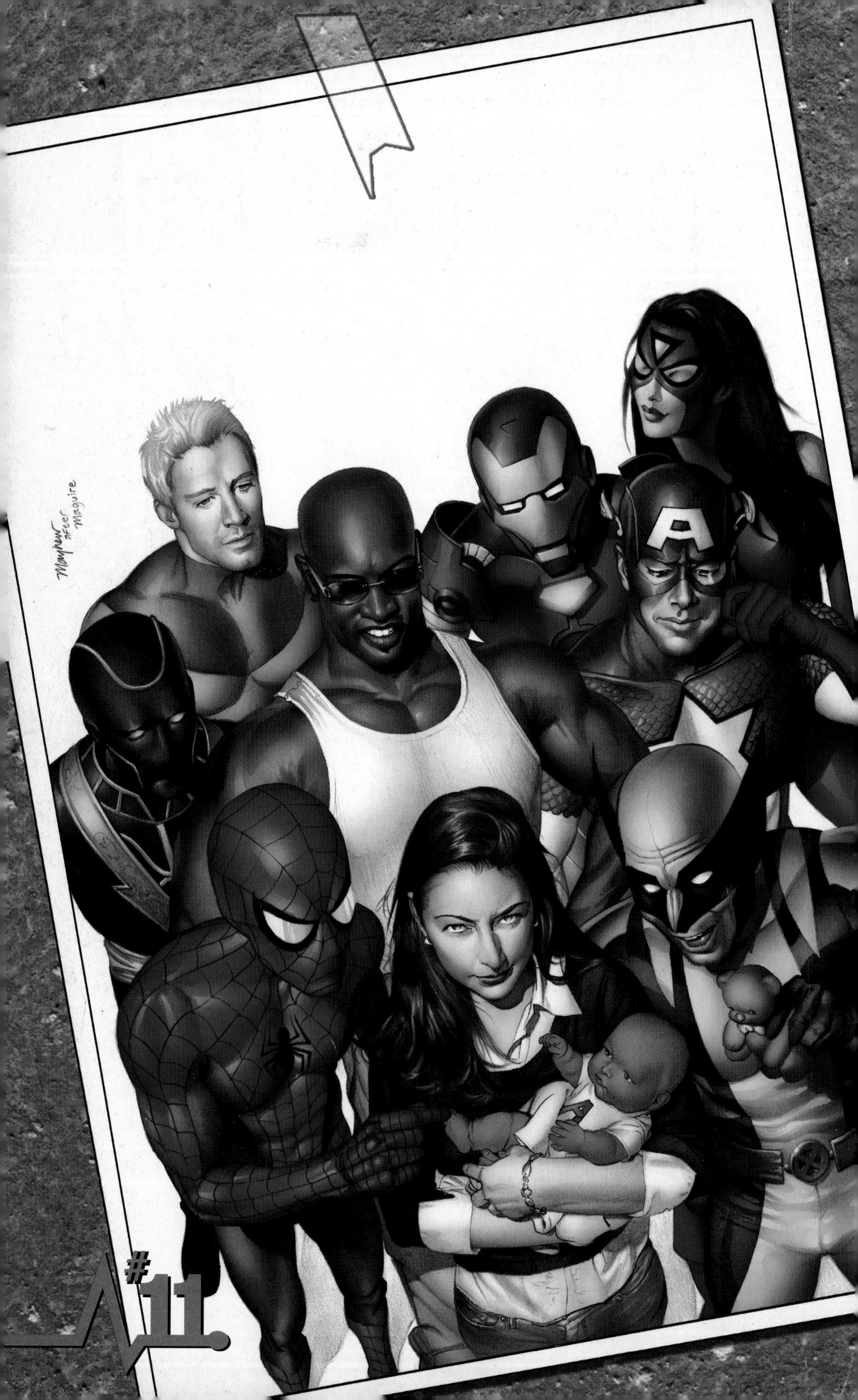
#11

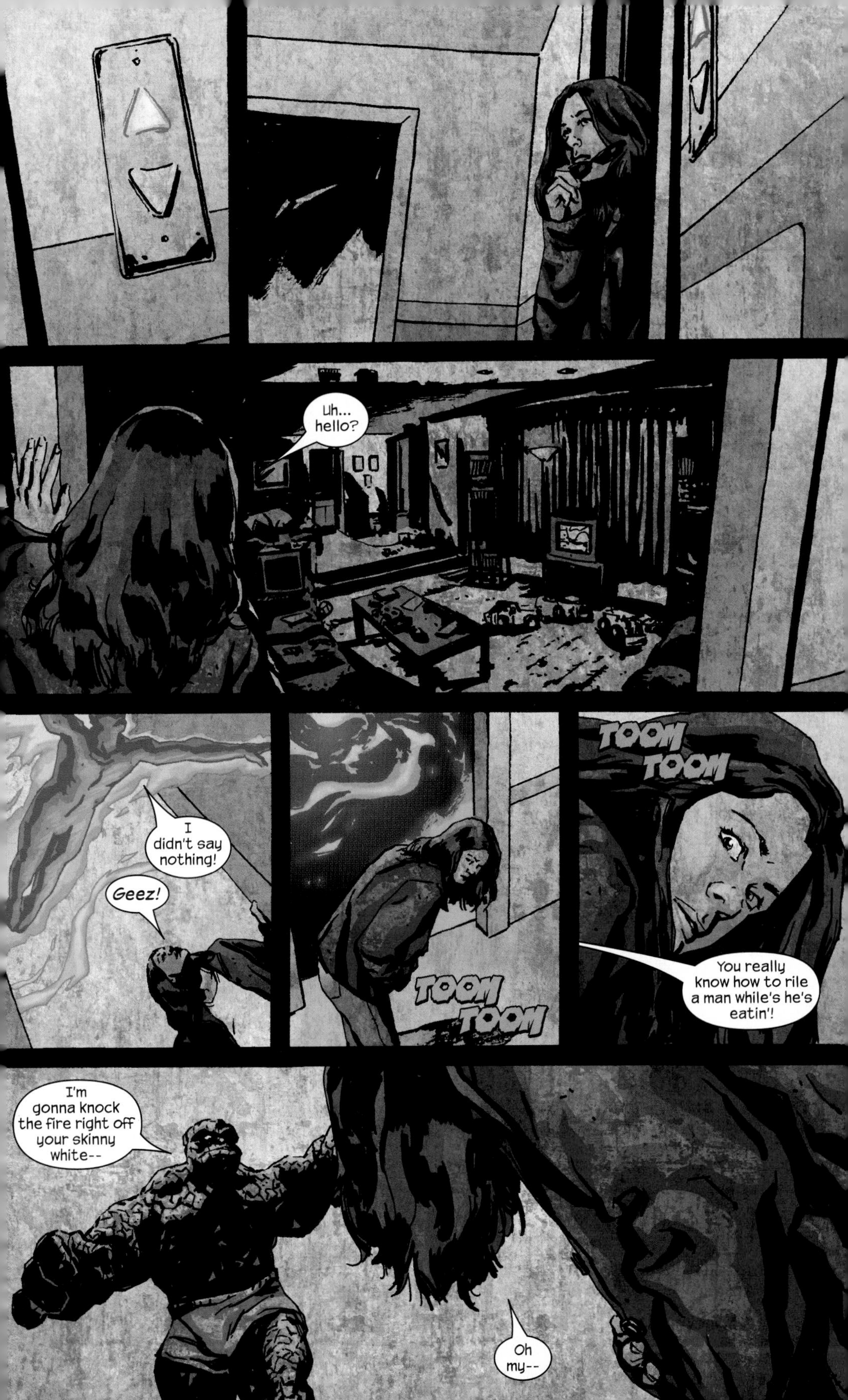
Uh... hello?
I didn't say nothing!
Geez!
TOOM TOOM
TOOM TOOM
You really know how to rile a man while's he's eatin'!
I'm gonna knock the fire right off your skinny white--
Oh my--

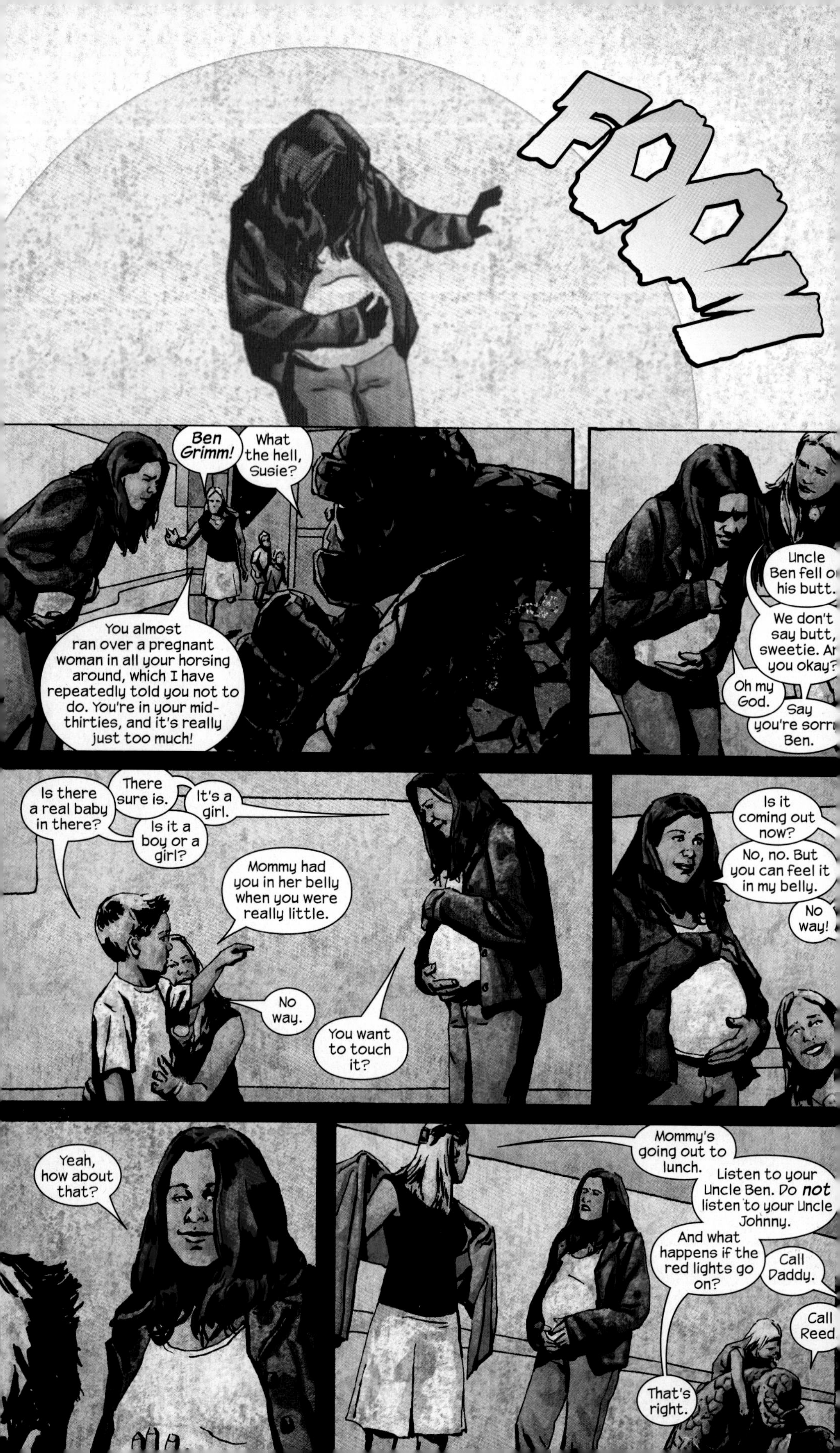
FOOOM
Ben Grimm!
What the hell, Susie?
You almost ran over a pregnant woman in all your horsing around, which I have repeatedly told you not to do. You're in your mid-thirties, and it's really just too much!
Uncle Ben fell o
his butt.
We don't say butt, sweetie. Ar you okay?
Oh my God.
Say you're sorr
Ben.
Is there a real baby in there?
There sure is.
It's a girl.
Is it a boy or a girl?
Mommy had you in her belly when you were really little.
No way.
You want to touch it?
Is it coming out now?
No, no. But you can feel it in my belly.
No way!
Yeah, how about that?
Mommy's going out to lunch.
Listen to your Uncle Ben. Do **not** listen to your Uncle Johnny.
And what happens if the red lights go on?
Call Daddy.
Call Reed.
That's right.

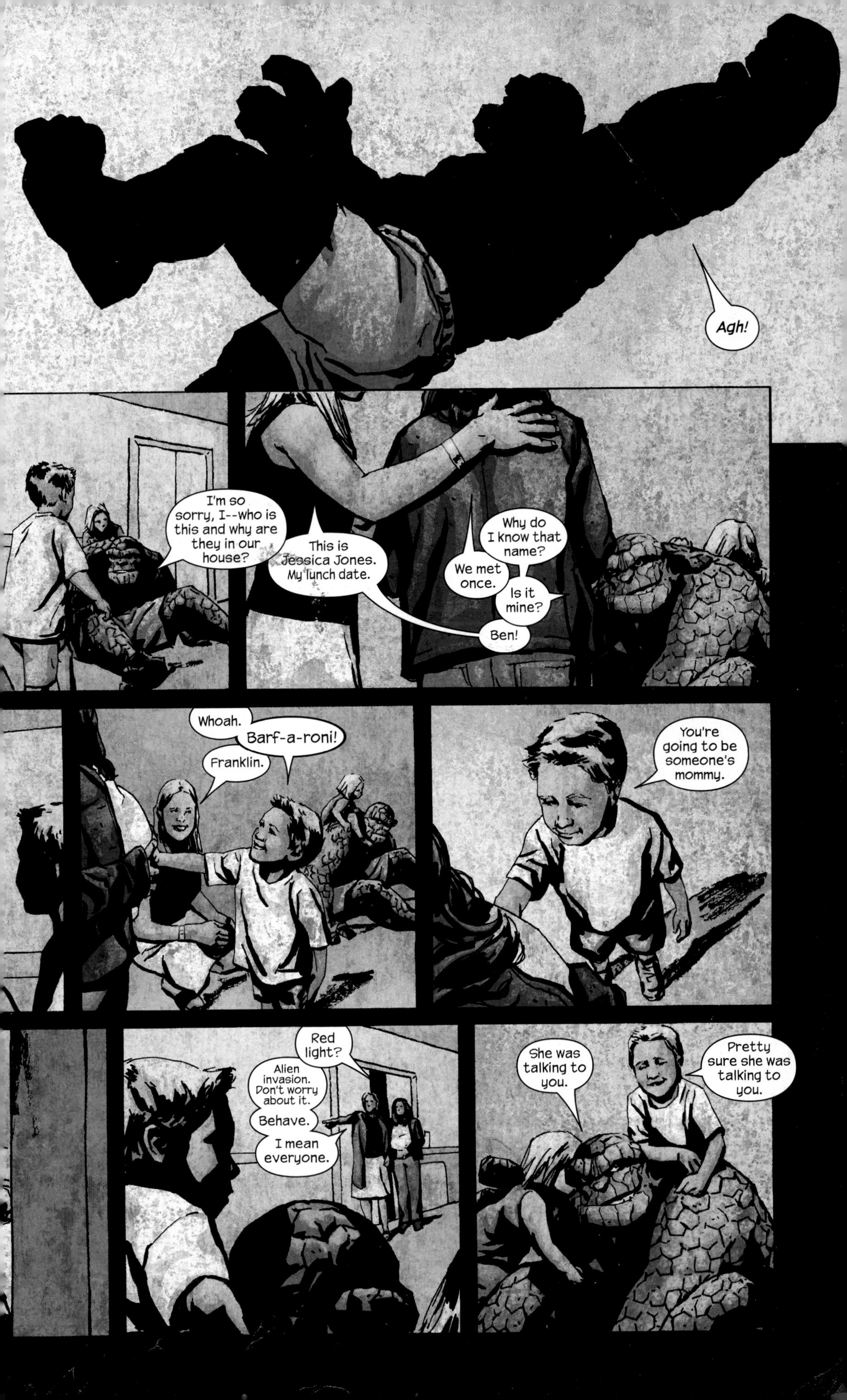
Agh!
I'm so sorry, I--who is this and why are they in our house?
This is Jessica Jones. My lunch date.
Why do I know that name?
We met once.
Is it mine?
Ben!
Whoah.
Barf-a-roni!
Franklin.
You're going to be someone's mommy.
Red light?
Alien invasion. Don't worry about it.
Behave.
I mean everyone.
She was talking to you.
Pretty sure she was talking to you.

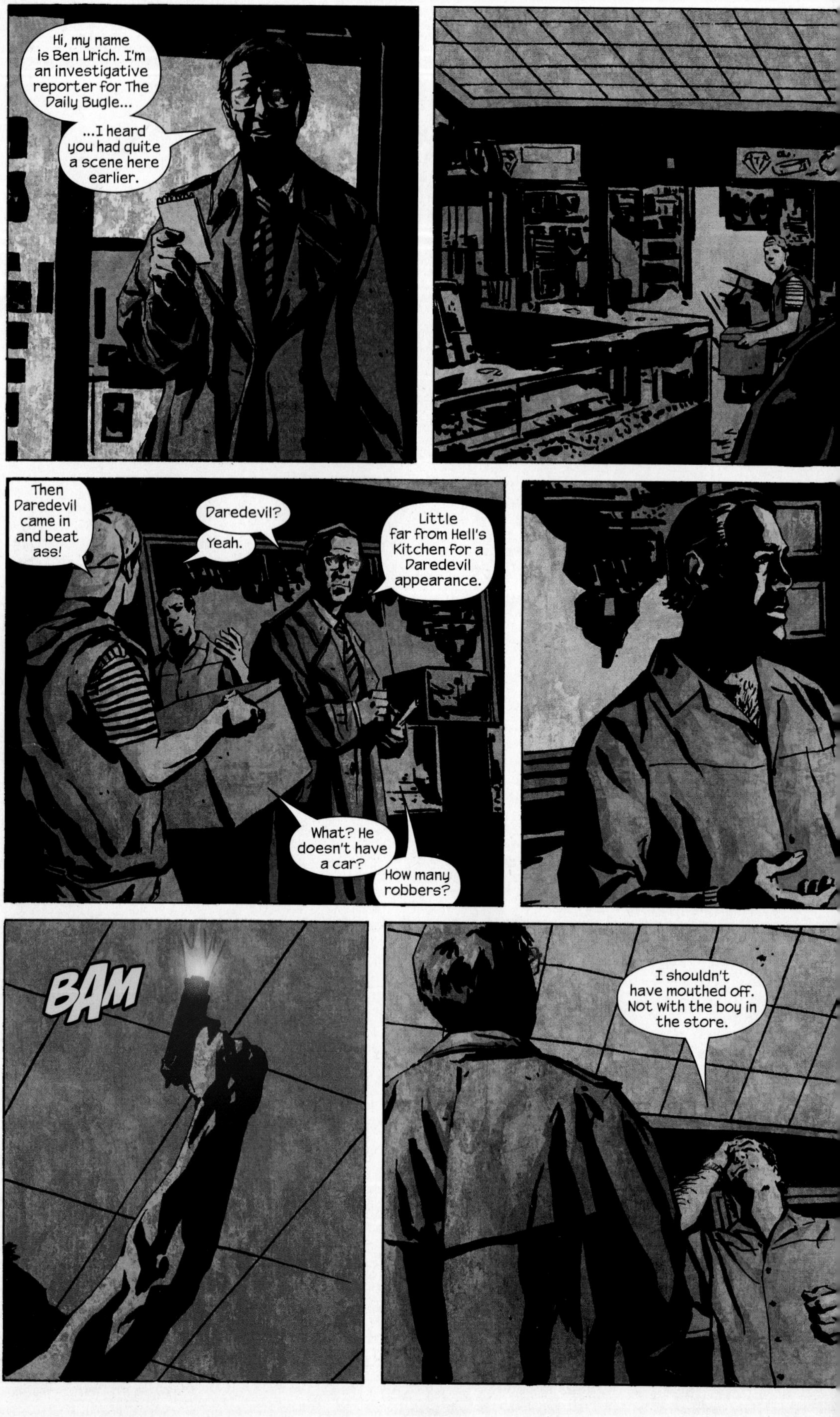
Hi, my name is Ben Urich. I'm an investigative reporter for The Daily Bugle...
...I heard you had quite a scene here earlier.
Then Daredevil came in and beat ass!
Daredevil?
Yeah.
Little far from Hell's Kitchen for a Daredevil appearance.
What? He doesn't have a car?
How many robbers?
BAM
I shouldn't have mouthed off. Not with the boy in the store.

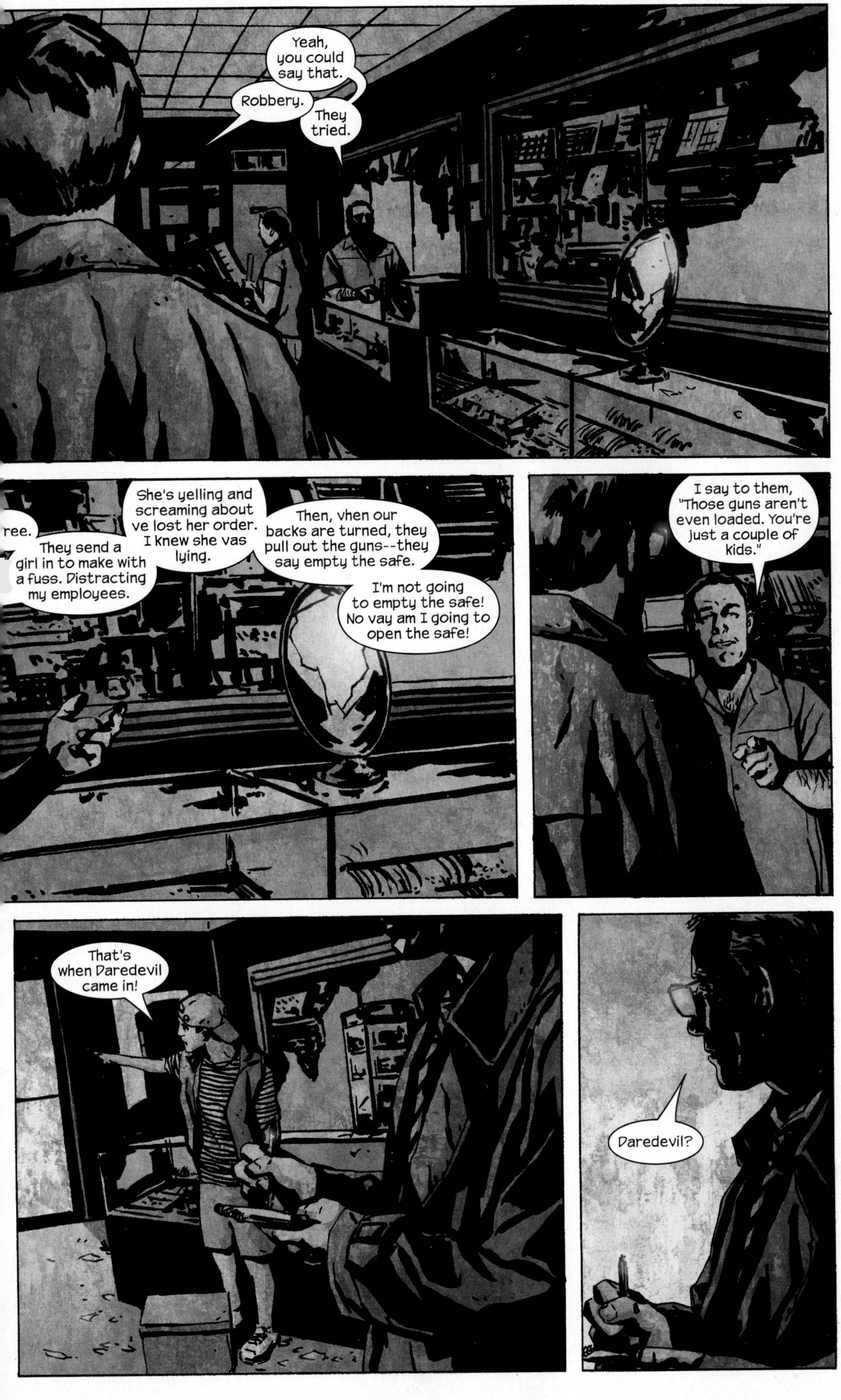
Yeah, you could say that.
Robbery.
They tried.
ree.
They send a girl in to make with a fuss. Distracting my employees.
She's yelling and screaming about ve lost her order. I knew she vas lying.
Then, vhen our backs are turned, they pull out the guns--they say empty the safe.
I'm not going to empty the safe! No vay am I going to open the safe!
I say to them, "Those guns aren't even loaded. You're just a couple of kids."
That's when Daredevil came in!
Daredevil?

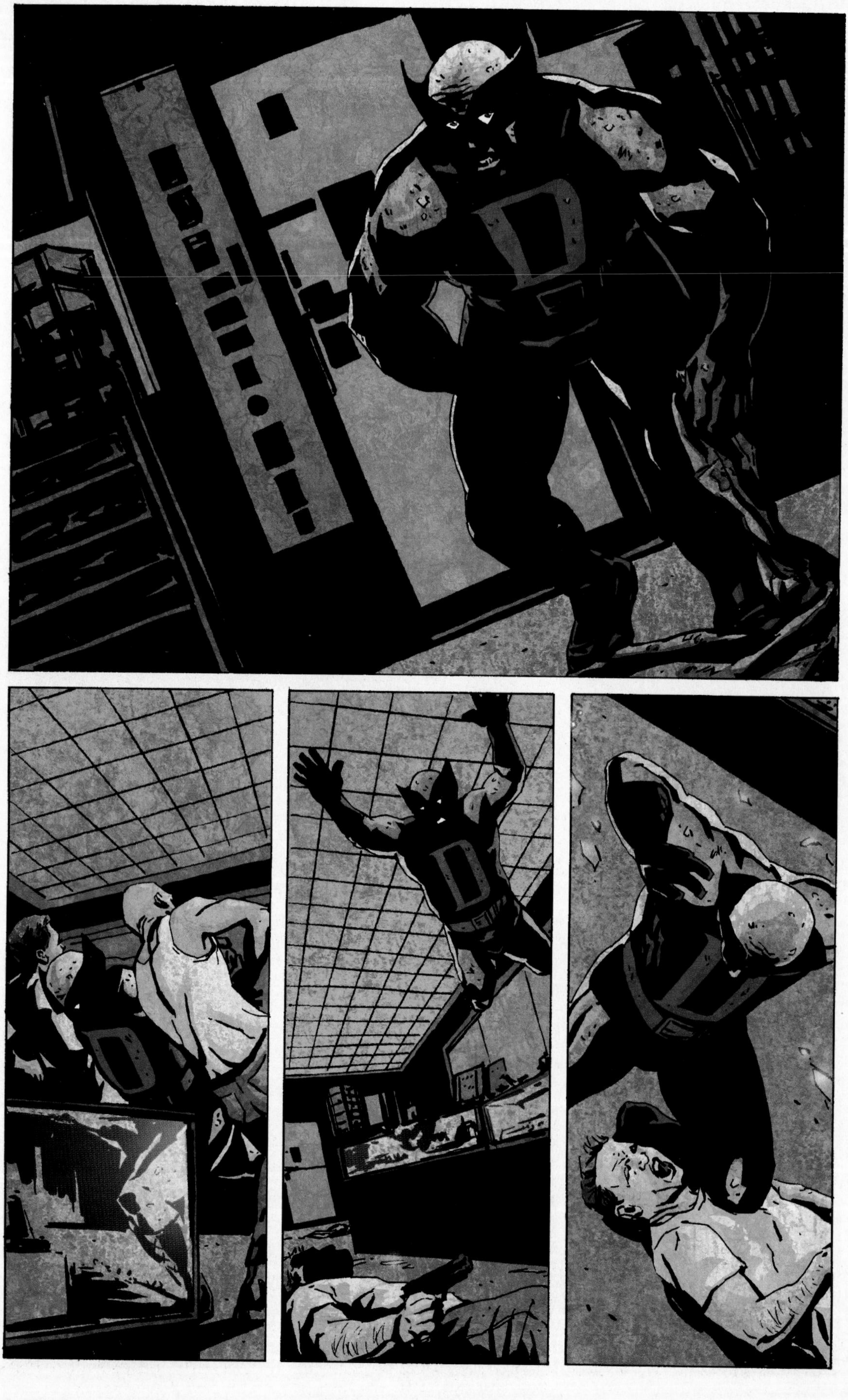

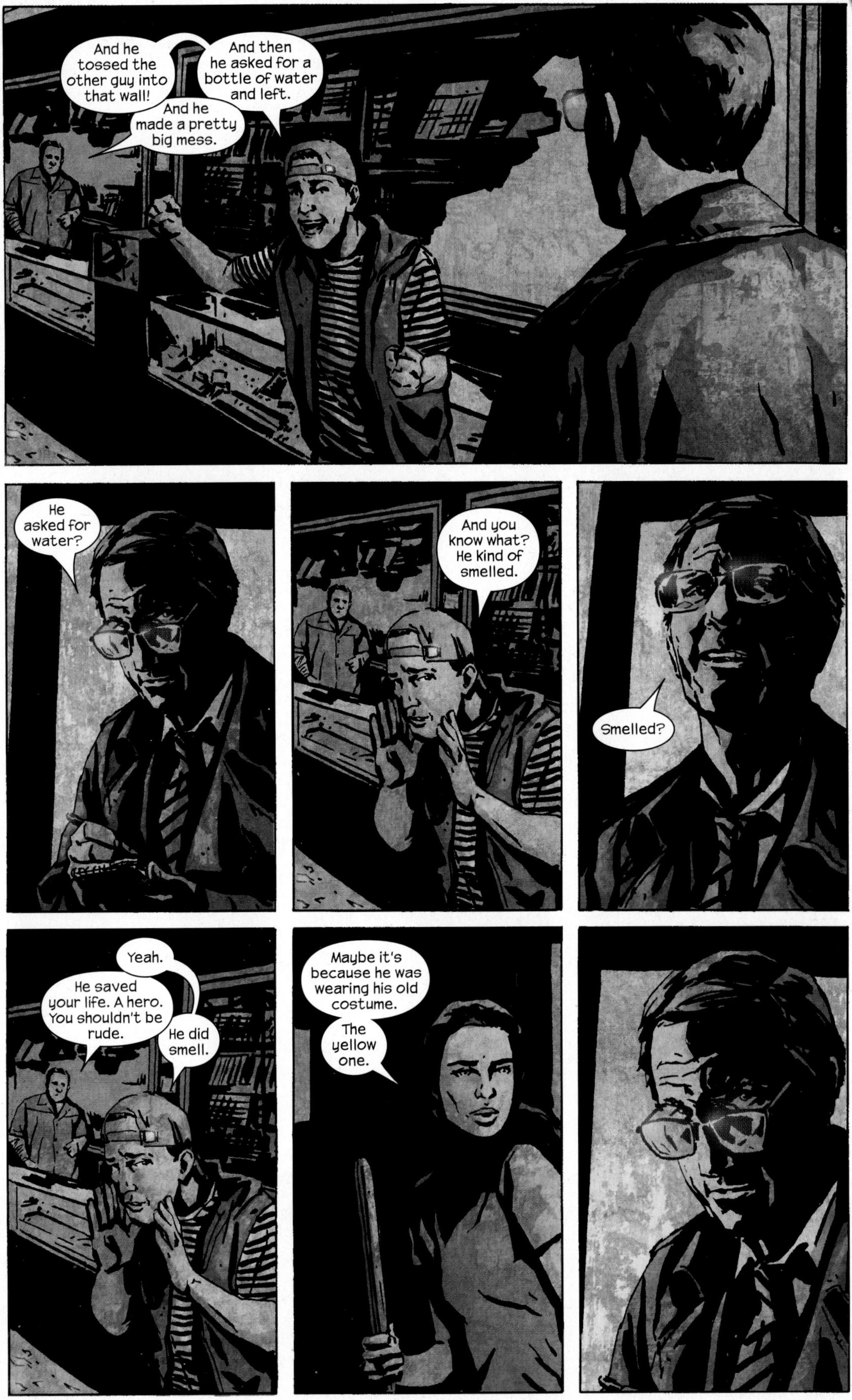
And he tossed the other guy into that wall!
And he made a pretty big mess.
And then he asked for a bottle of water and left.
He asked for water?
And you know what? He kind of smelled.
Smelled?
Yeah.
He saved your life. A hero. You shouldn't be rude.
He did smell.
Maybe it's because he was wearing his old costume.
The yellow one.

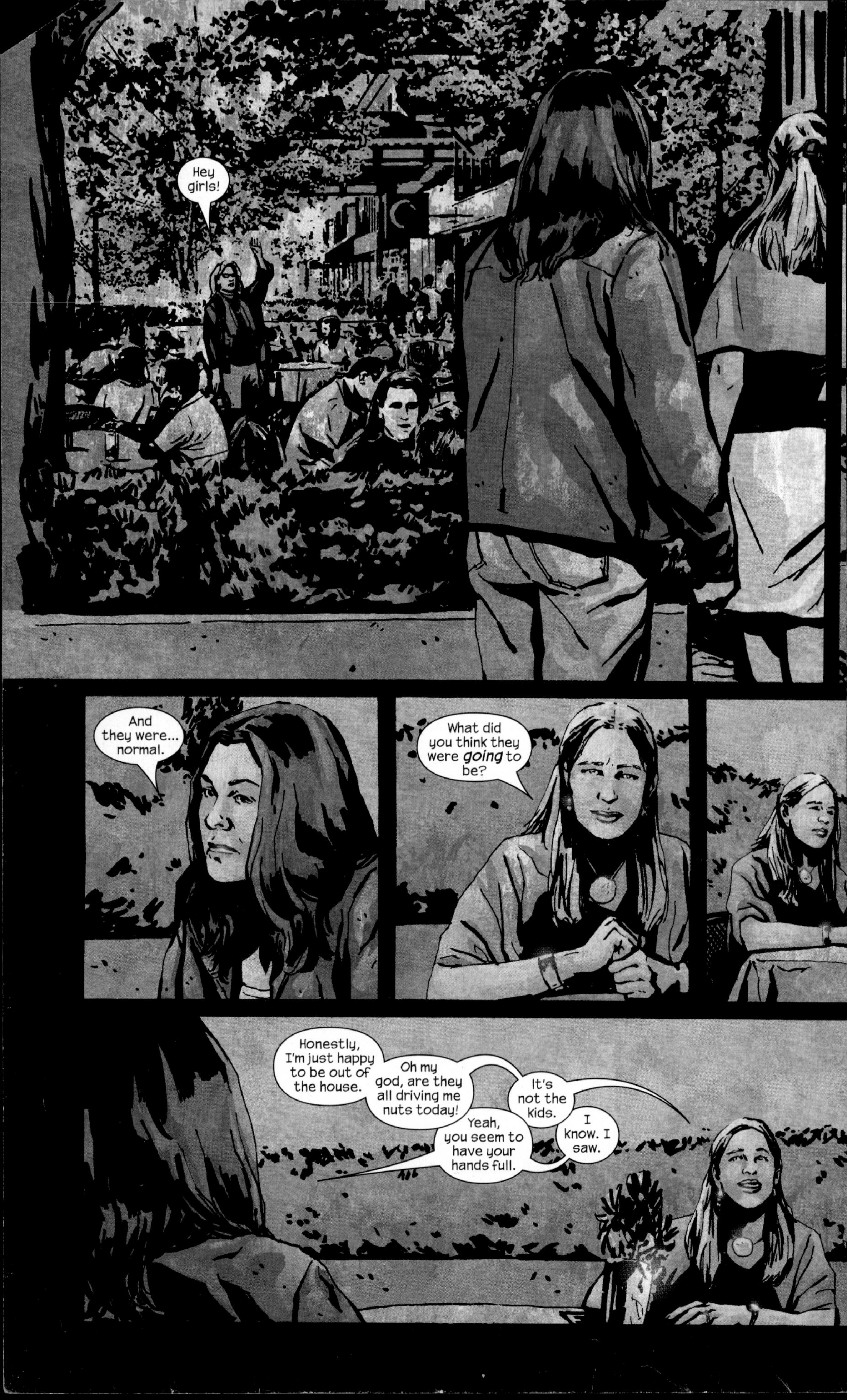
Hey girls!
And they were... normal.
What did you think they were *going* to be?
Honestly, I'm just happy to be out of the house.
Oh my god, are they all driving me nuts today!
It's not the kids.
Yeah, you seem to have your hands full.
I know. I saw.

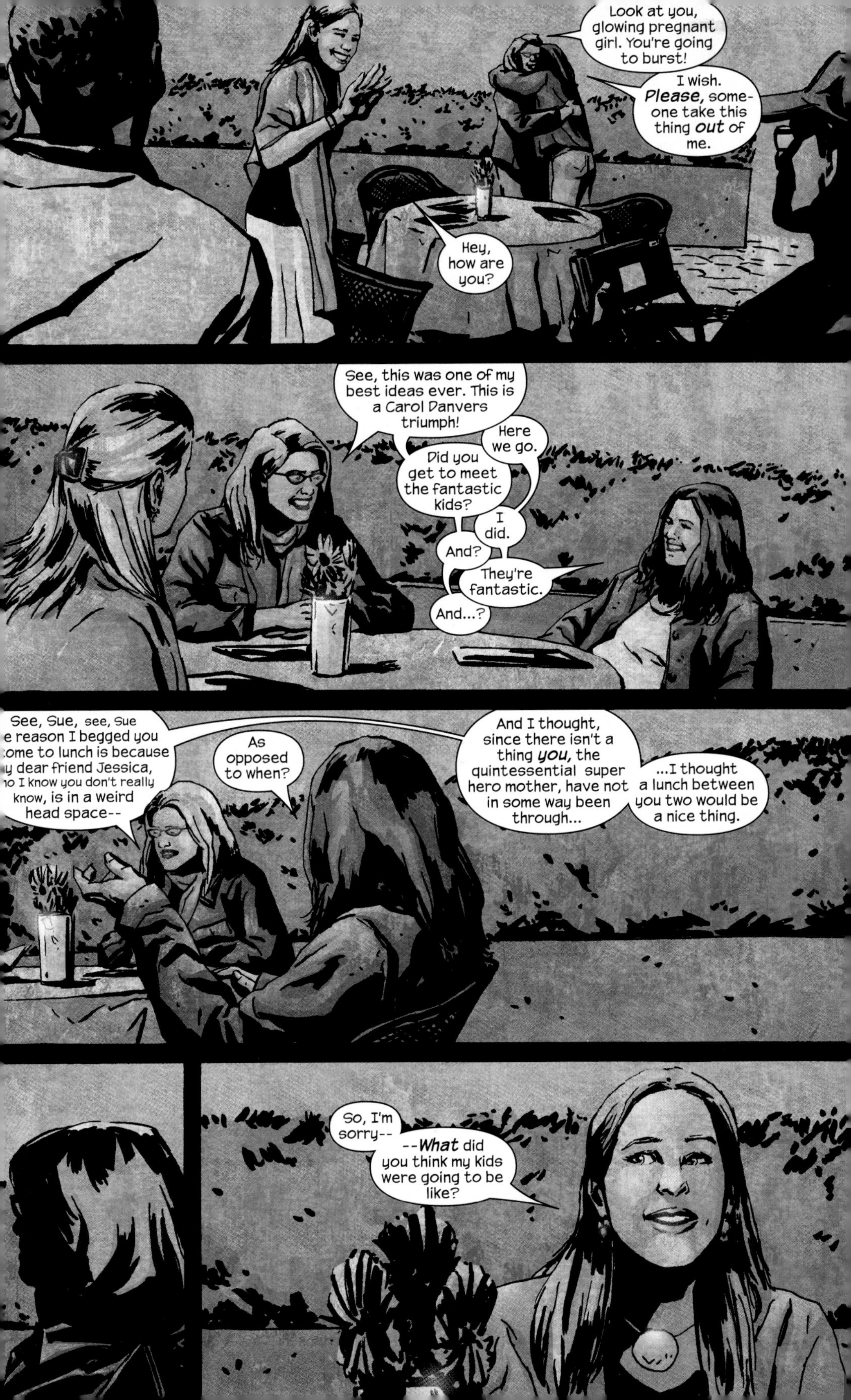
Look at you, glowing pregnant girl. You're going to burst!
I wish. *Please,* some-one take this thing *out* of me.
Hey, how are you?
See, this was one of my best ideas ever. This is a Carol Danvers triumph!
Here we go.
Did you get to meet the fantastic kids?
I did.
And?
They're fantastic.
And...?
See, Sue, see, Sue
e reason I begged you
ome to lunch is because
y dear friend Jessica,
o I know you don't really
know, is in a weird
head space--
As opposed to when?
And I thought, since there isn't a thing *you,* the quintessential super hero mother, have not in some way been through...
...I thought a lunch between you two would be a nice thing.
So, I'm sorry--
--*What* did you think my kids were going to be like?

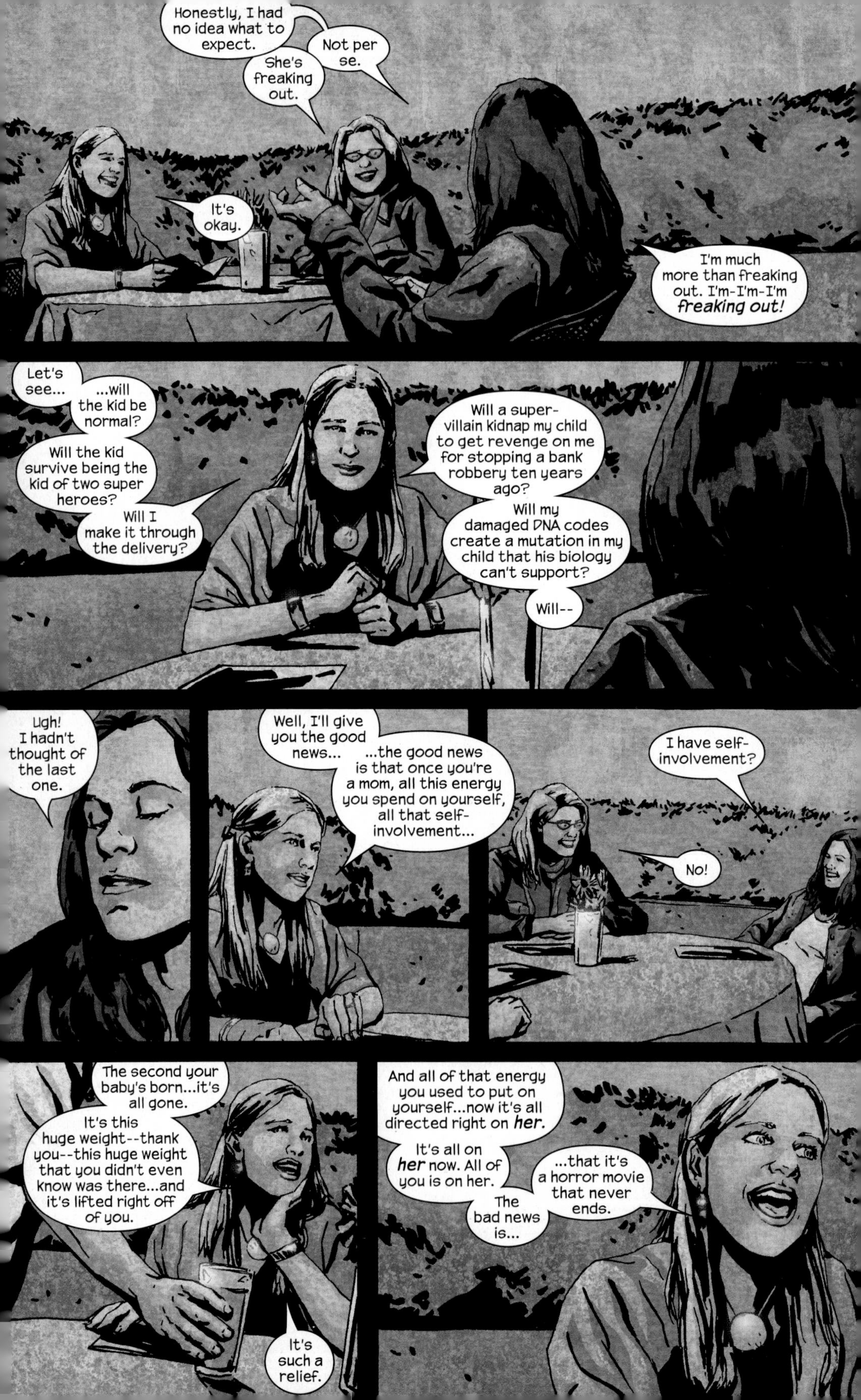
Honestly, I had no idea what to expect.
Not per se.
She's freaking out.
It's okay.
I'm much more than freaking out. I'm-I'm-I'm *freaking out!*
Let's see...
...will the kid be normal?
Will the kid survive being the kid of two super heroes?
Will I make it through the delivery?
Will a super-villain kidnap my child to get revenge on me for stopping a bank robbery ten years ago?
Will my damaged DNA codes create a mutation in my child that his biology can't support?
Will--
Ugh! I hadn't thought of the last one.
Well, I'll give you the good news...
...the good news is that once you're a mom, all this energy you spend on yourself, all that self-involvement...
I have self-involvement?
No!
The second your baby's born...it's all gone.
It's this huge weight--thank you--this huge weight that you didn't even know was there...and it's lifted right off of you.
It's such a relief.
And all of that energy you used to put on yourself...now it's all directed right on *her.*
It's all on *her* now. All of you is on her.
The bad news is...
...that it's a horror movie that never ends.

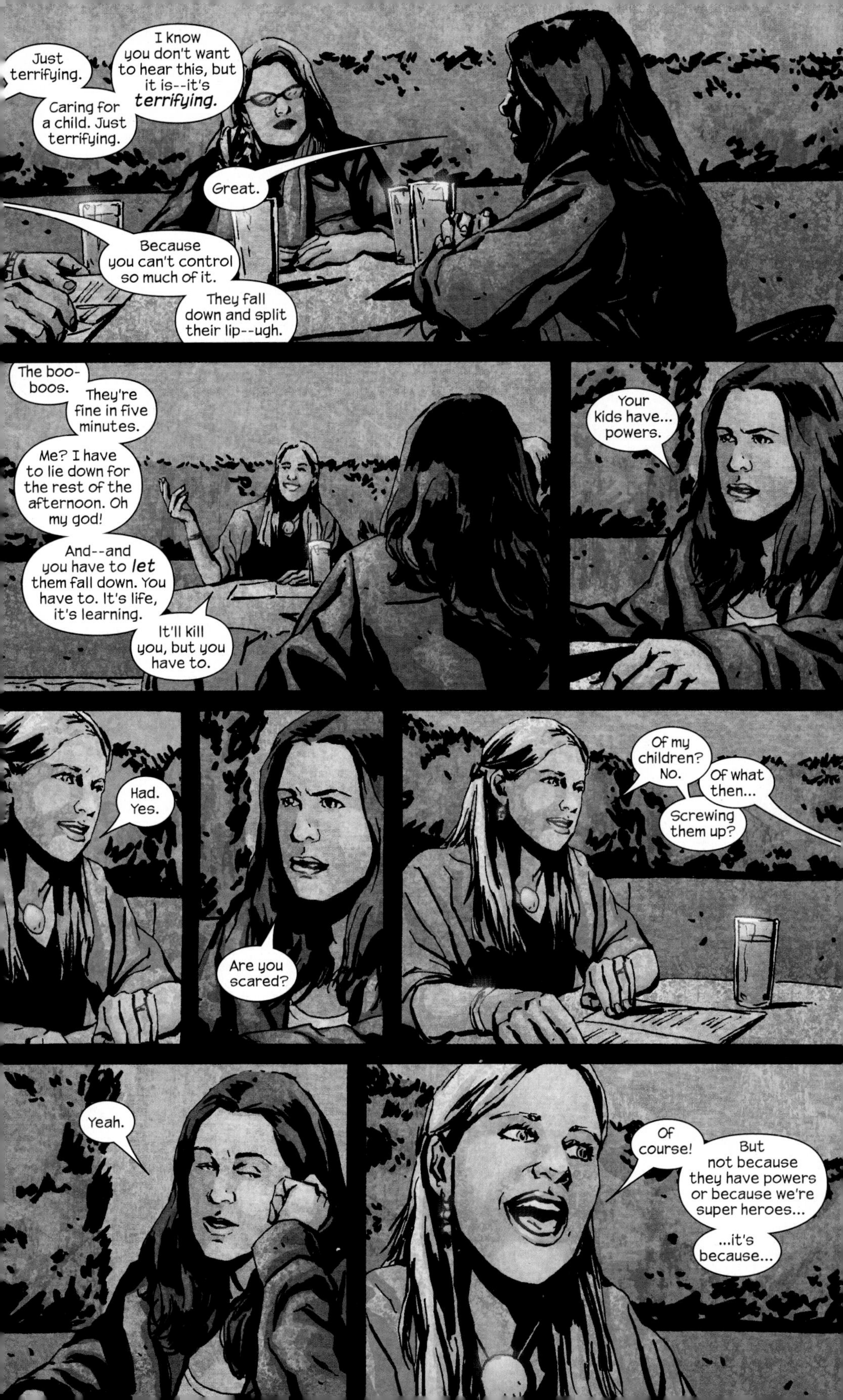
Just terrifying.
I know you don't want to hear this, but it is--it's *terrifying.*
Caring for a child. Just terrifying.
Great.
Because you can't control so much of it.
They fall down and split their lip--ugh.
The boo-boos.
They're fine in five minutes.
Me? I have to lie down for the rest of the afternoon. Oh my god!
And--and you have to *let* them fall down. You have to. It's life, it's learning.
It'll kill you, but you have to.
Your kids have... powers.
Had. Yes.
Are you scared?
Of my children? No.
Of what then...
Screwing them up?
Yeah.
Of course!
But not because they have powers or because we're super heroes...
...it's because...

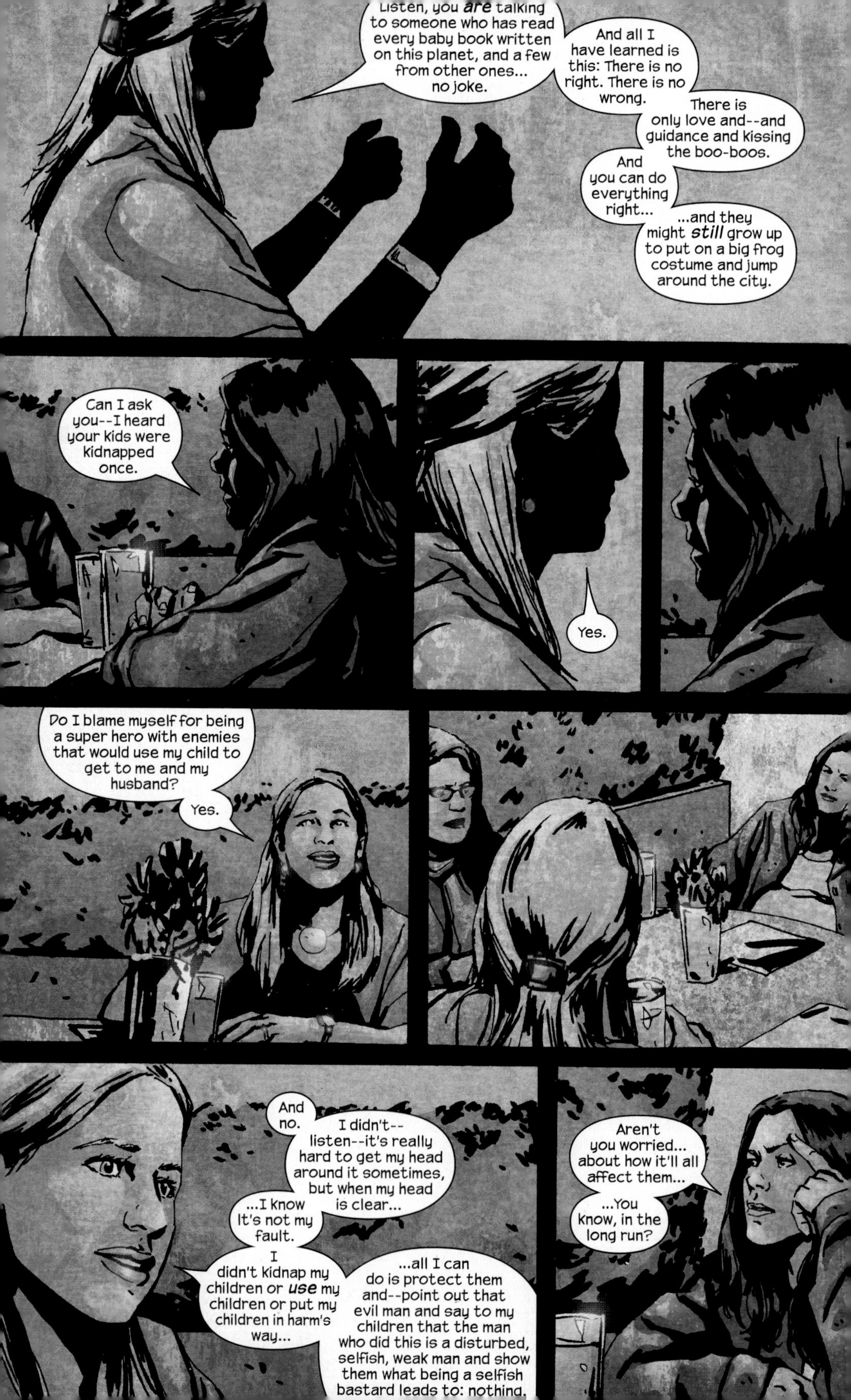

Listen, you are talking to someone who has read every baby book written on this planet, and a few from other ones... no joke.
And all I have learned is this: There is no right. There is no wrong.
There is only love and--and guidance and kissing the boo-boos.
And you can do everything right...
...and they might still grow up to put on a big frog costume and jump around the city.
Can I ask you--I heard your kids were kidnapped once.
Yes.
Do I blame myself for being a super hero with enemies that would use my child to get to me and my husband?
Yes.
And no.
I didn't--listen--it's really hard to get my head around it sometimes, but when my head is clear...
...I know it's not my fault.
I didn't kidnap my children or use my children or put my children in harm's way...
...all I can do is protect them and--point out that evil man and say to my children that the man who did this is a disturbed, selfish, weak man and show them what being a selfish bastard leads to: nothing.
Aren't you worried... about how it'll all affect them...
...You know, in the long run?

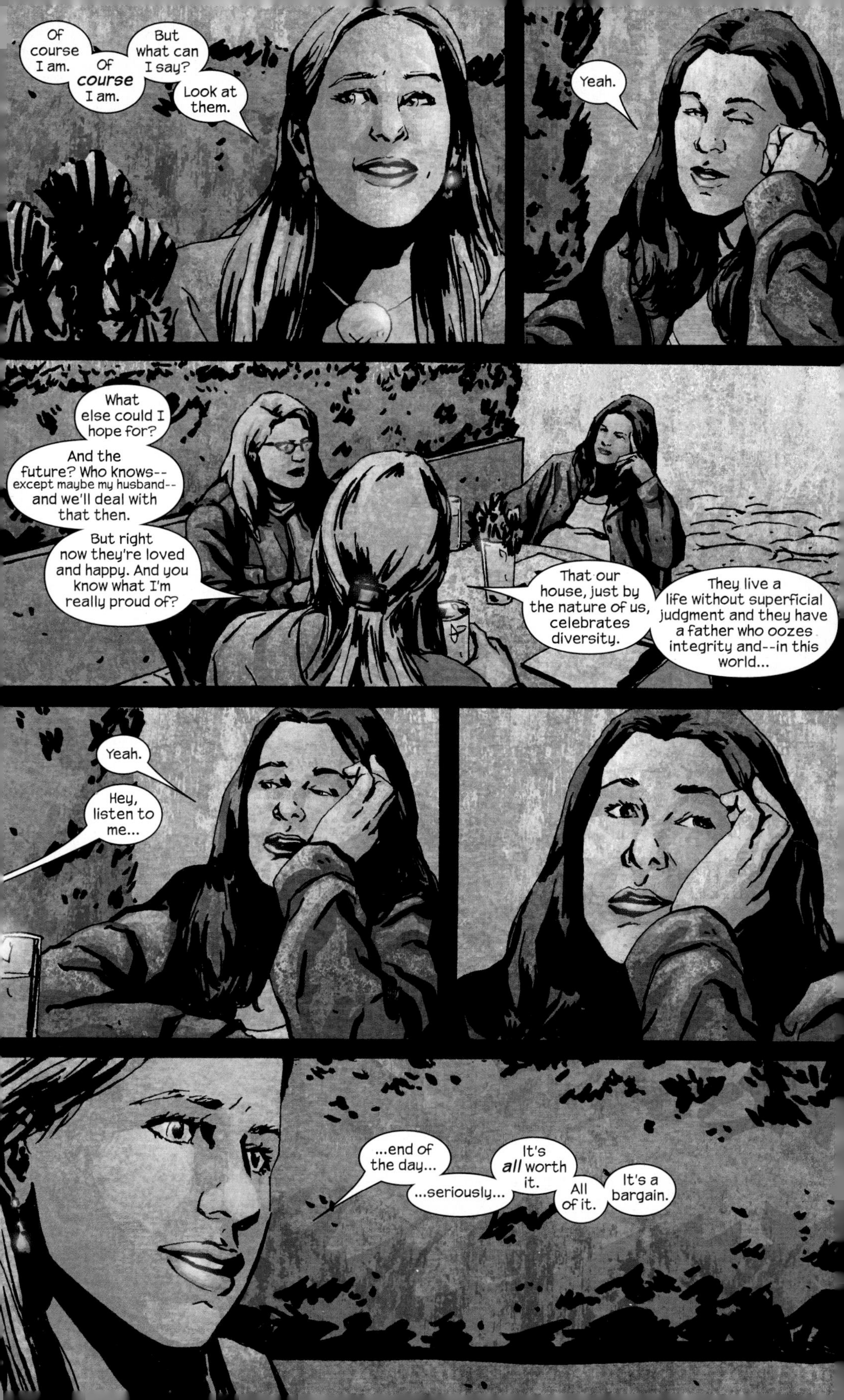
Of course I am.
Of *course* I am.
But what can I say?
Look at them.
Yeah.
What else could I hope for?
And the future? Who knows--except maybe my husband--and we'll deal with that then.
But right now they're loved and happy. And you know what I'm really proud of?
That our house, just by the nature of us, celebrates diversity.
They live a life without superficial judgment and they have a father who oozes integrity and--in this world...
Yeah.
Hey, listen to me...
...end of the day...
...seriously...
It's *all* worth it.
All of it.
It's a bargain.

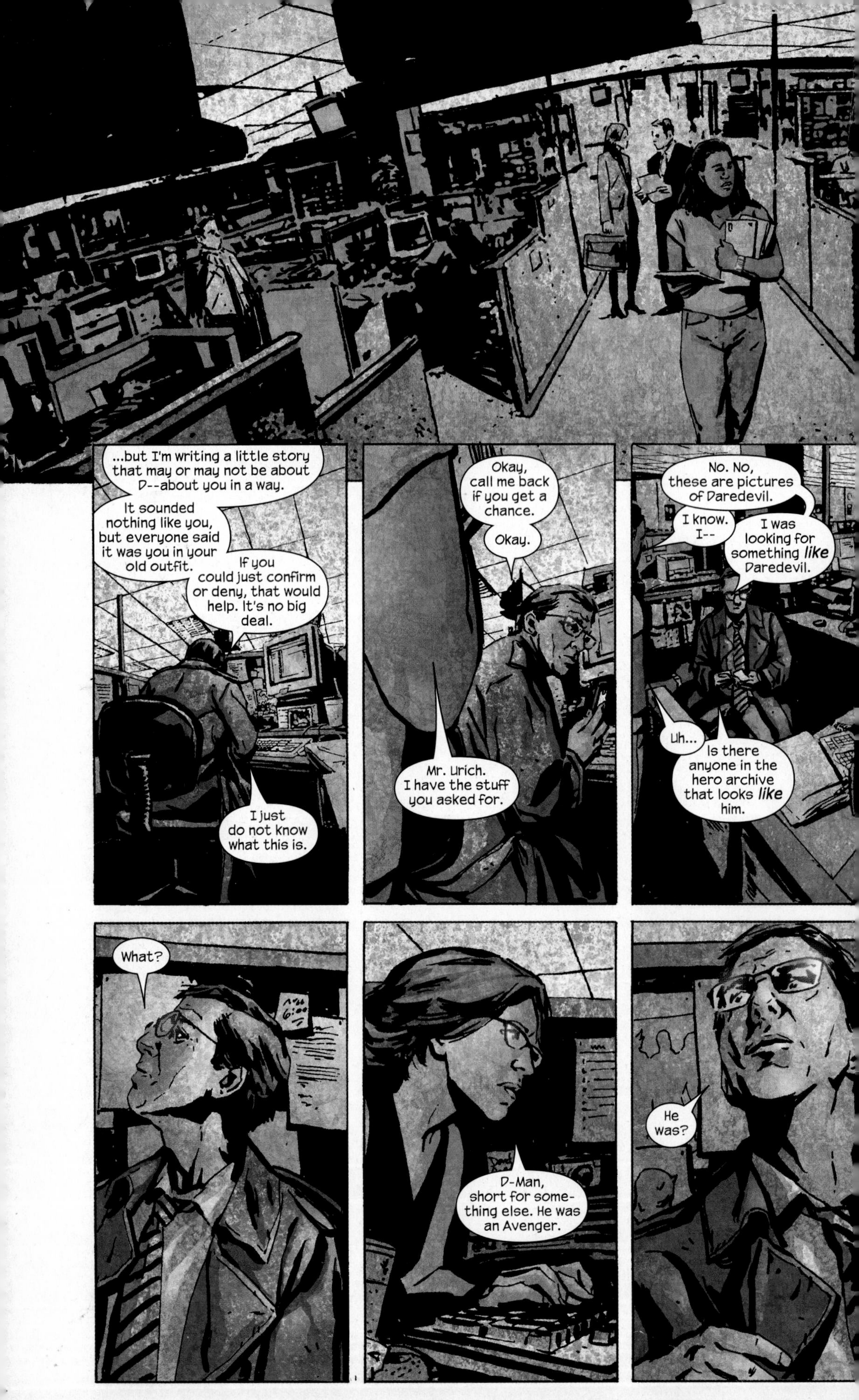
...but I'm writing a little story that may or may not be about D--about you in a way.
It sounded nothing like you, but everyone said it was you in your old outfit.
If you could just confirm or deny, that would help. It's no big deal.
I just do not know what this is.
Okay, call me back if you get a chance.
Okay.
Mr. Urich. I have the stuff you asked for.
No. No, these are pictures of Daredevil.
I know. I--
I was looking for something *like* Daredevil.
Uh...
Is there anyone in the hero archive that looks *like* him.
What?
D-Man, short for something else. He was an Avenger.
He was?

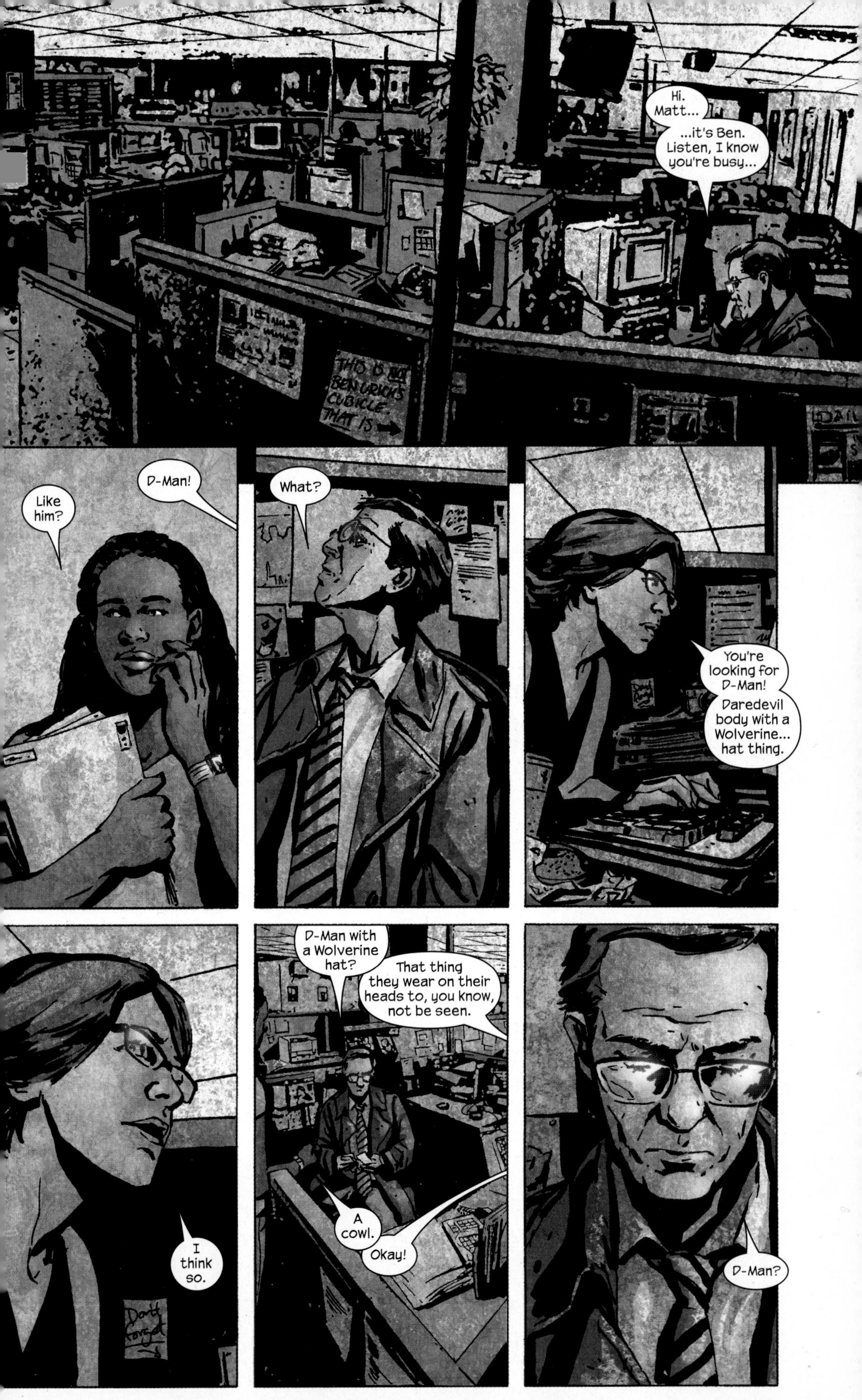
Hi. Matt...
...it's Ben. Listen, I know you're busy...
THIS IS NOT BEN URICH'S CUBICLE THAT IS →
D-Man!
Like him?
What?
You're looking for D-Man!
Daredevil body with a Wolverine... hat thing.
I think so.
D-Man with a Wolverine hat?
That thing they wear on their heads to, you know, not be seen.
A cowl.
Okay!
D-Man?

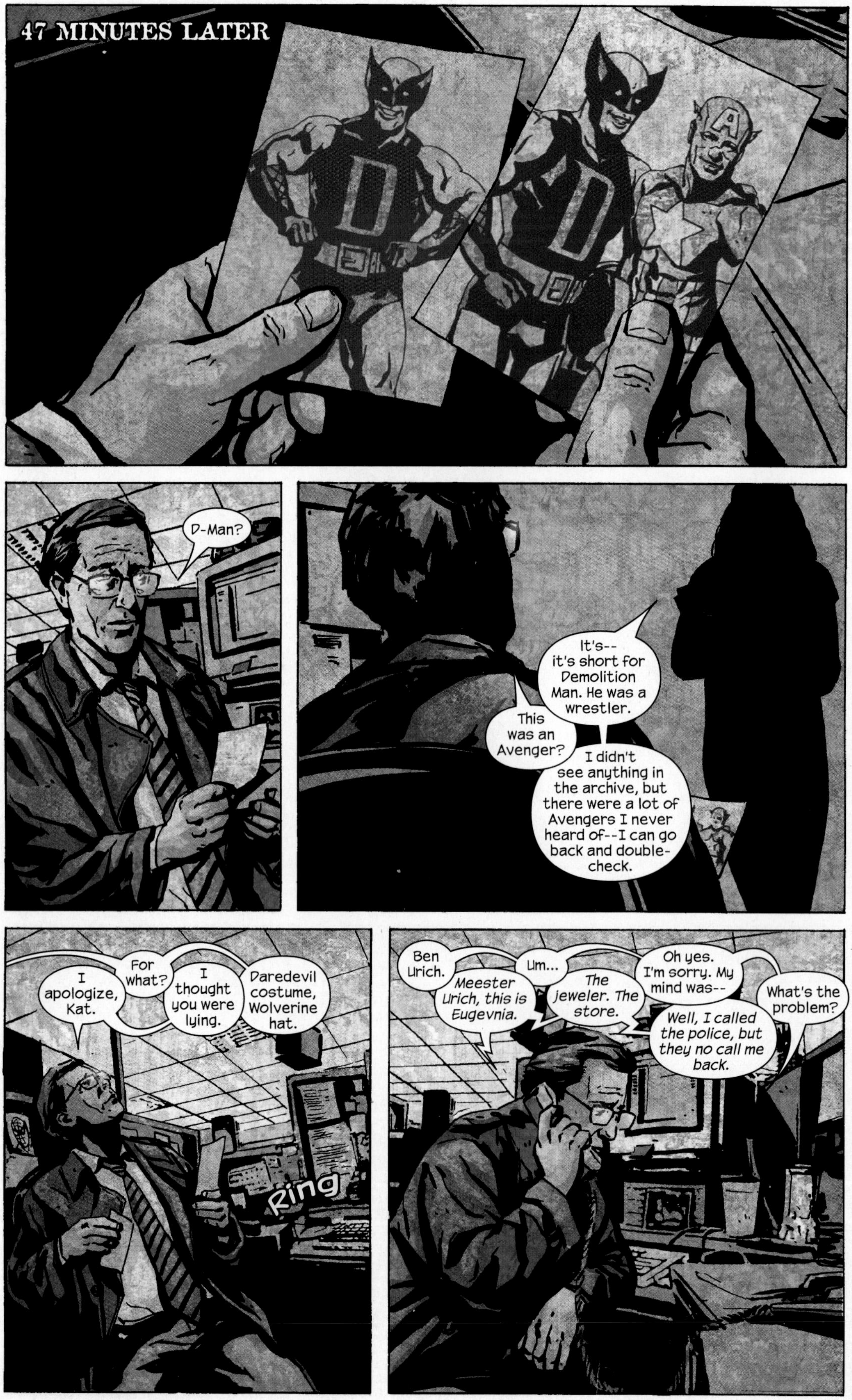
47 MINUTES LATER
D-Man?
It's--
it's short for Demolition Man. He was a wrestler.
This was an Avenger?
I didn't see anything in the archive, but there were a lot of Avengers I never heard of--I can go back and double-check.
I apologize, Kat.
For what?
I thought you were lying.
Daredevil costume, Wolverine hat.
Ring
Ben Urich.
Meester Urich, this is Eugevnia.
Um...
The jeweler. The store.
Oh yes. I'm sorry. My mind was--
Well, I called the police, but they no call me back.
What's the problem?

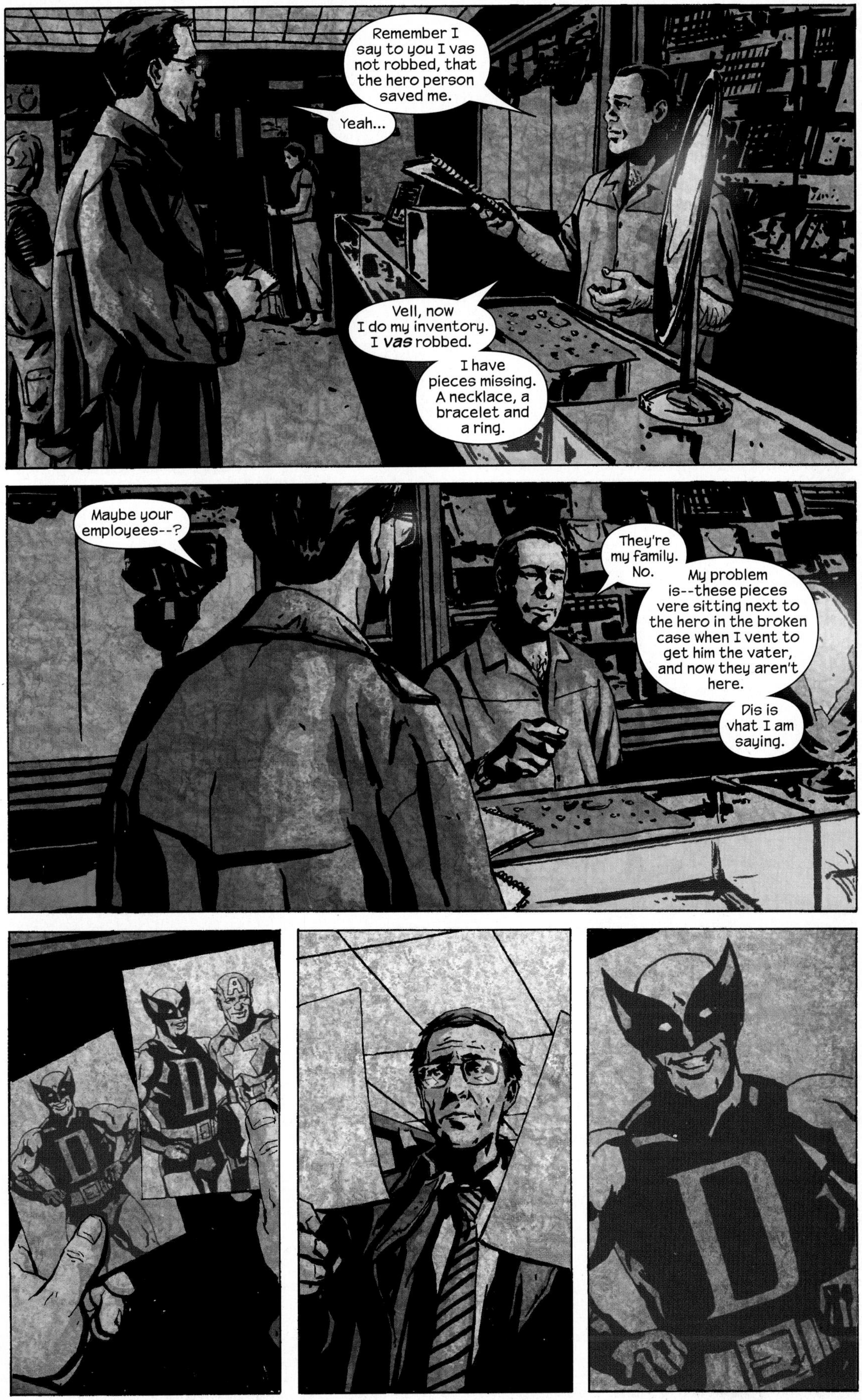
Remember I say to you I vas not robbed, that the hero person saved me.
Yeah...
Vell, now I do my inventory. I *vas* robbed.
I have pieces missing. A necklace, a bracelet and a ring.
Maybe your employees--?
They're my family. No.
My problem is--these pieces vere sitting next to the hero in the broken case when I vent to get him the vater, and now they aren't here.
Dis is vhat I am saying.

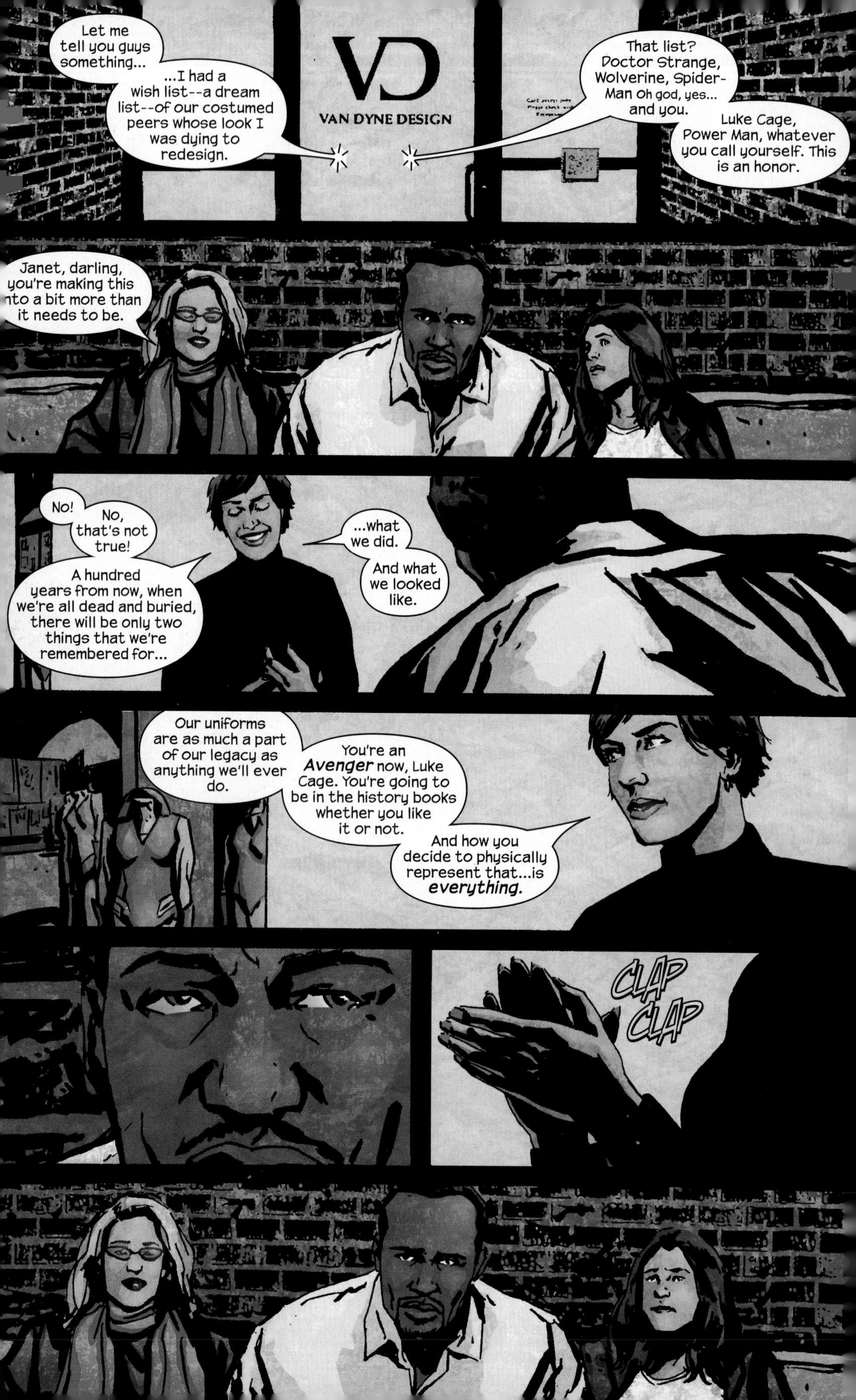

Let me tell you guys something...
...I had a wish list--a dream list--of our costumed peers whose look I was dying to redesign.
VAN DYNE DESIGN
That list? Doctor Strange, Wolverine, Spider-Man Oh god, yes... and you.
Luke Cage, Power Man, whatever you call yourself. This is an honor.
Janet, darling, you're making this into a bit more than it needs to be.
No!
No, that's not true!
A hundred years from now, when we're all dead and buried, there will be only two things that we're remembered for...
...what we did.
And what we looked like.
Our uniforms are as much a part of our legacy as anything we'll ever do.
You're an *Avenger* now, Luke Cage. You're going to be in the history books whether you like it or not.
And how you decide to physically represent that...is *everything.*
CLAP CLAP

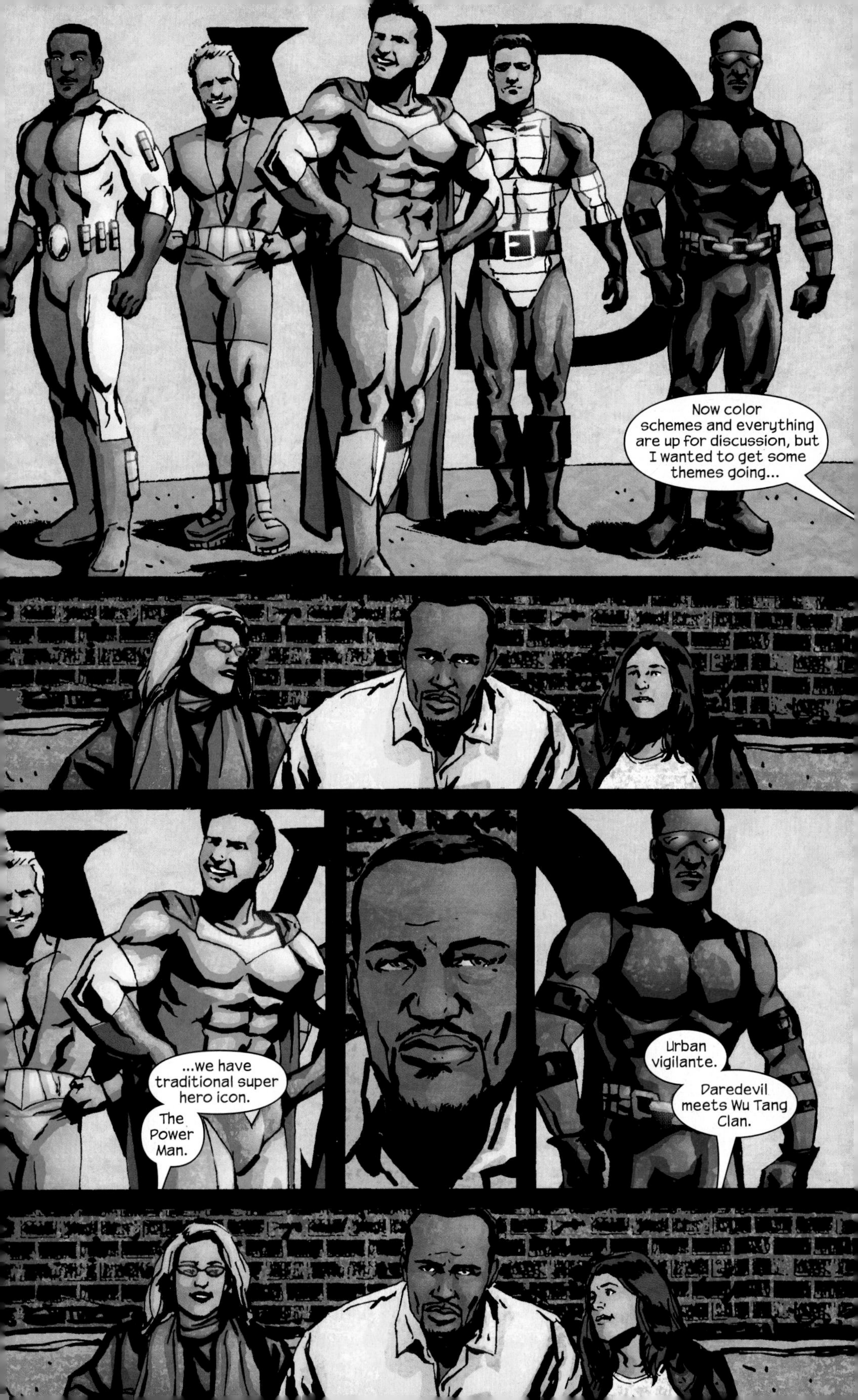
Now color schemes and everything are up for discussion, but I wanted to get some themes going...
...we have traditional super hero icon.
The Power Man.
Urban vigilante.
Daredevil meets Wu Tang Clan.

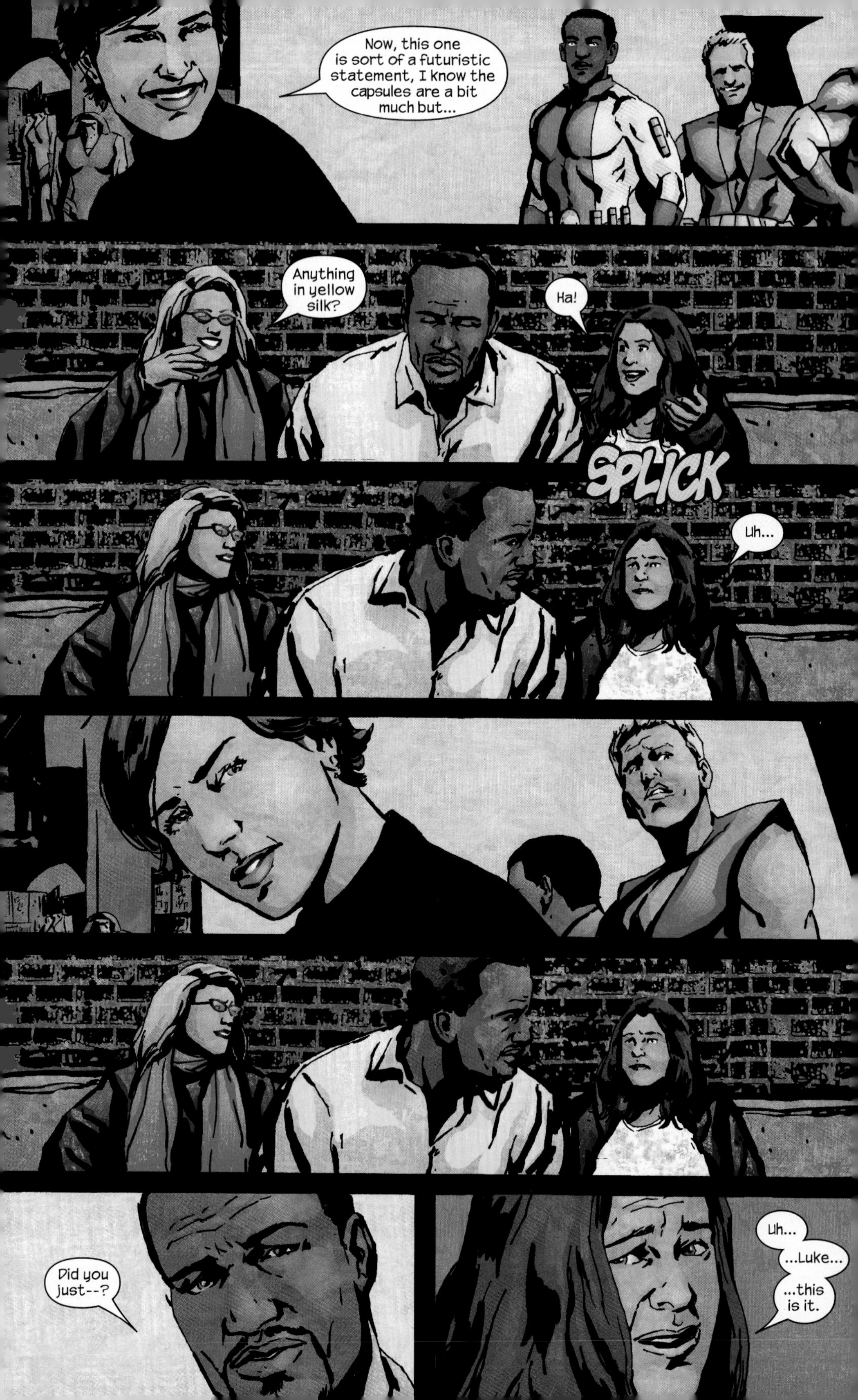
Now, this one is sort of a futuristic statement, I know the capsules are a bit much but...
Anything in yellow silk?
Ha!
SPLICK
Uh...
Did you just--?
Uh...
...Luke...
...this is it.

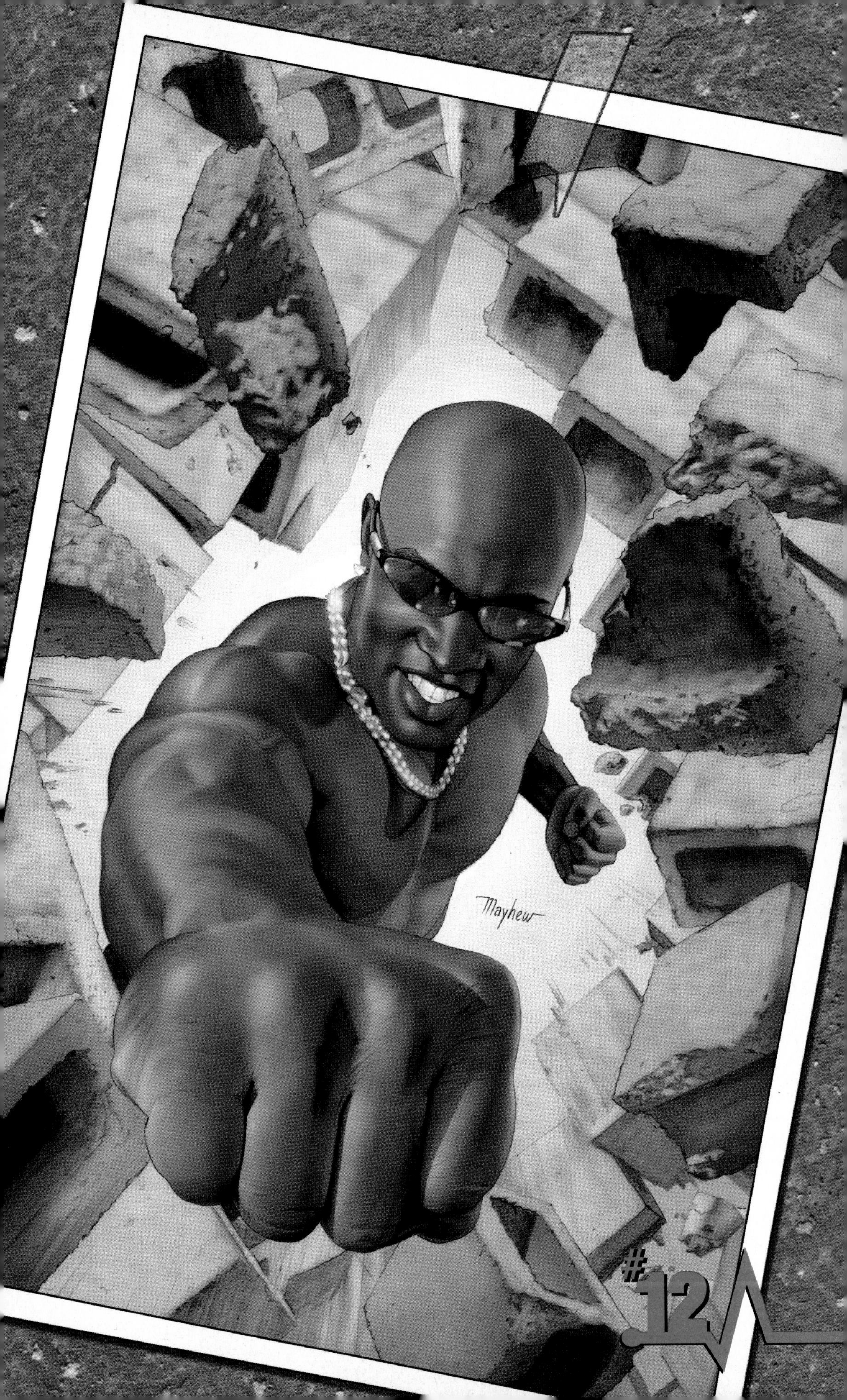
Mayhew
#12

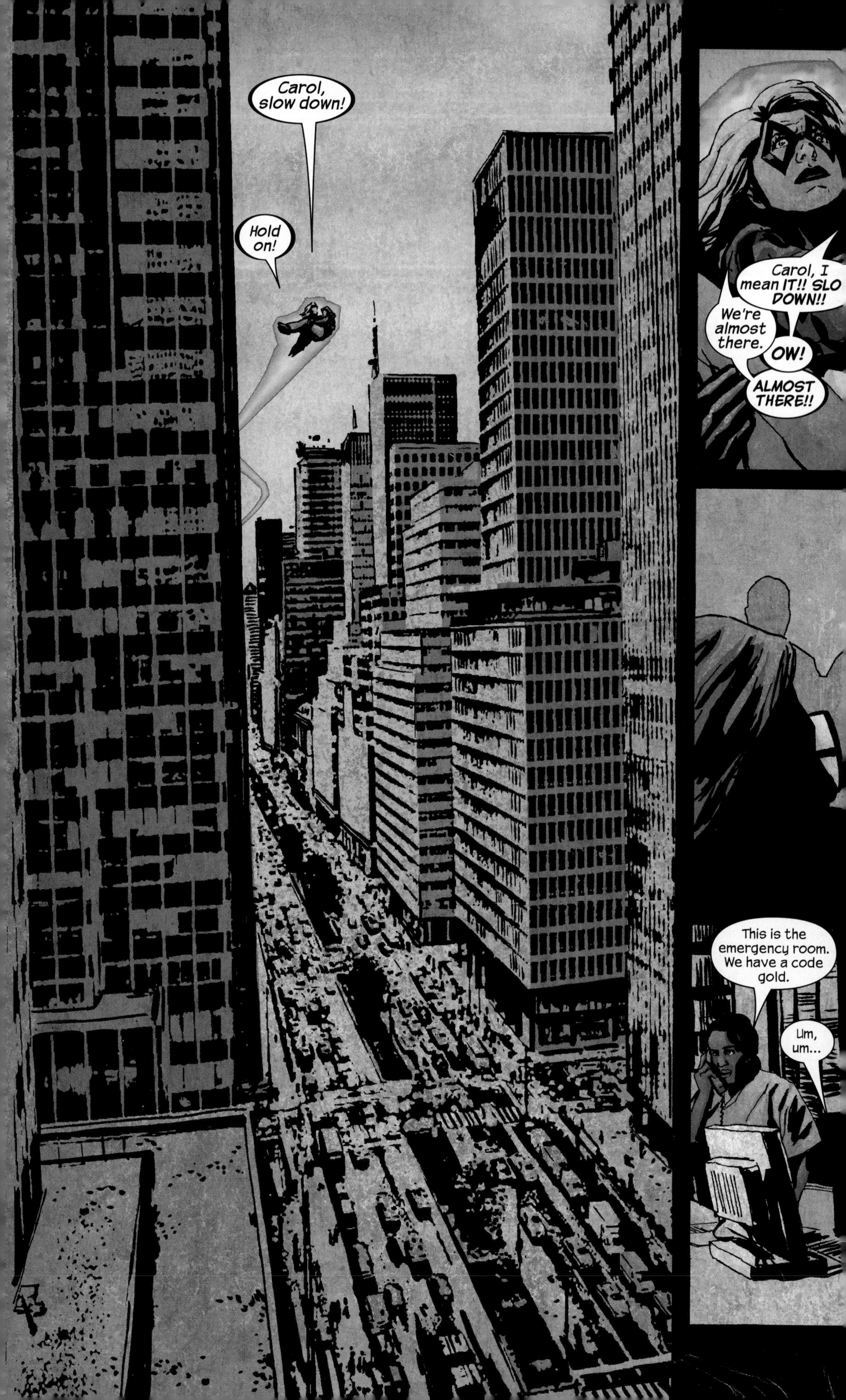
Carol, slow down!
Hold on!
Carol, I mean IT!! SLO DOWN!!
We're almost there.
OW!
ALMOST THERE!!
This is the emergency room. We have a code gold.
Um, um...

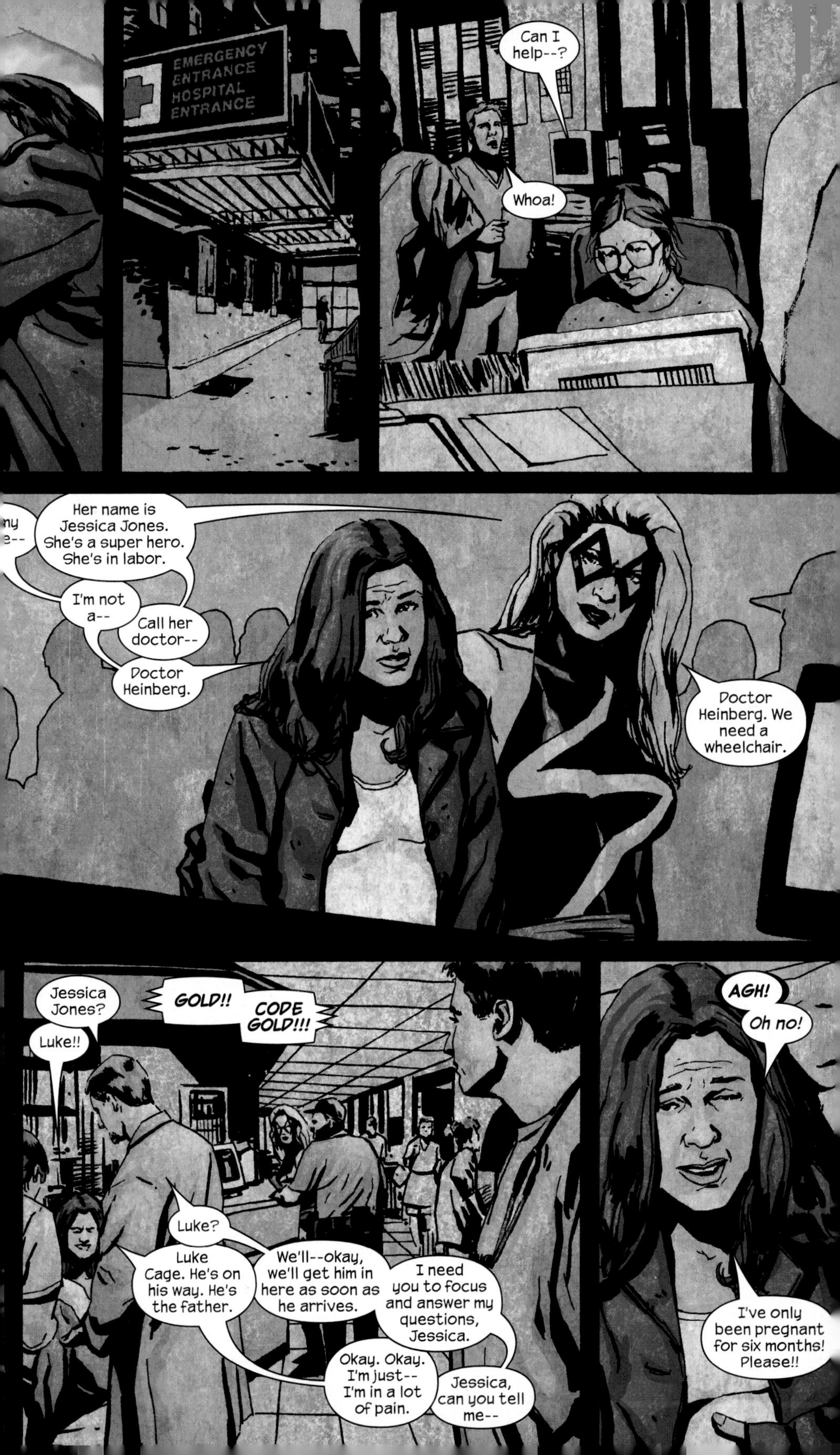
EMERGENCY ENTRANCE HOSPITAL ENTRANCE
Can I help--?
Whoa!
Her name is Jessica Jones. She's a super hero. She's in labor.
I'm not a--
Call her doctor--
Doctor Heinberg.
Doctor Heinberg. We need a wheelchair.
Jessica Jones?
Luke!!
GOLD!!
CODE GOLD!!!
Luke?
Luke Cage. He's on his way. He's the father.
We'll--okay, we'll get him in here as soon as he arrives.
I need you to focus and answer my questions, Jessica.
Okay. Okay. I'm just-- I'm in a lot of pain.
Jessica, can you tell me--
AGH!
Oh no!
I've only been pregnant for six months! Please!!

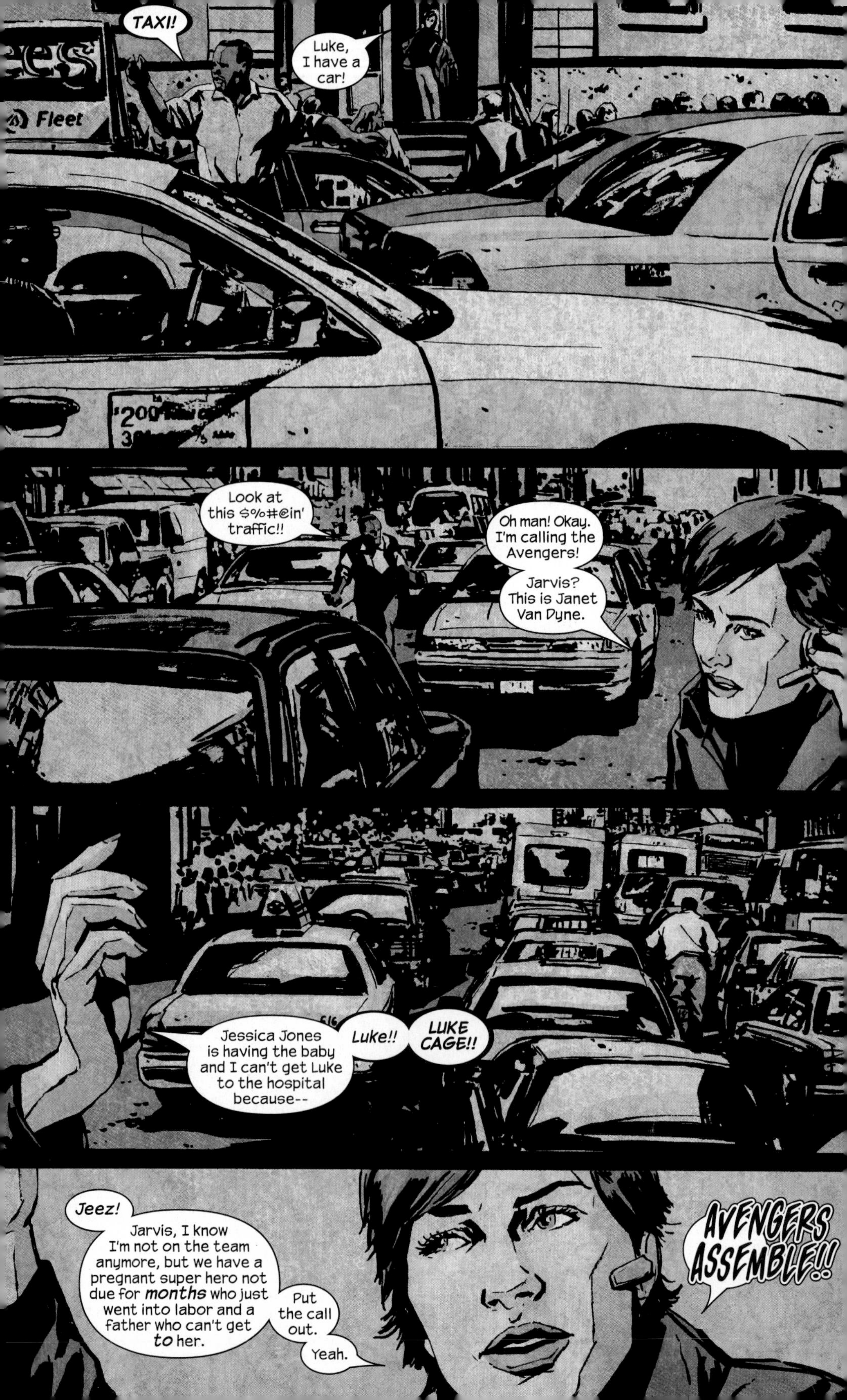

TAXI!
Luke, I have a car!
Fleet
Look at this $%#@in' traffic!!
Oh man! Okay. I'm calling the Avengers!
Jarvis? This is Janet Van Dyne.
Jessica Jones is having the baby and I can't get Luke to the hospital because--
Luke!!
LUKE CAGE!!
Jeez!
Jarvis, I know I'm not on the team anymore, but we have a pregnant super hero not due for *months* who just went into labor and a father who can't get *to* her.
Put the call out.
Yeah.
AVENGERS ASSEMBLE!!

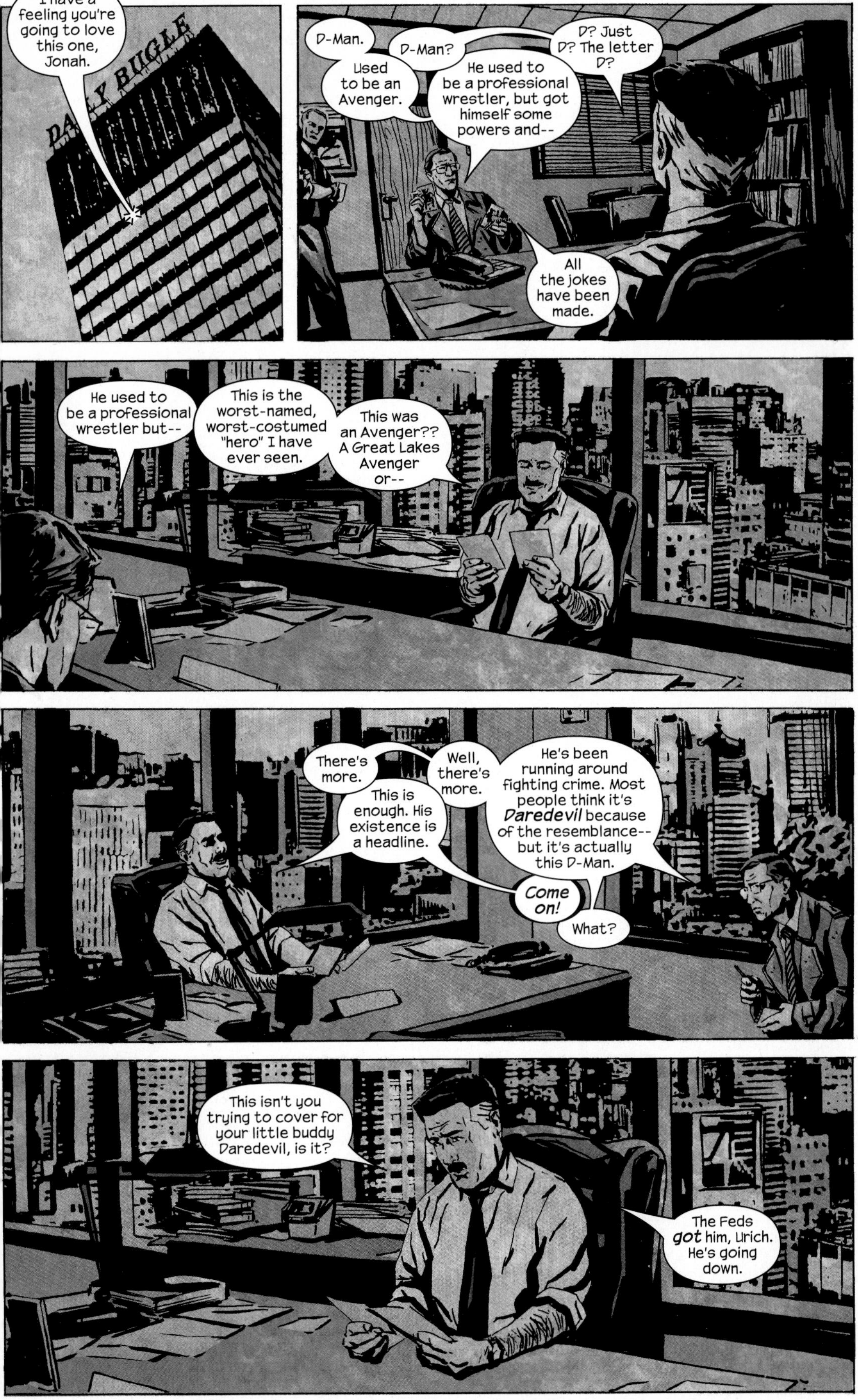

I have a feeling you're going to love this one, Jonah.
DAILY BUGLE
D-Man.
D-Man?
D? Just D? The letter D?
Used to be an Avenger.
He used to be a professional wrestler, but got himself some powers and--
All the jokes have been made.
He used to be a professional wrestler but--
This is the worst-named, worst-costumed "hero" I have ever seen.
This was an Avenger?? A Great Lakes Avenger or--
There's more.
Well, there's more.
He's been running around fighting crime. Most people think it's *Daredevil* because of the resemblance-- but it's actually this D-Man.
This is enough. His existence is a headline.
Come on!
What?
This isn't you trying to cover for your little buddy Daredevil, is it?
The Feds ***got*** him, Urich. He's going down.

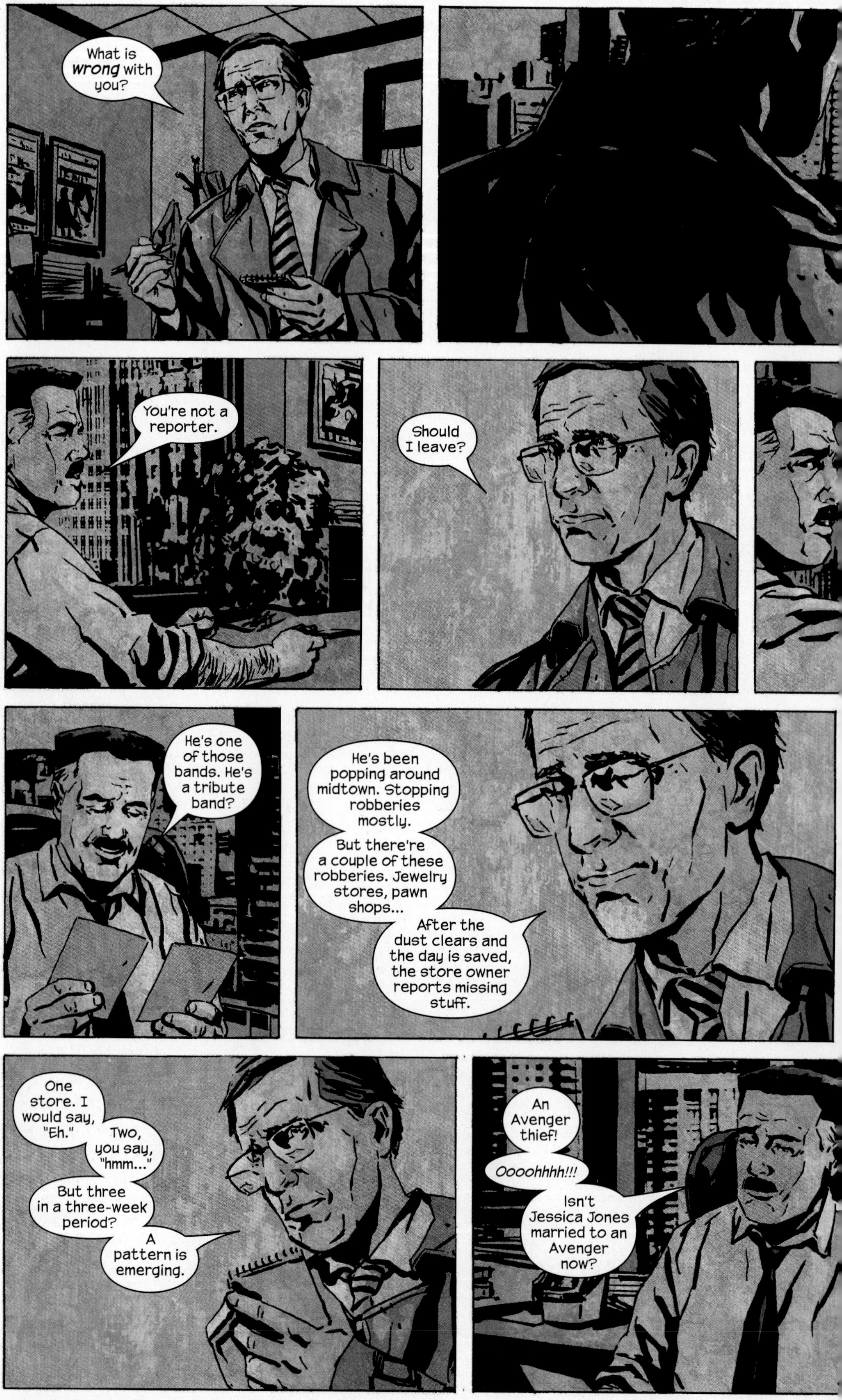
What is *wrong* with you?
You're not a reporter.
Should I leave?
He's one of those bands. He's a tribute band?
He's been popping around midtown. Stopping robberies mostly.
But there're a couple of these robberies. Jewelry stores, pawn shops...
After the dust clears and the day is saved, the store owner reports missing stuff.
One store. I would say, "Eh."
Two, you say, "hmm..."
But three in a three-week period?
A pattern is emerging.
An Avenger thief!
Oooohhhh!!!
Isn't Jessica Jones married to an Avenger now?

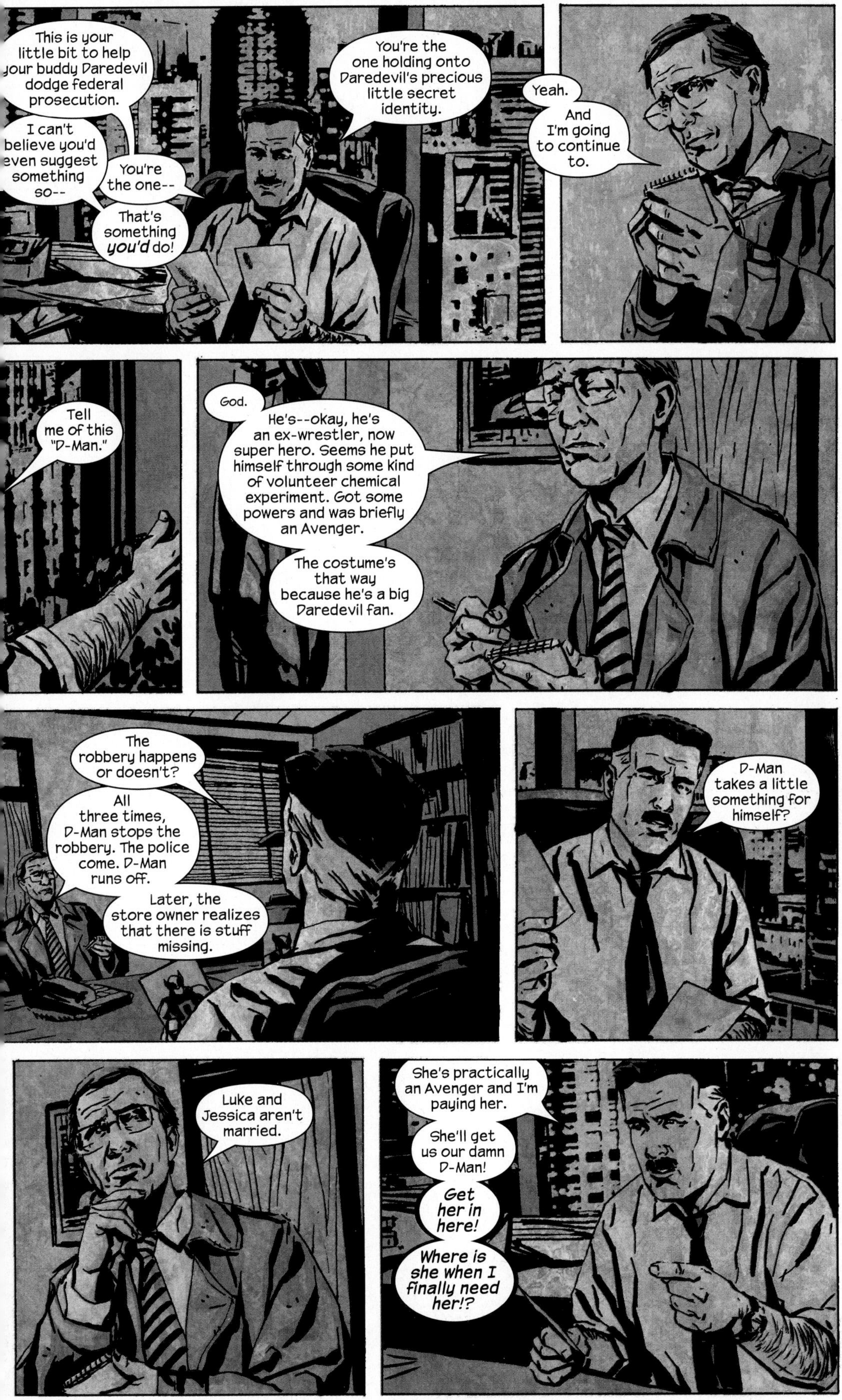

This is your little bit to help your buddy Daredevil dodge federal prosecution.
I can't believe you'd even suggest something so--
You're the one--
That's something *you'd* do!
You're the one holding onto Daredevil's precious little secret identity.
Yeah.
And I'm going to continue to.
Tell me of this "D-Man."
God.
He's--okay, he's an ex-wrestler, now super hero. Seems he put himself through some kind of volunteer chemical experiment. Got some powers and was briefly an Avenger.
The costume's that way because he's a big Daredevil fan.
The robbery happens or doesn't?
All three times, D-Man stops the robbery. The police come. D-Man runs off.
Later, the store owner realizes that there is stuff missing.
D-Man takes a little something for himself?
Luke and Jessica aren't married.
She's practically an Avenger and I'm paying her.
She'll get us our damn D-Man!
Get her in here!
Where is she when I finally need her!?

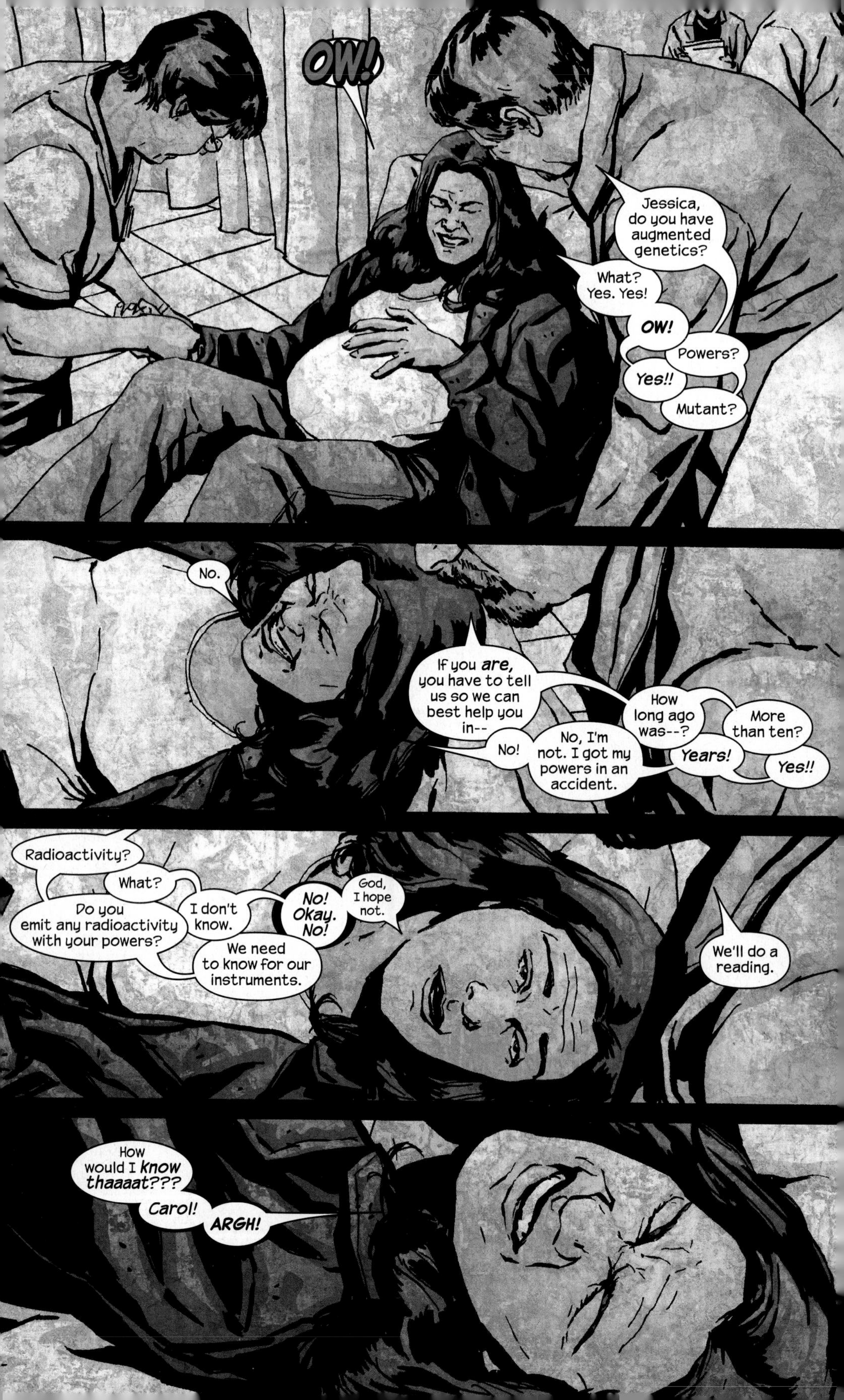
OW!
Jessica, do you have augmented genetics?
What? Yes. Yes!
OW!
Powers?
Yes!!
Mutant?
No.
If you are, you have to tell us so we can best help you in--
No!
No, I'm not. I got my powers in an accident.
How long ago was--?
More than ten?
Years!
Yes!!
Radioactivity?
What?
Do you emit any radioactivity with your powers?
I don't know.
We need to know for our instruments.
No! Okay. No!
God, I hope not.
We'll do a reading.
How would I know thaaaat???
Carol!
ARGH!

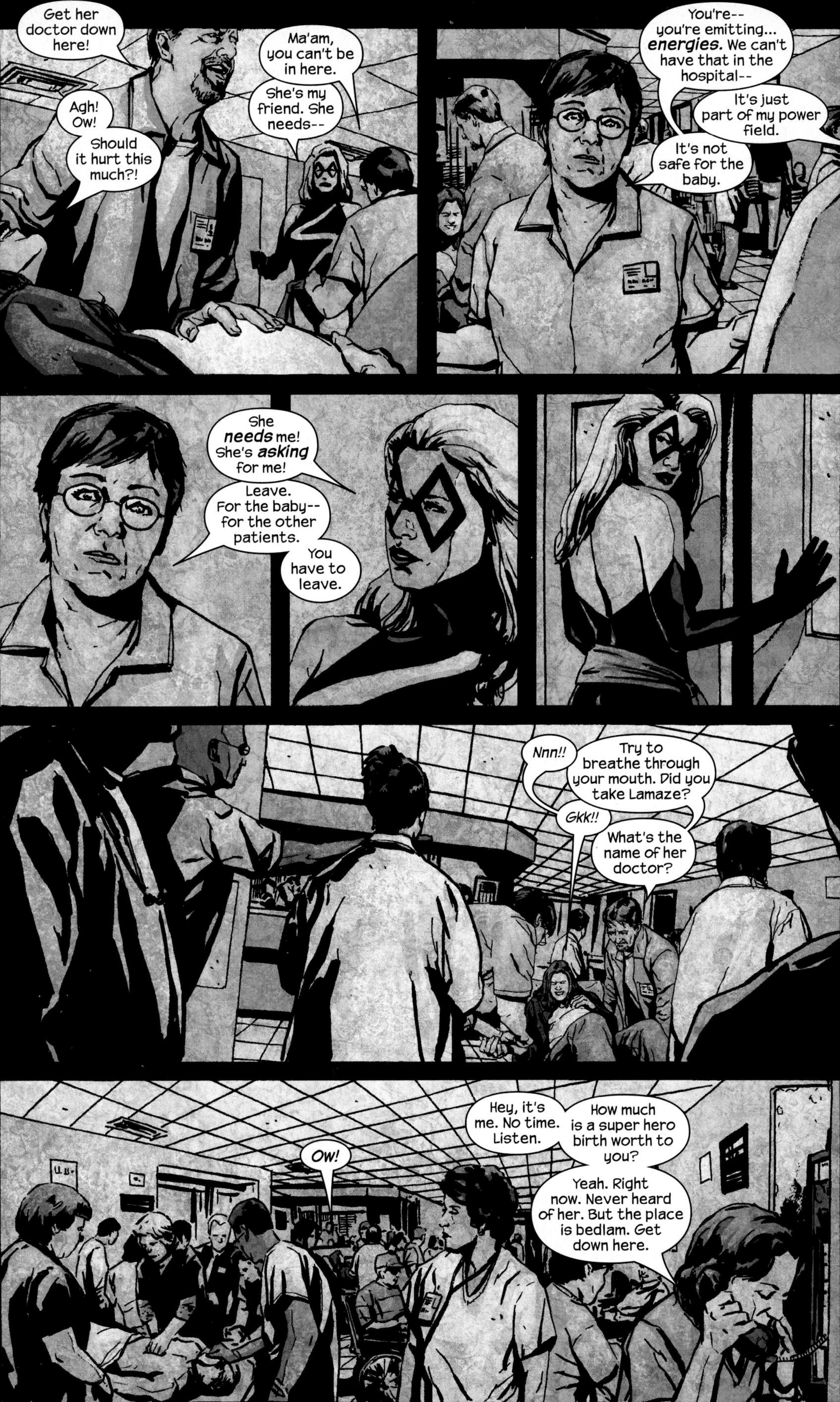
Get her doctor down here!
Ma'am, you can't be in here.
She's my friend. She needs--
Agh! Ow!
Should it hurt this much?!
You're-- you're emitting... **energies.** We can't have that in the hospital--
It's just part of my power field.
It's not safe for the baby.
She **needs** me! She's **asking** for me!
Leave. For the baby-- for the other patients.
You have to leave.
Nnn!!
Try to breathe through your mouth. Did you take Lamaze?
Gkk!!
What's the name of her doctor?
Ow!
Hey, it's me. No time. Listen.
How much is a super hero birth worth to you?
Yeah. Right now. Never heard of her. But the place is bedlam. Get down here.

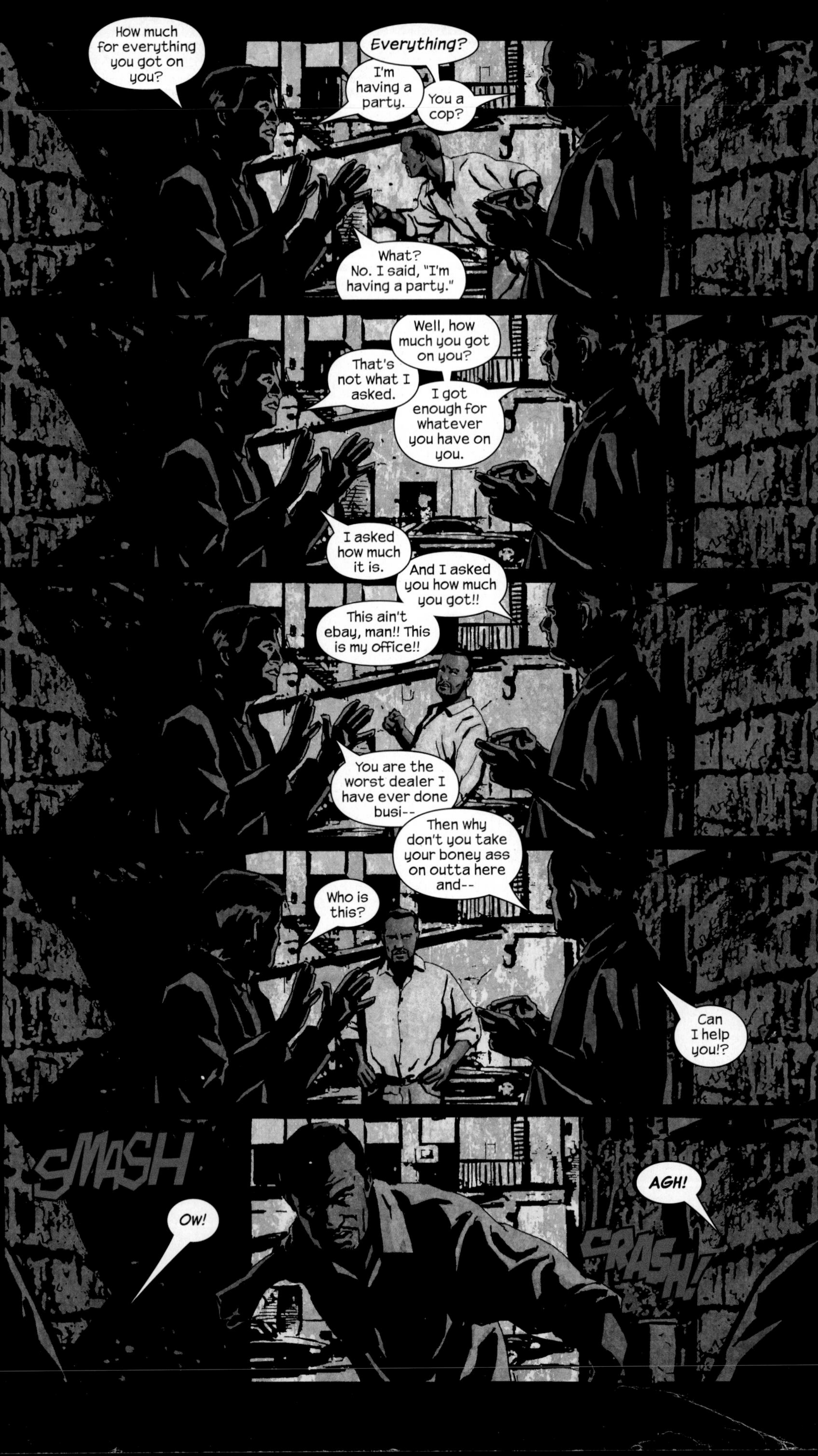
How much for everything you got on you?
Everything?
I'm having a party.
You a cop?
What? No. I said, "I'm having a party."
Well, how much you got on you?
That's not what I asked.
I got enough for whatever you have on you.
I asked how much it is.
And I asked you how much you got!!
This ain't ebay, man!! This is my office!!
You are the worst dealer I have ever done busi--
Then why don't you take your boney ass on outta here and--
Who is this?
Can I help you!?
SMASH
OW!
AGH!
CRASH!

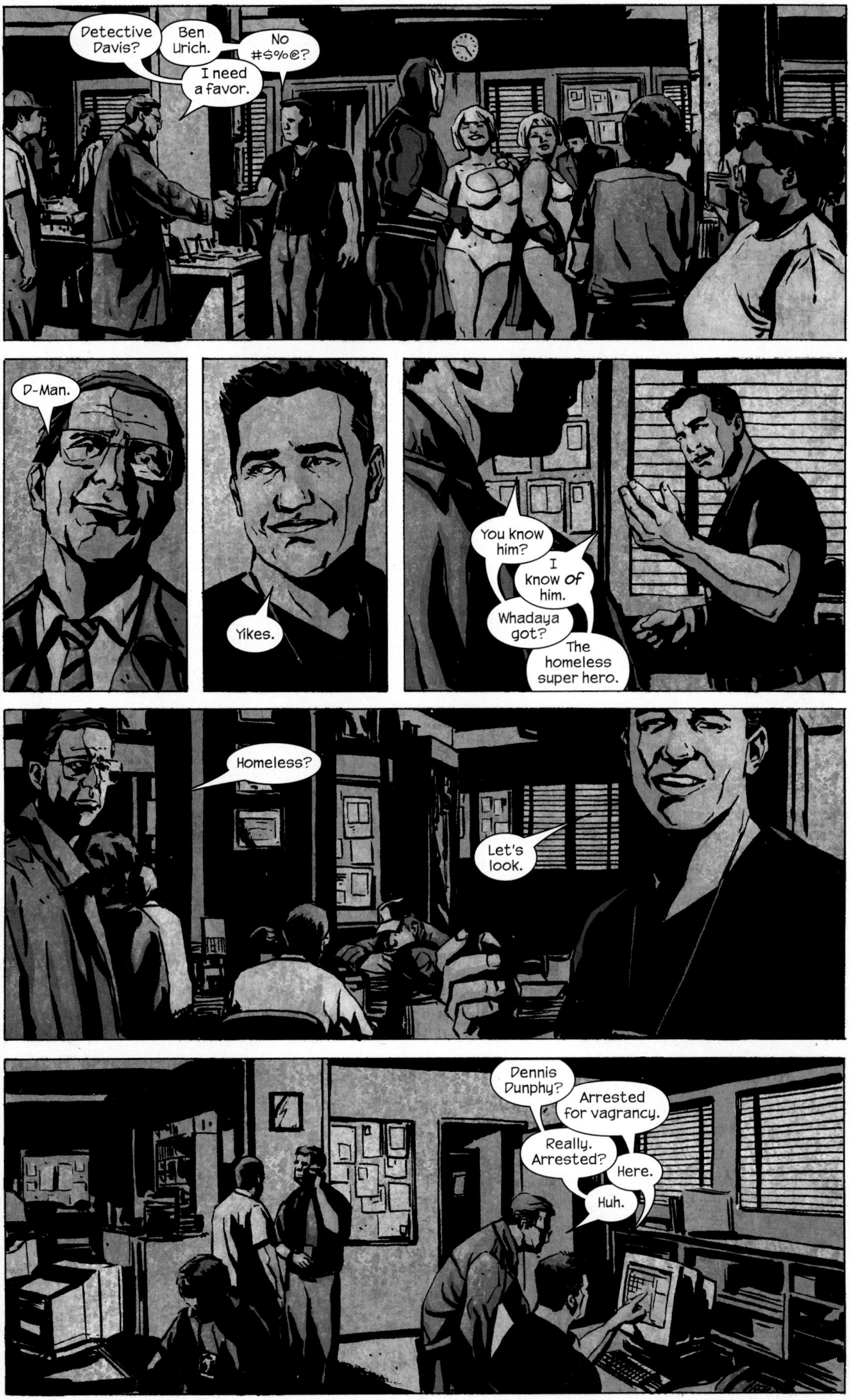
Detective Davis?
Ben Urich.
No #$%@?
I need a favor.
D-Man.
Yikes.
You know him?
I know *of* him.
Whadaya got?
The homeless super hero.
Homeless?
Let's look.
Dennis Dunphy?
Arrested for vagrancy.
Really. Arrested?
Here.
Huh.

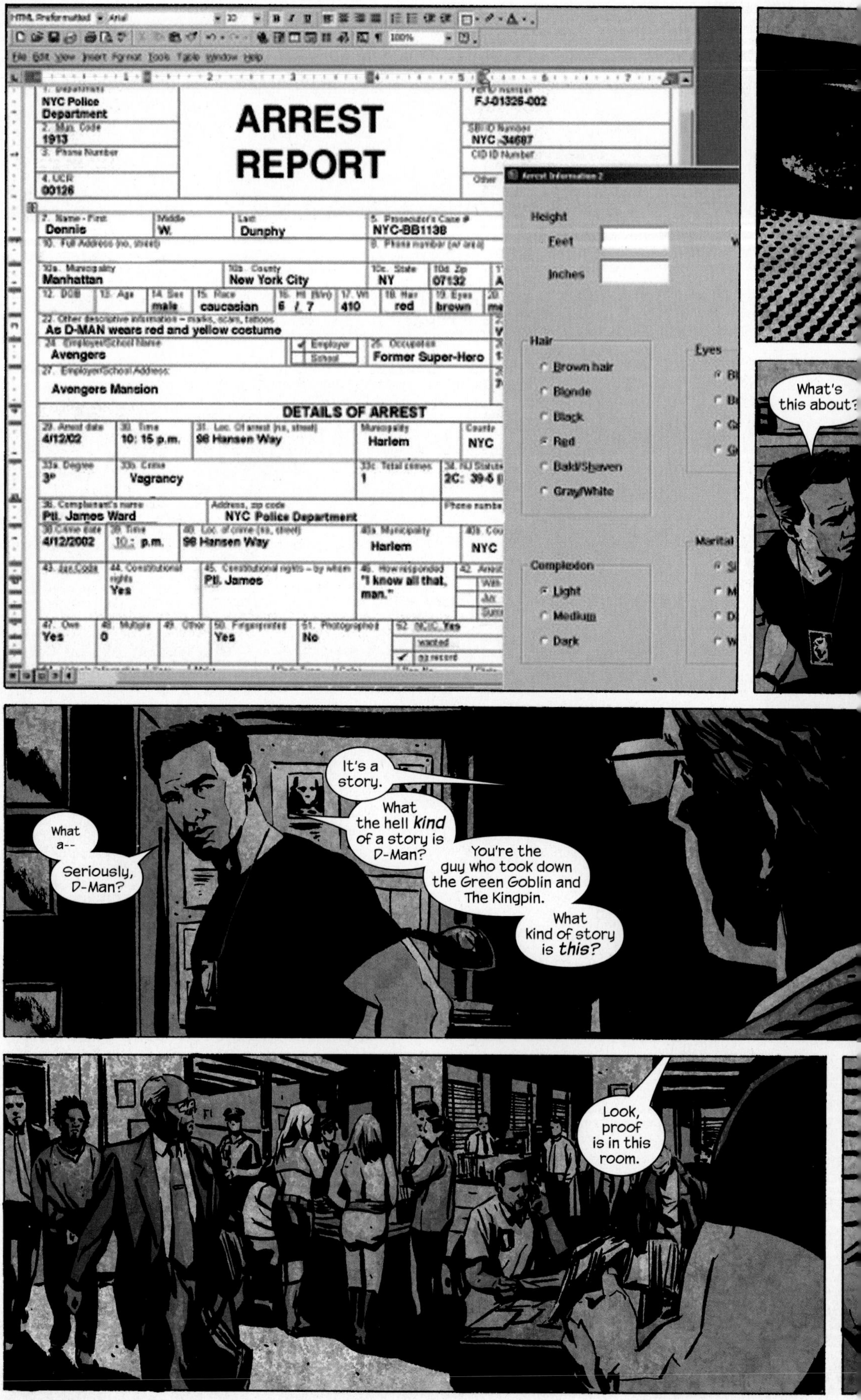
NYC Police Department
1913
00126
ARREST REPORT
FJ-01326-002
NYC 34687
Arrest Information 2
Height
Feet
Inches
Dennis
W.
Dunphy
NYC-BB1138
Manhattan
New York City
NY
07132
male
caucasian
6 / 7
410
red
brown
As D-MAN wears red and yellow costume
Avengers
Employer
School
Former Super-Hero
Avengers Mansion
DETAILS OF ARREST
4/12/02
10: 15 p.m.
98 Hansen Way
Harlem
NYC
3rd
Vagrancy
1
2C: 39-5
Ptl. James Ward
NYC Police Department
4/12/2002
10: p.m.
98 Hansen Way
Harlem
NYC
Yes
Ptl. James
"I know all that, man."
Yes
0
Yes
No
wanted
no record
Hair
Brown hair
Blonde
Black
Red
Bald/Shaven
Gray/White
Eyes
Complexion
Light
Medium
Dark
Marital
What's this about?
It's a story.
What the hell kind of a story is D-Man?
What a--
Seriously, D-Man?
You're the guy who took down the Green Goblin and The Kingpin.
What kind of story is this?
Look, proof is in this room.

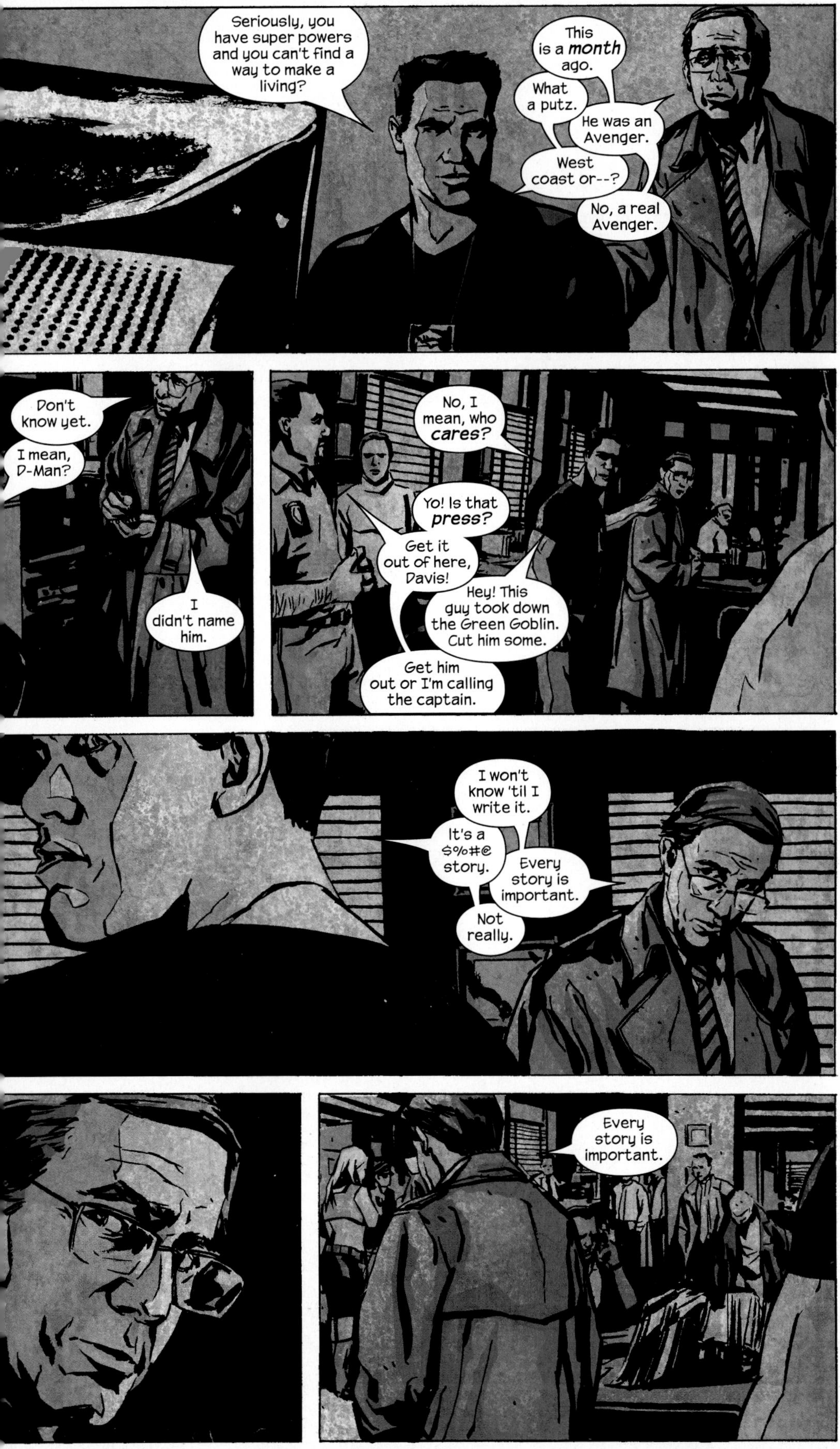

Seriously, you have super powers and you can't find a way to make a living?
This is a month ago.
What a putz.
He was an Avenger.
West coast or--?
No, a real Avenger.
Don't know yet.
I mean, D-Man?
I didn't name him.
No, I mean, who cares?
Yo! Is that press?
Get it out of here, Davis!
Hey! This guy took down the Green Goblin. Cut him some.
Get him out or I'm calling the captain.
I won't know 'til I write it.
It's a $%#@ story.
Every story is important.
Not really.
Every story is important.

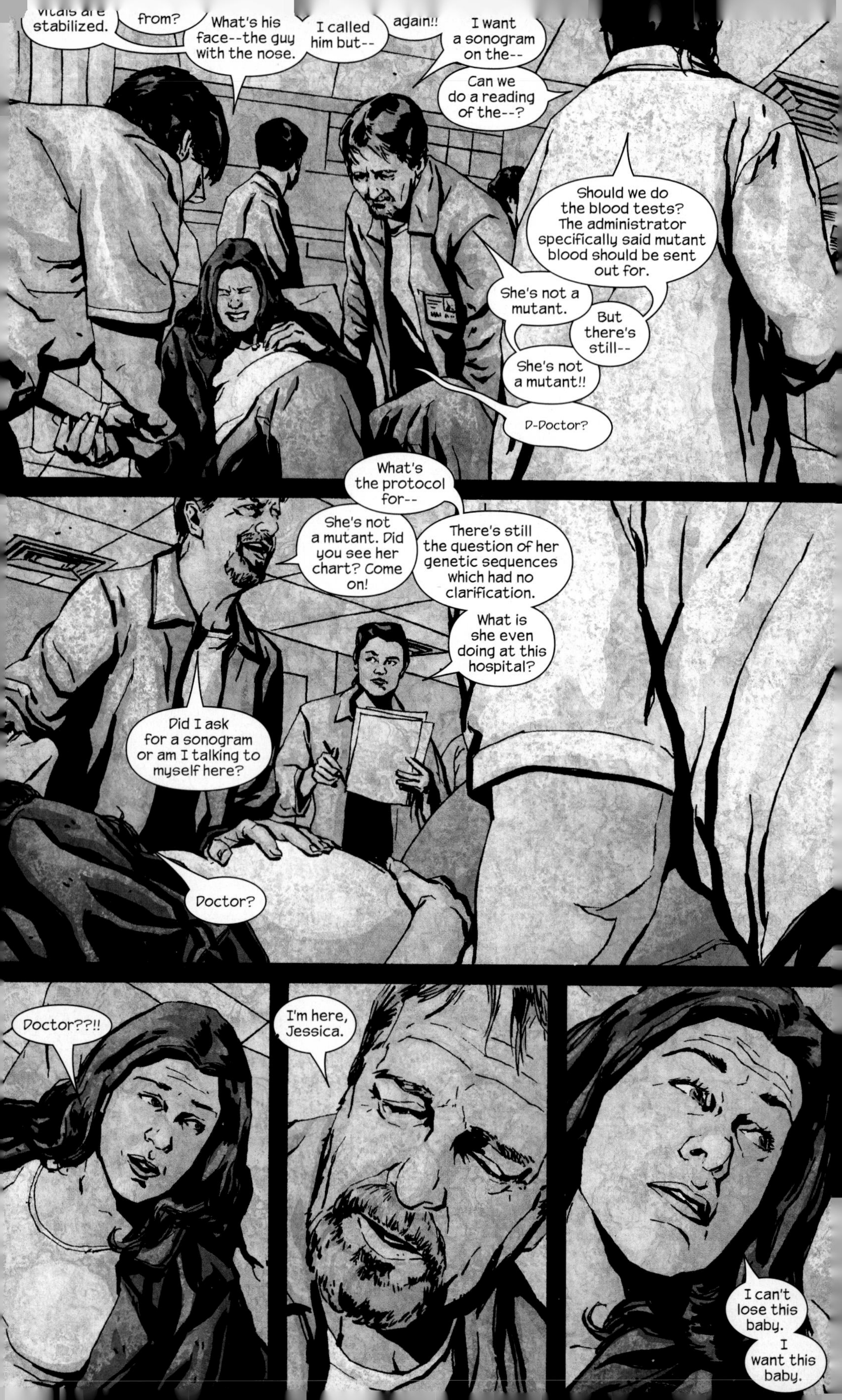
vitals are stabilized.
from?
What's his face--the guy with the nose.
I called him but--
again!!
I want a sonogram on the--
Can we do a reading of the--?
Should we do the blood tests? The administrator specifically said mutant blood should be sent out for.
She's not a mutant.
But there's still--
She's not a mutant!!
D-Doctor?
What's the protocol for--
She's not a mutant. Did you see her chart? Come on!
There's still the question of her genetic sequences which had no clarification.
What is she even doing at this hospital?
Did I ask for a sonogram or am I talking to myself here?
Doctor?
Doctor??!!
I'm here, Jessica.
I can't lose this baby.
I want this baby.

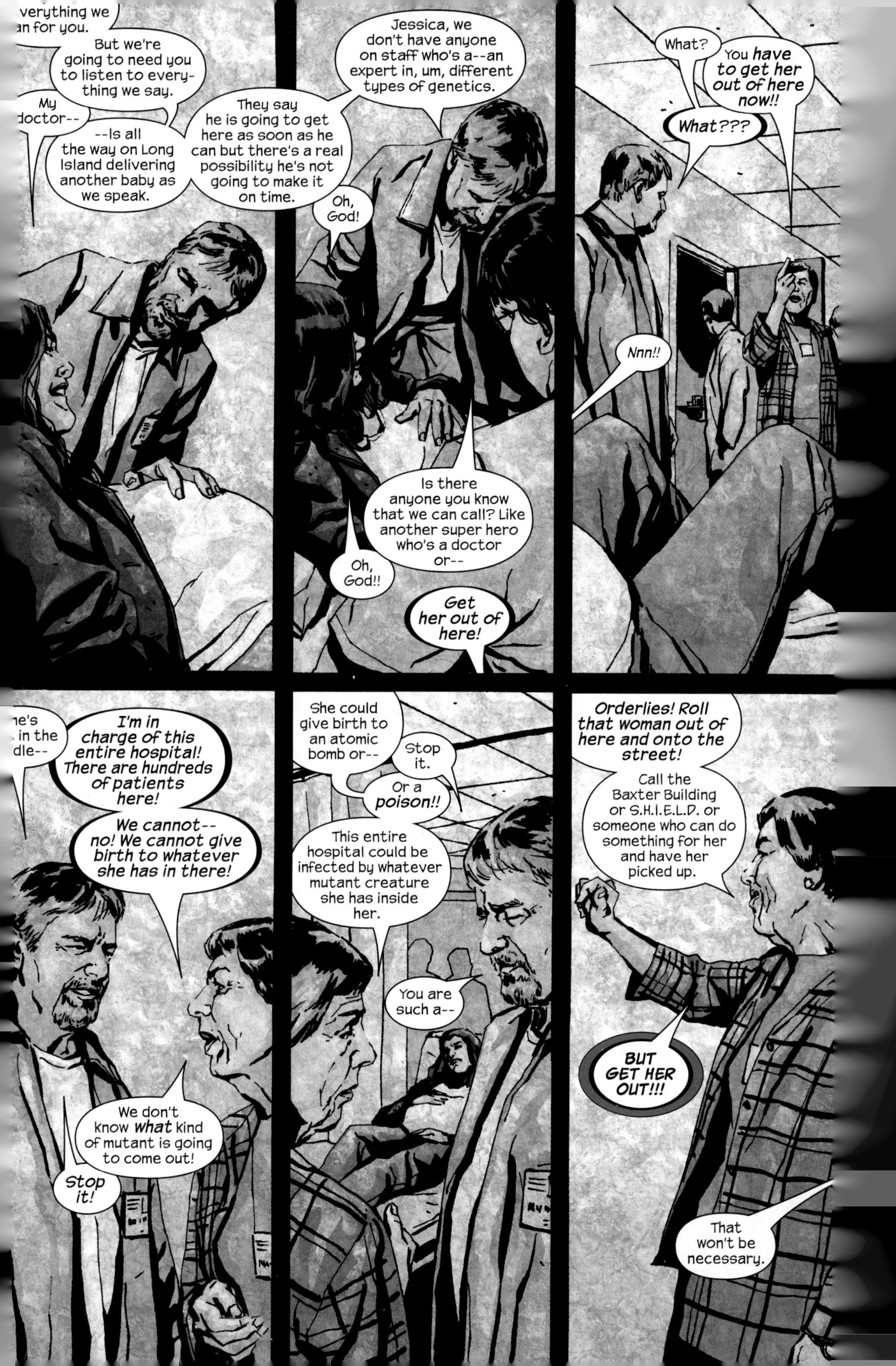

verything we
an for you.
But we're going to need you to listen to every-thing we say.
My doctor--
--Is all the way on Long Island delivering another baby as we speak.
They say he is going to get here as soon as he can but there's a real possibility he's not going to make it on time.
Jessica, we don't have anyone on staff who's a--an expert in, um, different types of genetics.
Oh, God!
Is there anyone you know that we can call? Like another super hero who's a doctor or--
Oh, God!!
Get her out of here!
What?
You have to get her out of here now!!
What???
Nnn!!
in the
dle--
I'm in charge of this entire hospital! There are hundreds of patients here!
We cannot-- no! We cannot give birth to whatever she has in there!
We don't know what kind of mutant is going to come out!
Stop it!
She could give birth to an atomic bomb or--
Stop it.
Or a poison!!
This entire hospital could be infected by whatever mutant creature she has inside her.
You are such a--
Orderlies! Roll that woman out of here and onto the street!
Call the Baxter Building or S.H.I.E.L.D. or someone who can do something for her and have her picked up.
BUT GET HER OUT!!!
That won't be necessary.

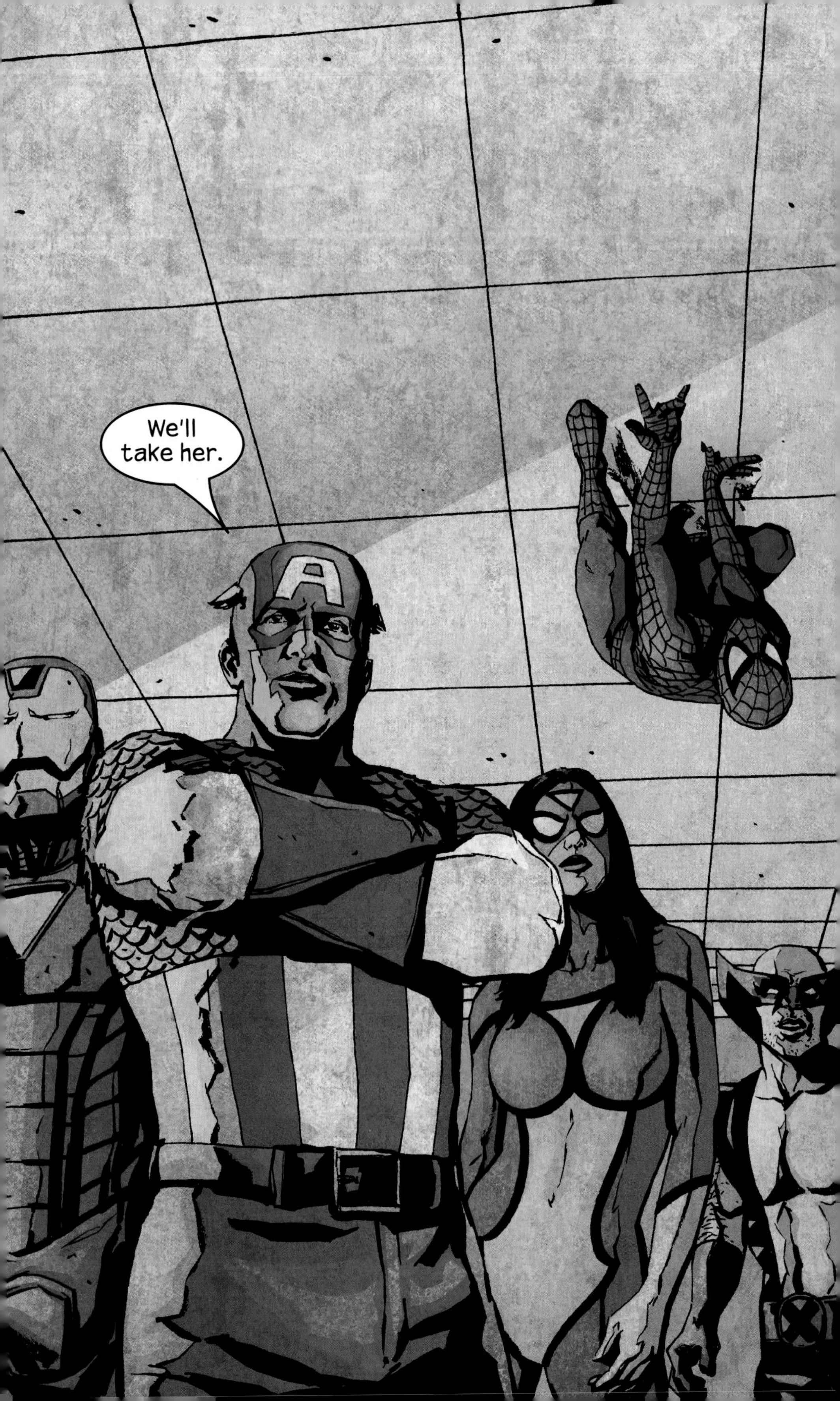
We'll take her.

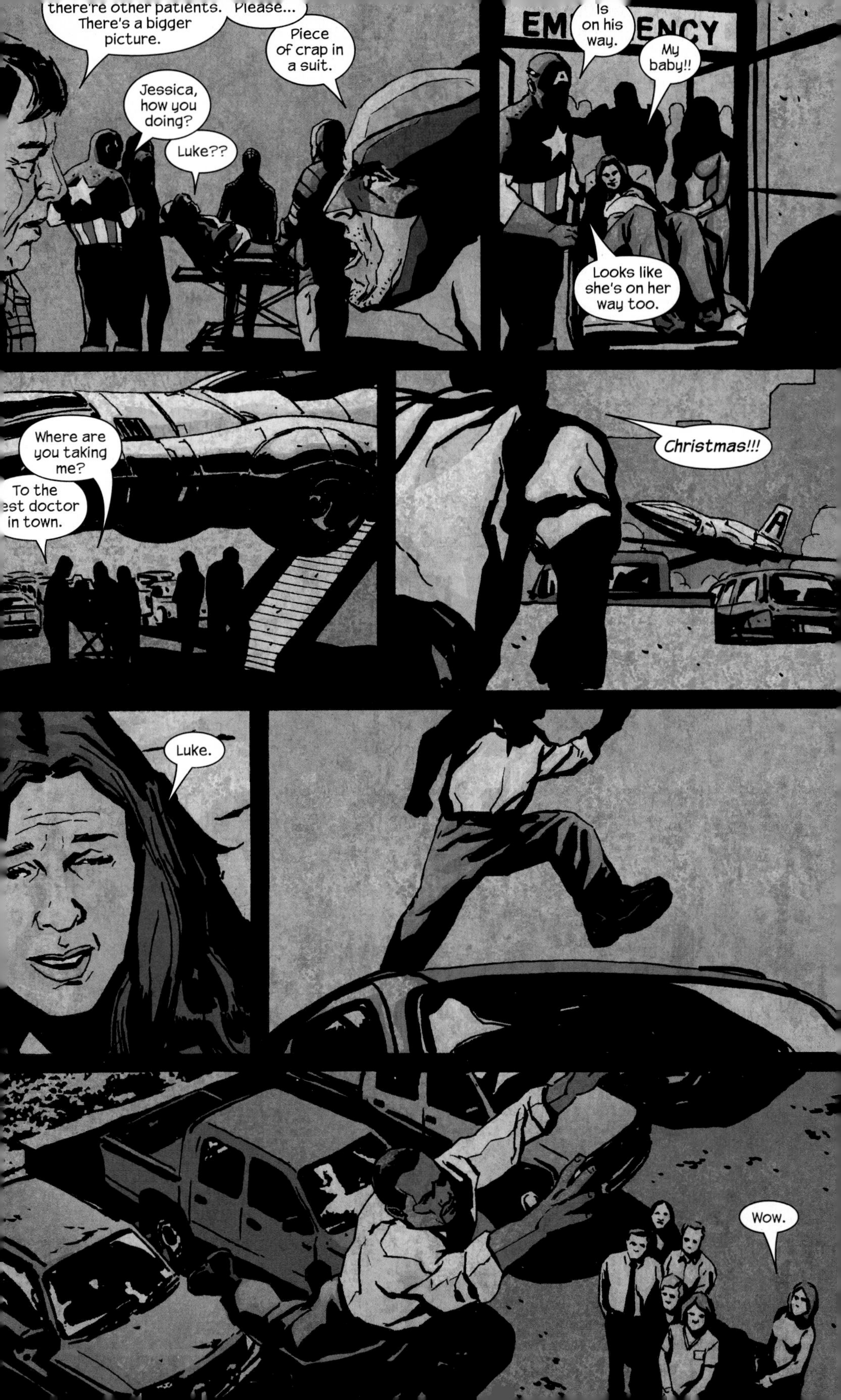
there're other patients. There's a bigger picture.
Please...
Piece of crap in a suit.
Jessica, how you doing?
Luke??
Is on his way.
My baby!!
Looks like she's on her way too.
Where are you taking me?
To the est doctor in town.
Christmas!!!
Luke.
Wow.

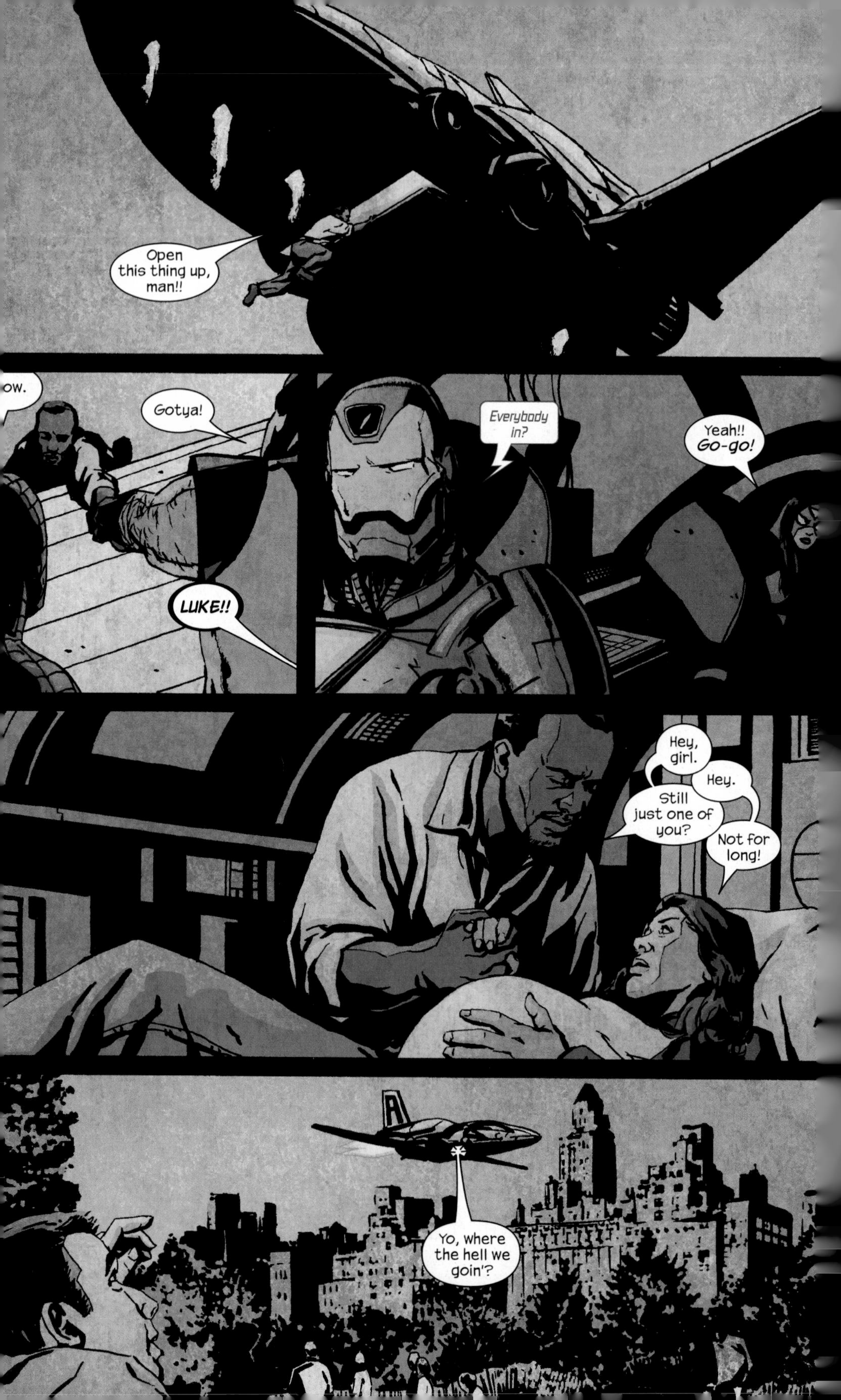

Open this thing up, man!!
ow.
Gotya!
LUKE!!
Everybody in?
Yeah!! Go-go!
Hey, girl.
Hey.
Still just one of you?
Not for long!
Yo, where the hell we goin'?

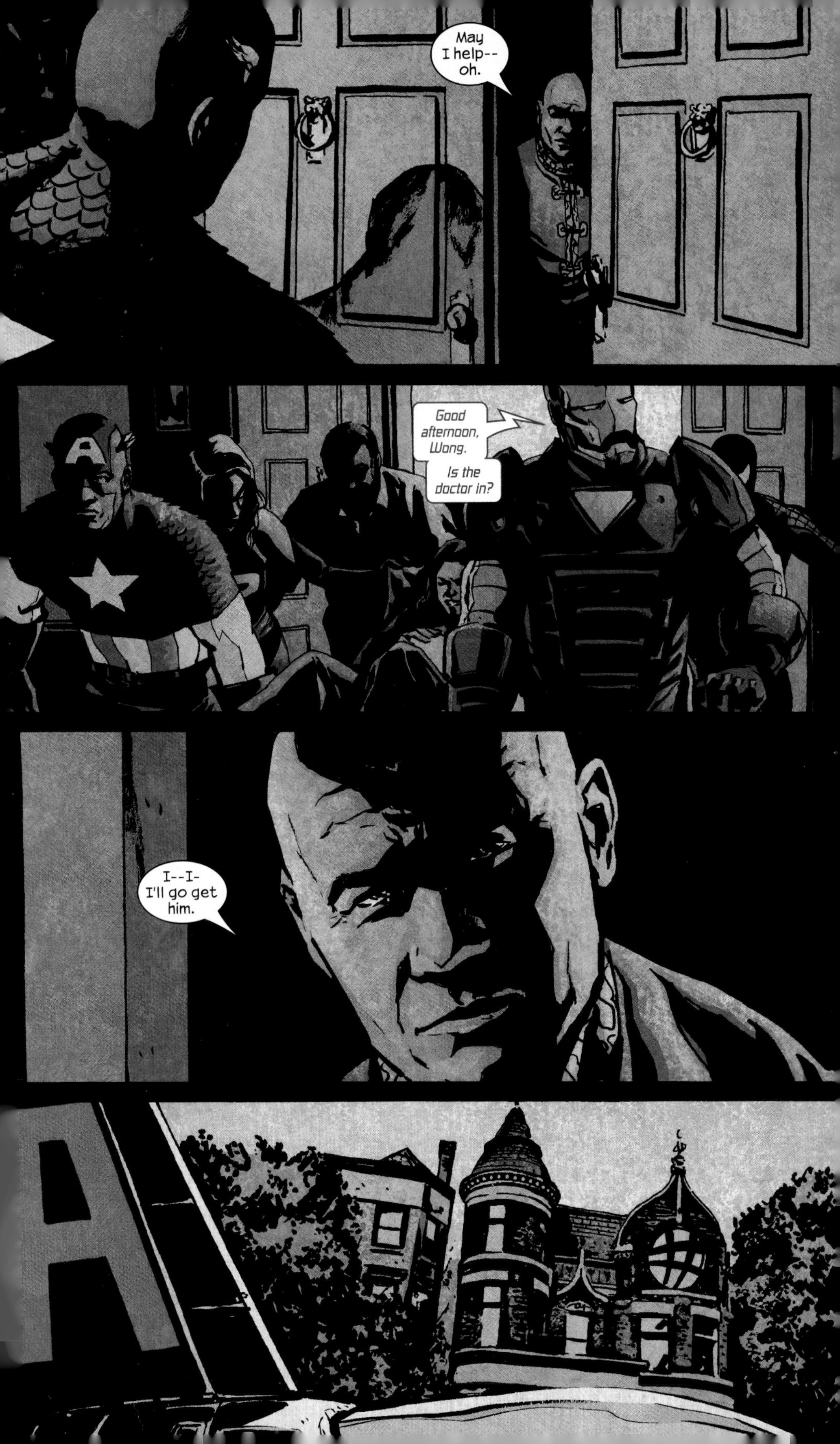
May I help-- oh.
Good afternoon, Wong.
Is the doctor in?
I--I- I'll go get him.

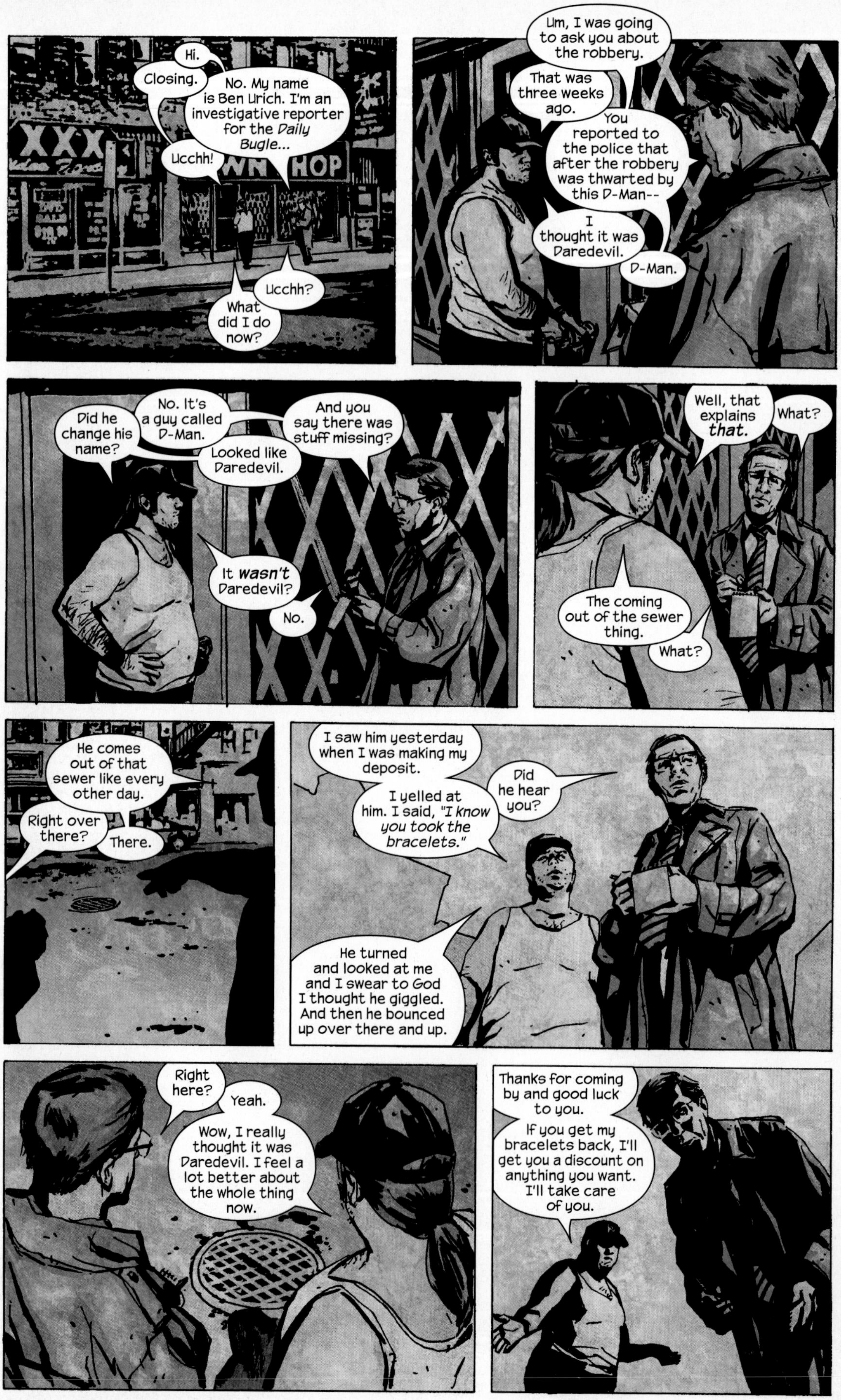
Hi.
Closing.
No. My name is Ben Urich. I'm an investigative reporter for the *Daily Bugle*...
Ucchh!
Ucchh?
What did I do now?
Um, I was going to ask you about the robbery.
That was three weeks ago.
You reported to the police that after the robbery was thwarted by this D-Man--
I thought it was Daredevil.
D-Man.
Did he change his name?
No. It's a guy called D-Man.
Looked like Daredevil.
And you say there was stuff missing?
It *wasn't* Daredevil?
No.
Well, that explains *that.*
What?
The coming out of the sewer thing.
What?
He comes out of that sewer like every other day.
Right over there?
There.
I saw him yesterday when I was making my deposit.
I yelled at him. I said, *"I know you took the bracelets."*
Did he hear you?
He turned and looked at me and I swear to God I thought he giggled. And then he bounced up over there and up.
Right here?
Yeah.
Wow, I really thought it was Daredevil. I feel a lot better about the whole thing now.
Thanks for coming by and good luck to you.
If you get my bracelets back, I'll get you a discount on anything you want. I'll take care of you.

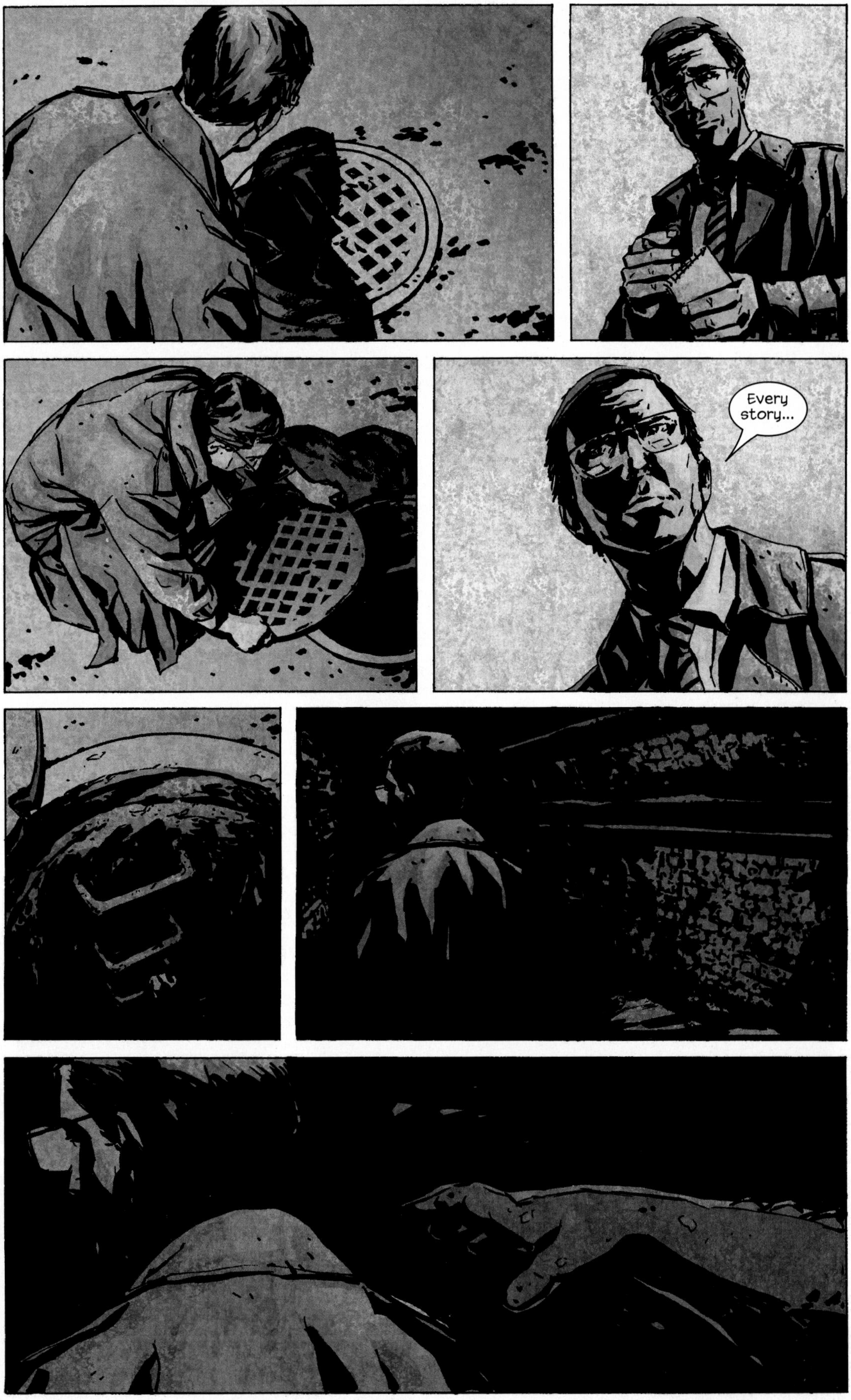
Every story...

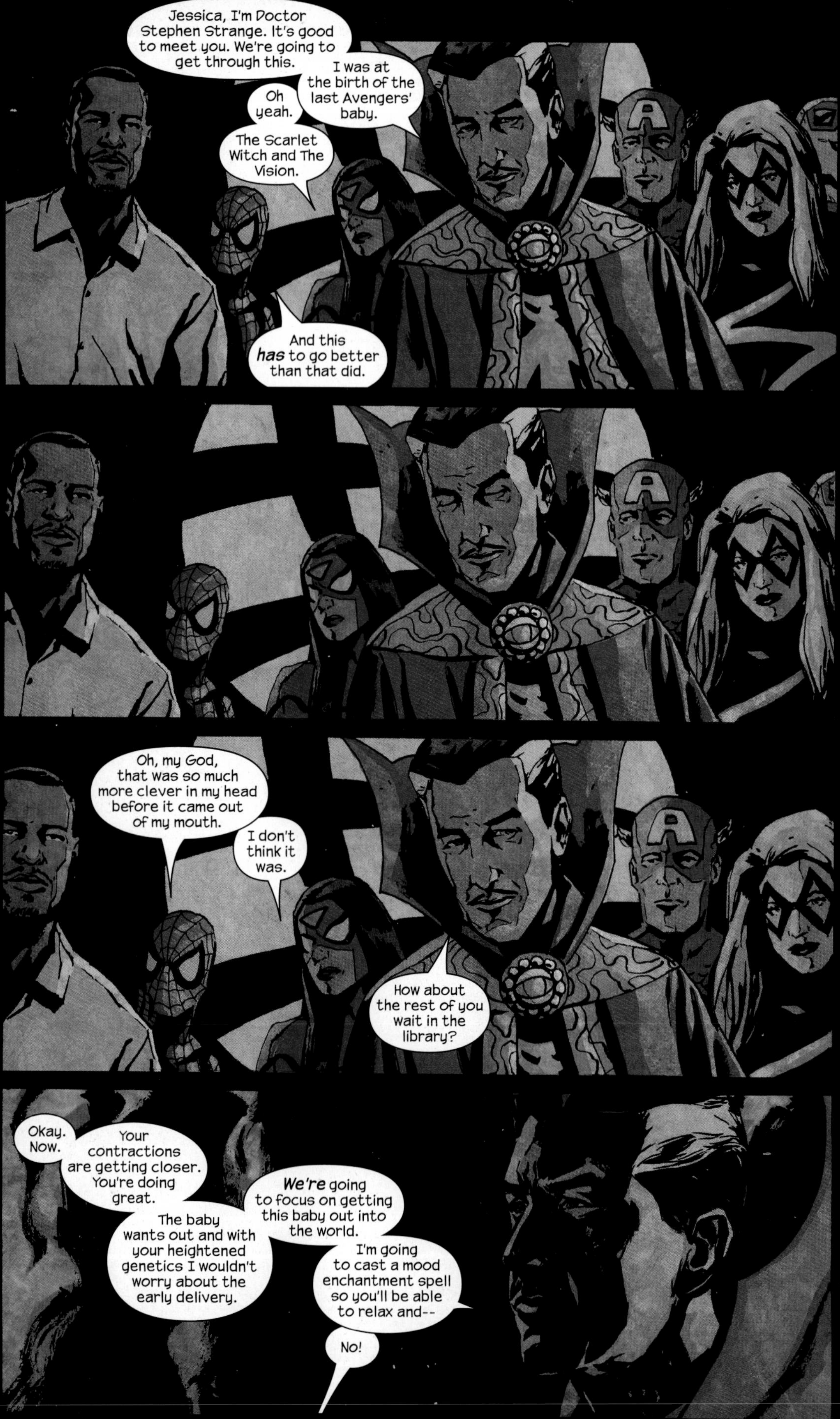
Jessica, I'm Doctor Stephen Strange. It's good to meet you. We're going to get through this.
I was at the birth of the last Avengers' baby.
Oh yeah.
The Scarlet Witch and The Vision.
And this *has* to go better than that did.
Oh, my God, that was so much more clever in my head before it came out of my mouth.
I don't think it was.
How about the rest of you wait in the library?
Okay. Now.
Your contractions are getting closer. You're doing great.
The baby wants out and with your heightened genetics I wouldn't worry about the early delivery.
We're going to focus on getting this baby out into the world.
I'm going to cast a mood enchantment spell so you'll be able to relax and--
No!

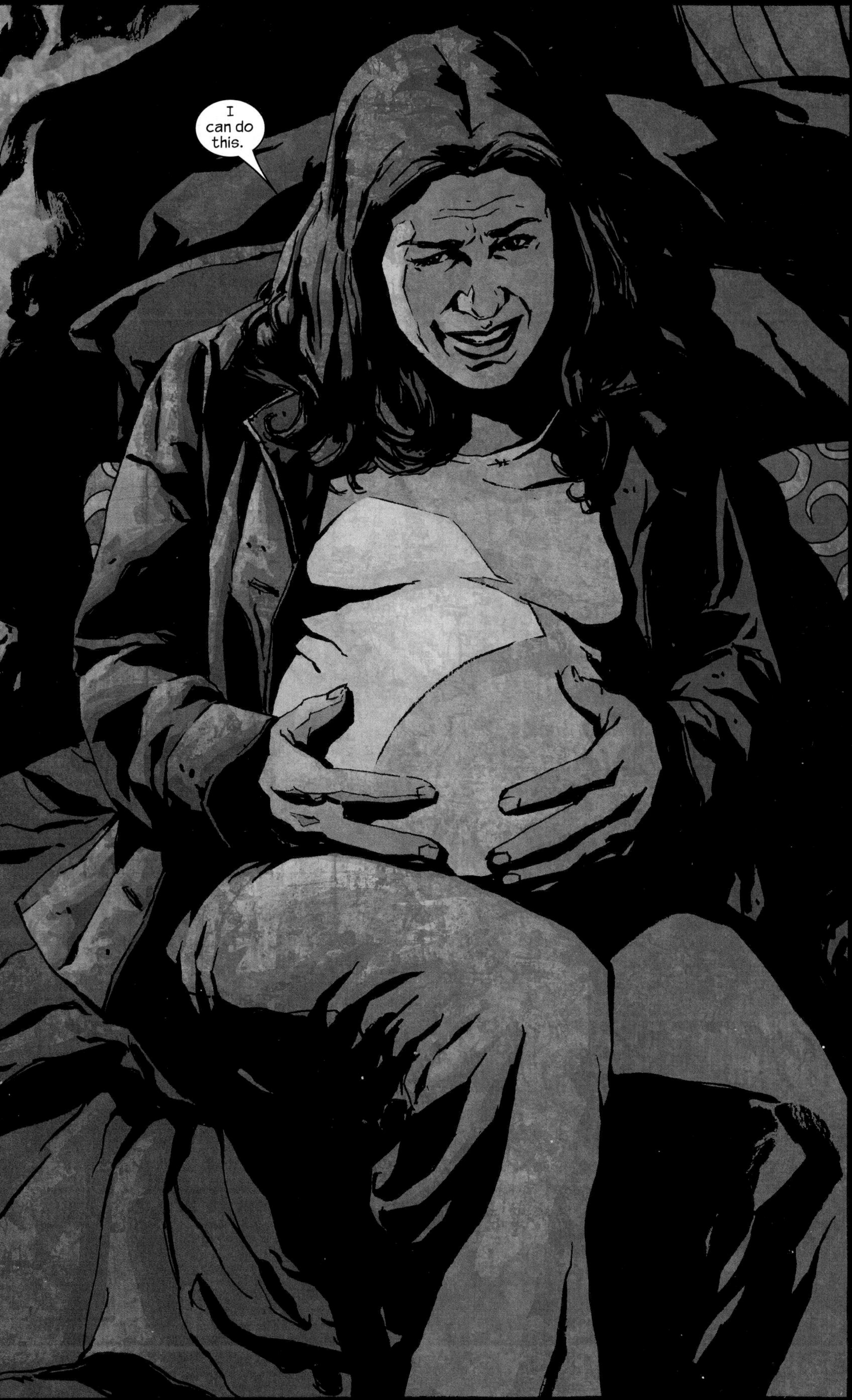
I can do this.

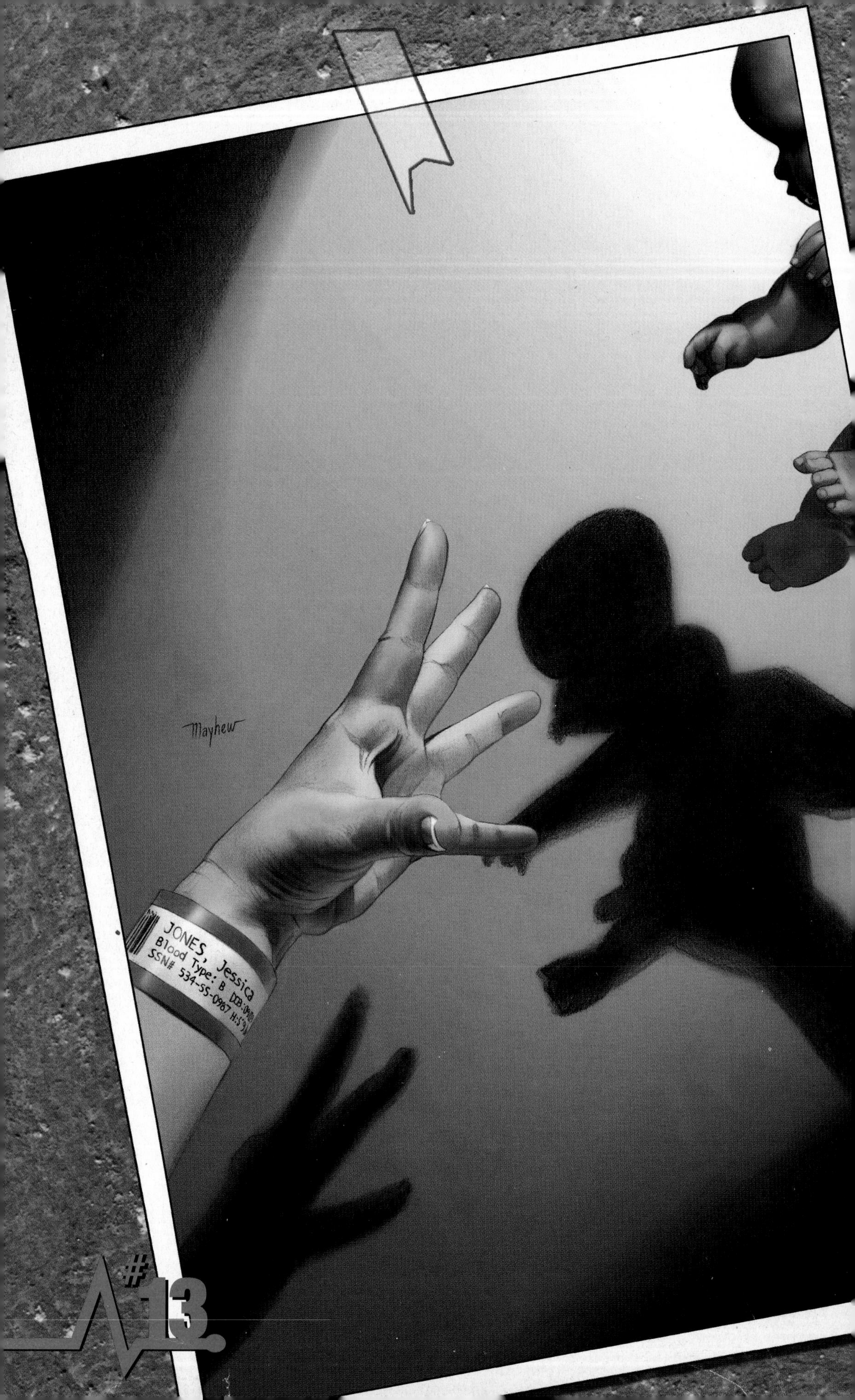
Mayhew
JONES, Jessica
Blood Type: B
SSN# 534-55-0987
#13

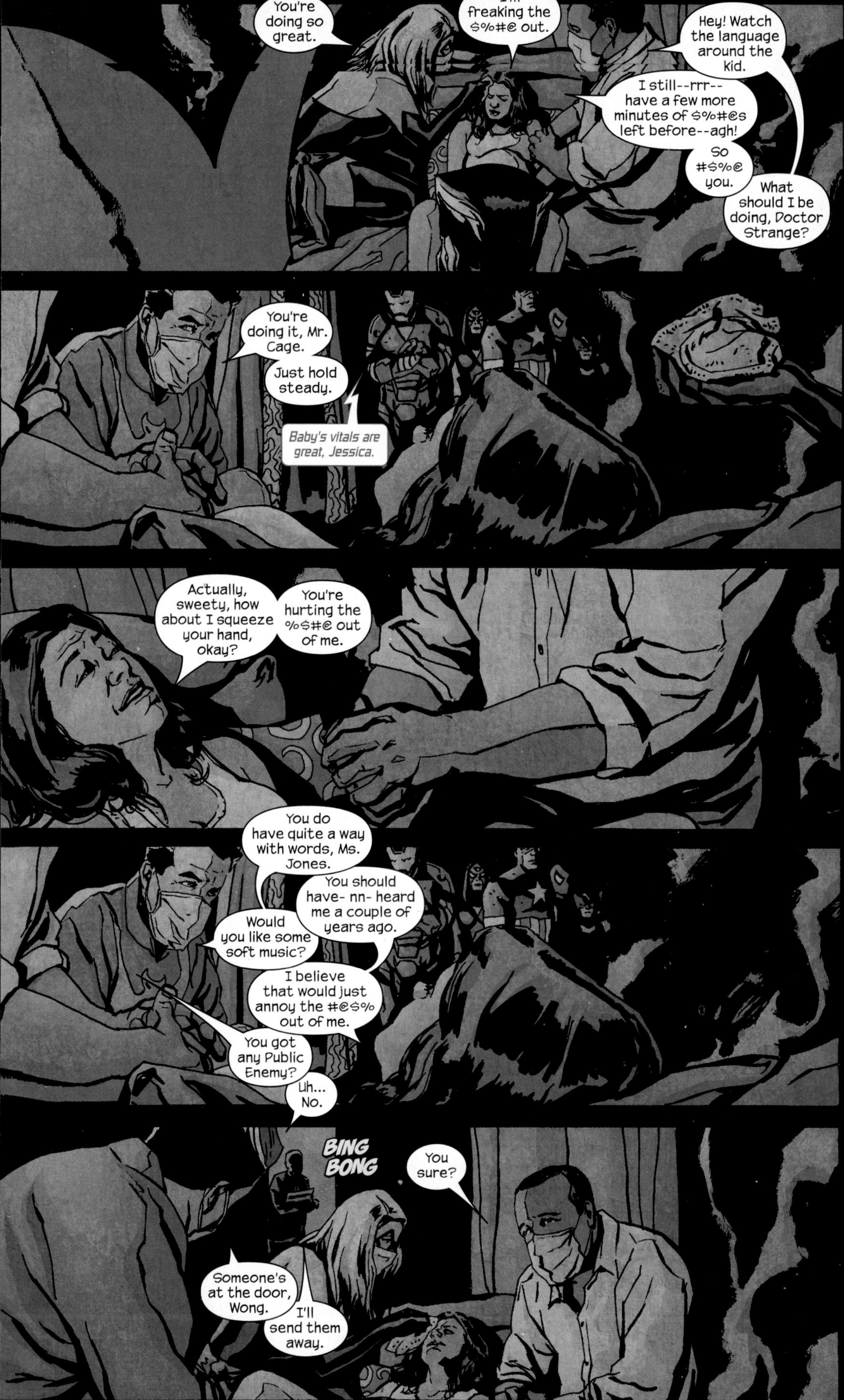
You're doing so great.
I'm freaking the $%#@ out.
Hey! Watch the language around the kid.
I still--rrr--have a few more minutes of $%#@s left before--agh!
So #$%@ you.
What should I be doing, Doctor Strange?
You're doing it, Mr. Cage.
Just hold steady.
Baby's vitals are great, Jessica.
Actually, sweety, how about I squeeze your hand, okay?
You're hurting the %$#@ out of me.
You do have quite a way with words, Ms. Jones.
You should have- nn- heard me a couple of years ago.
Would you like some soft music?
I believe that would just annoy the #@$% out of me.
You got any Public Enemy?
Uh... No.
BING BONG
You sure?
Someone's at the door, Wong.
I'll send them away.

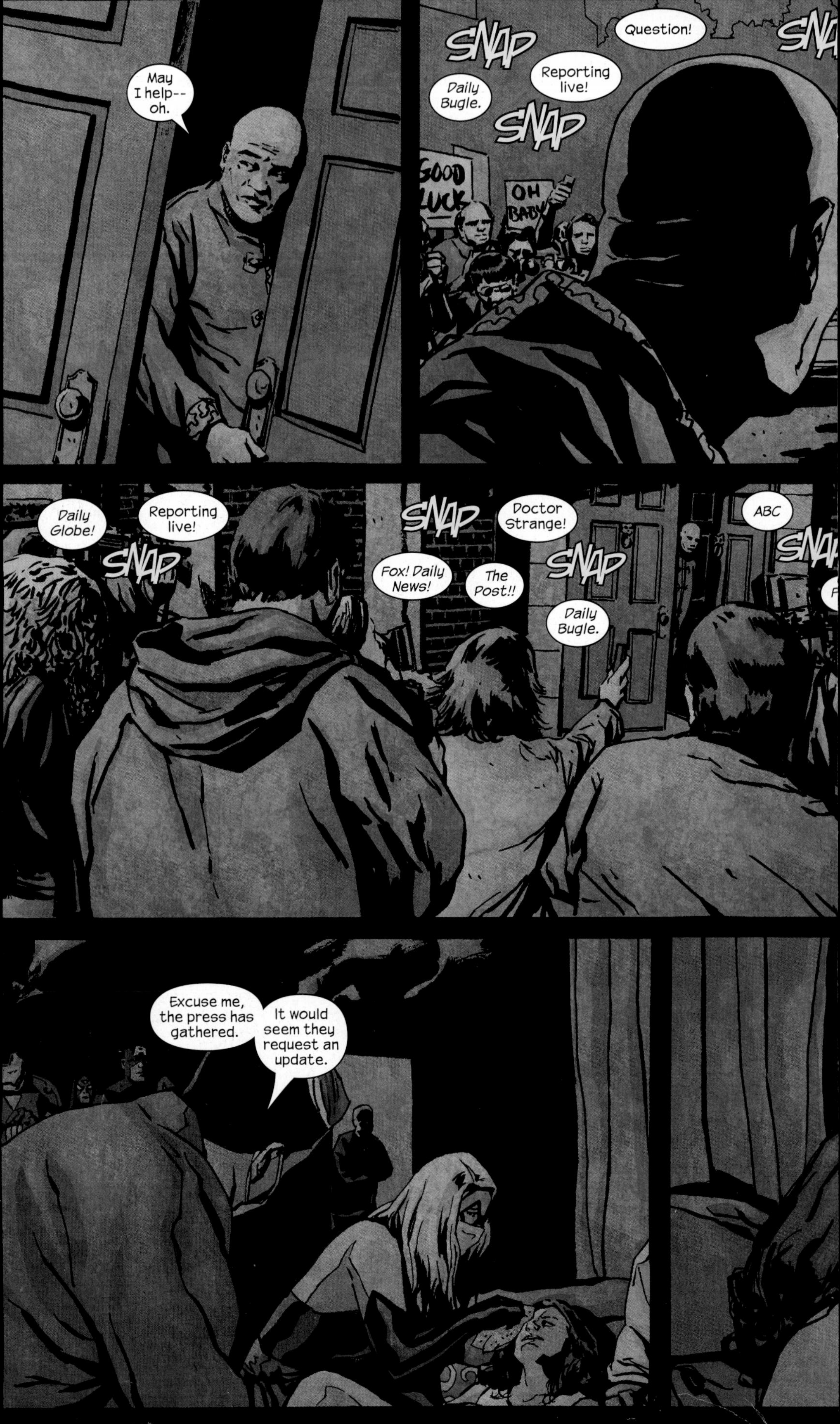

May I help--oh.
SNAP
Daily Bugle.
Reporting live!
SNAP
Question!
GOOD LUCK
OH BABY
Daily Globe!
Reporting live!
SNAP
SNAP
Fox! Daily News!
The Post!!
Doctor Strange!
SNAP
Daily Bugle.
ABC
Excuse me, the press has gathered.
It would seem they request an update.

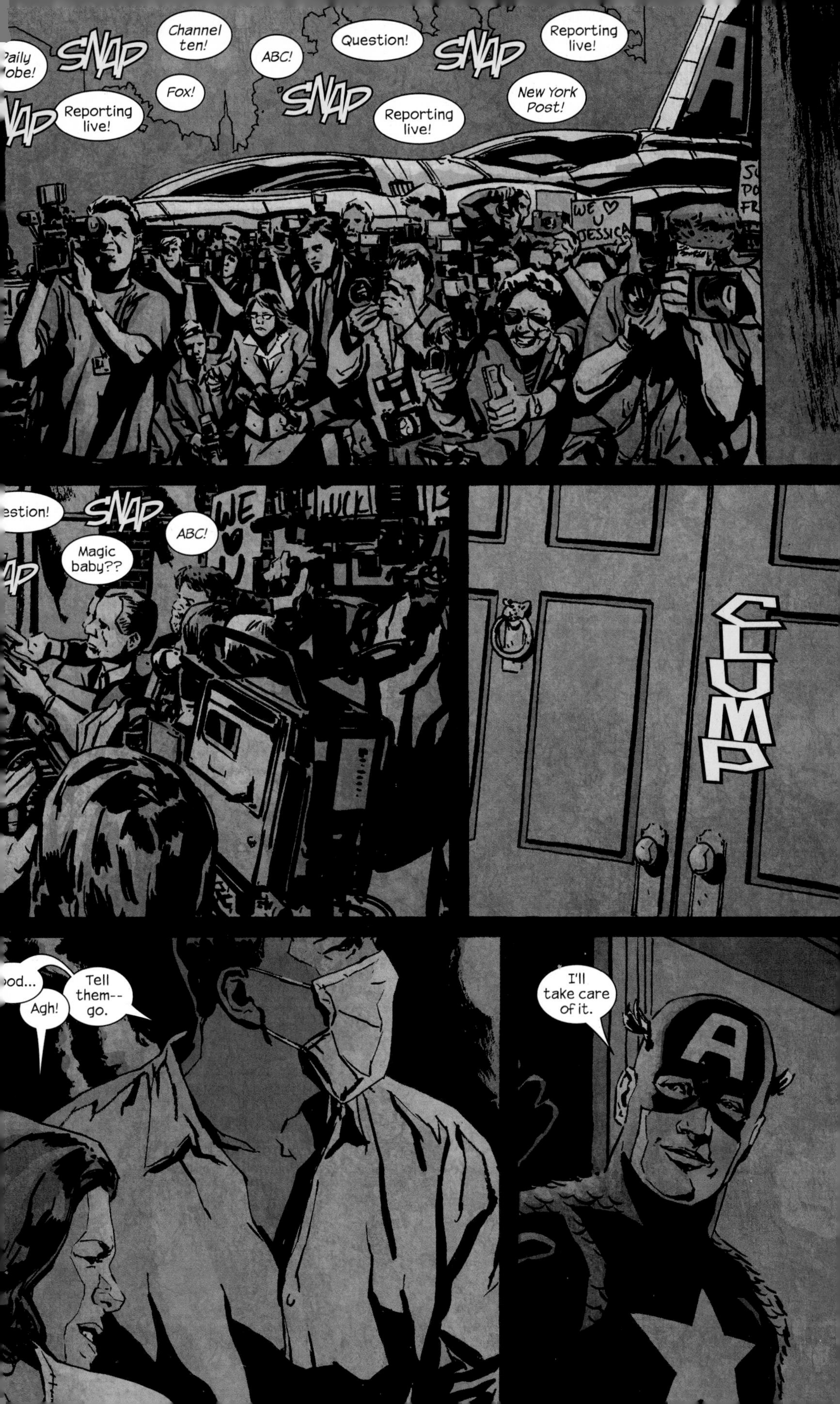

SNAP
Channel ten!
ABC!
Question!
SNAP
Reporting live!
Fox!
Reporting live!
SNAP
Reporting live!
New York Post!
WE ♥ U JESSICA
SNAP
ABC!
Magic baby??
CLUMP
Agh!
Tell them-- go.
I'll take care of it.

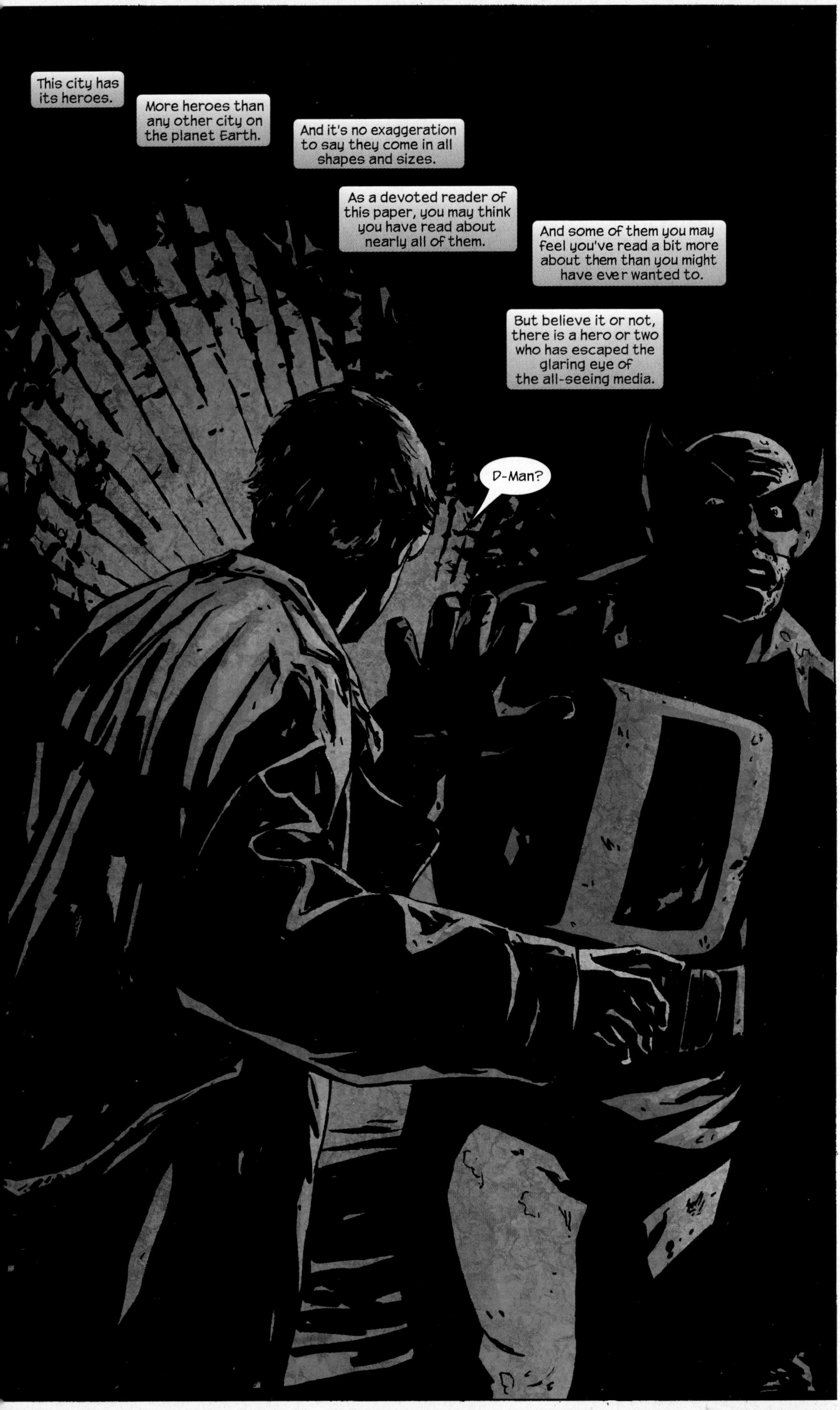
This city has its heroes.
More heroes than any other city on the planet Earth.
And it's no exaggeration to say they come in all shapes and sizes.
As a devoted reader of this paper, you may think you have read about nearly all of them.
And some of them you may feel you've read a bit more about them than you might have ever wanted to.
But believe it or not, there is a hero or two who has escaped the glaring eye of the all-seeing media.
D-Man?

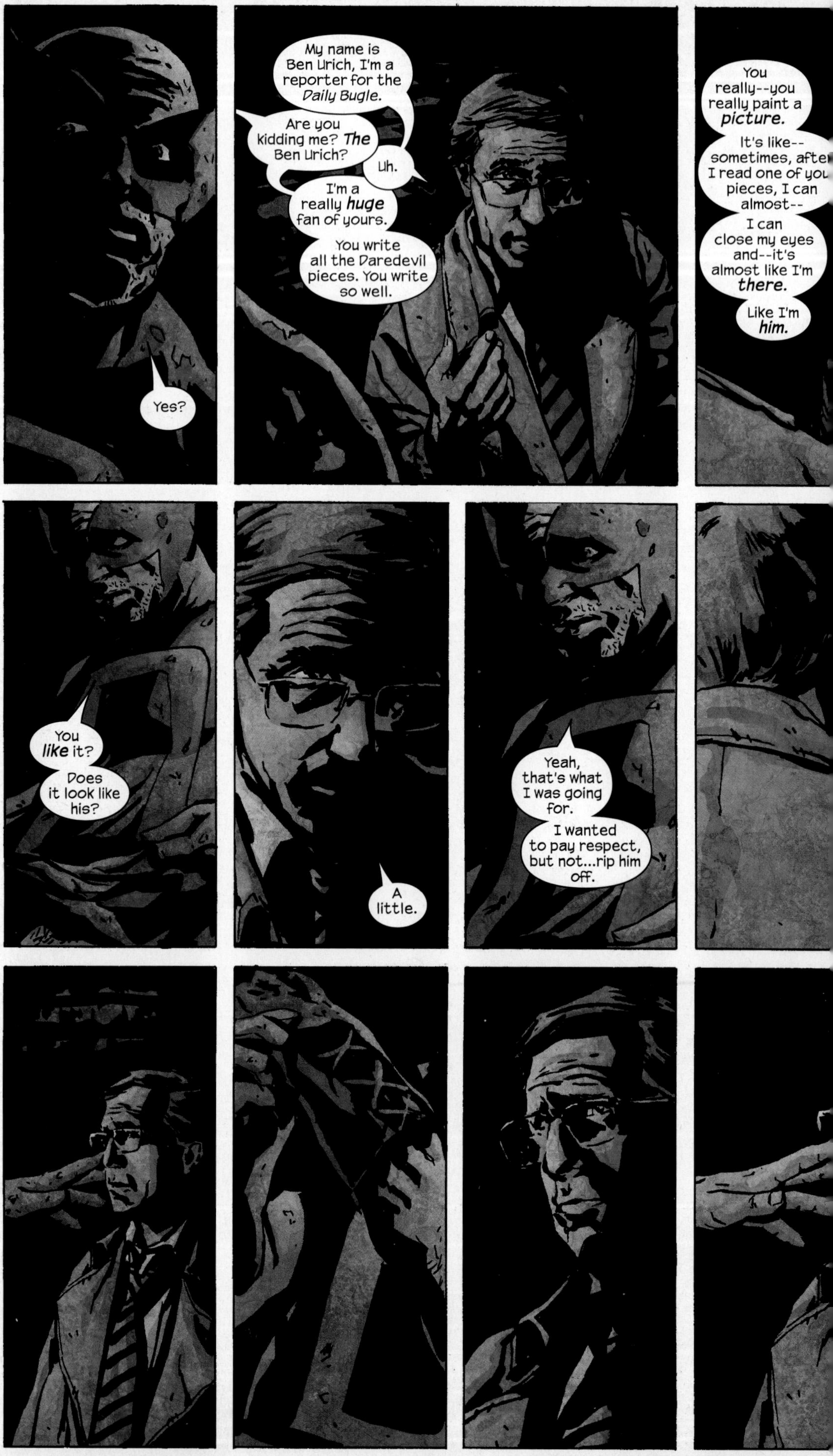
Yes?
My name is Ben Urich, I'm a reporter for the *Daily Bugle.*
Are you kidding me? *The* Ben Urich?
Uh.
I'm a really ***huge*** fan of yours.
You write all the Daredevil pieces. You write so well.
You really--you really paint a ***picture.***
It's like--sometimes, afte
I read one of you
pieces, I can almost--
I can close my eyes and--it's almost like I'm ***there.***
Like I'm ***him.***
You ***like*** it?
Does it look like his?
A little.
Yeah, that's what I was going for.
I wanted to pay respect, but not...rip him off.

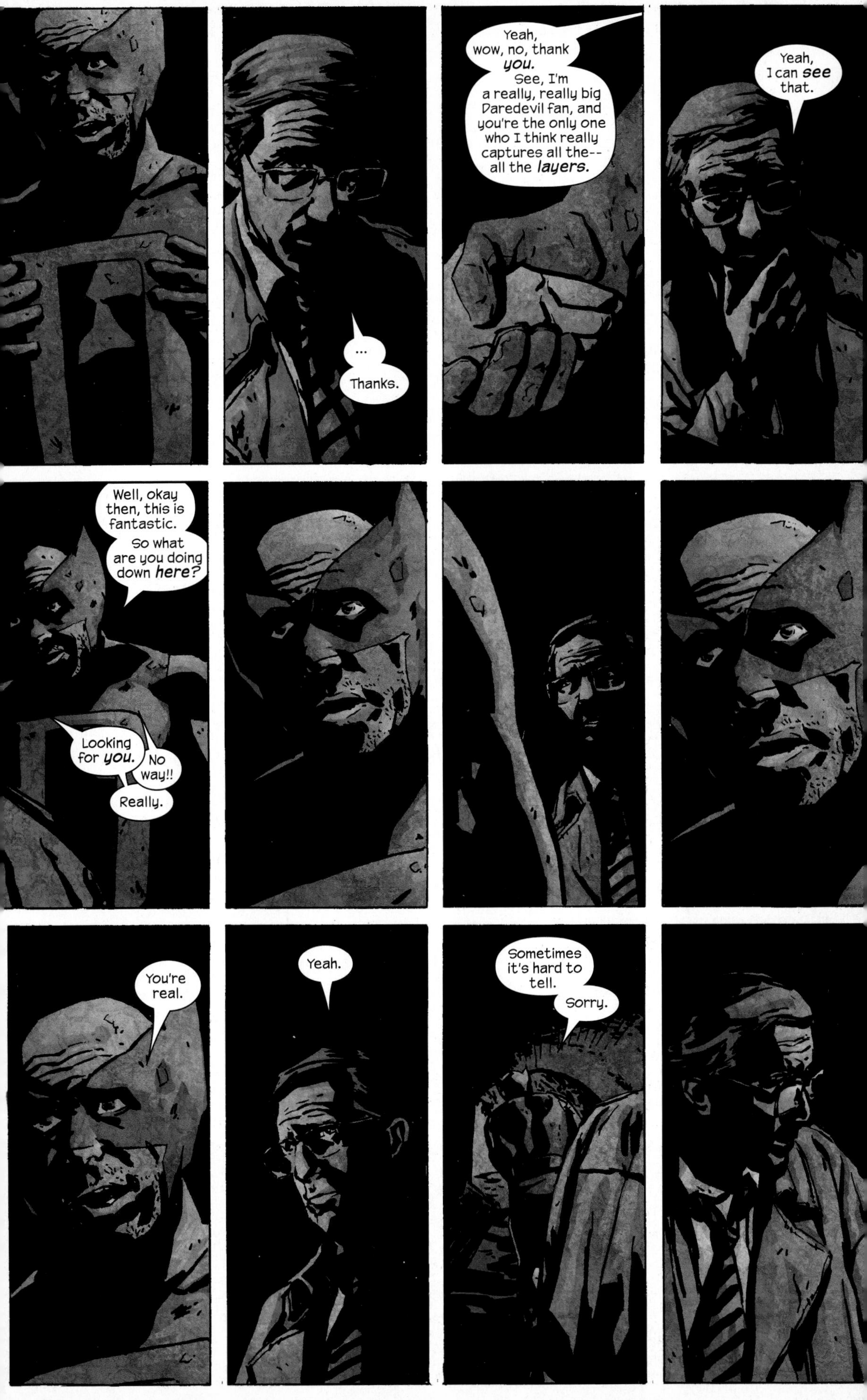
...
Thanks.
Yeah, wow, no, thank you.
See, I'm a really, really big Daredevil fan, and you're the only one who I think really captures all the-- all the layers.
Yeah, I can see that.
Well, okay then, this is fantastic.
So what are you doing down here?
Looking for you.
No way!!
Really.
You're real.
Yeah.
Sometimes it's hard to tell.
Sorry.

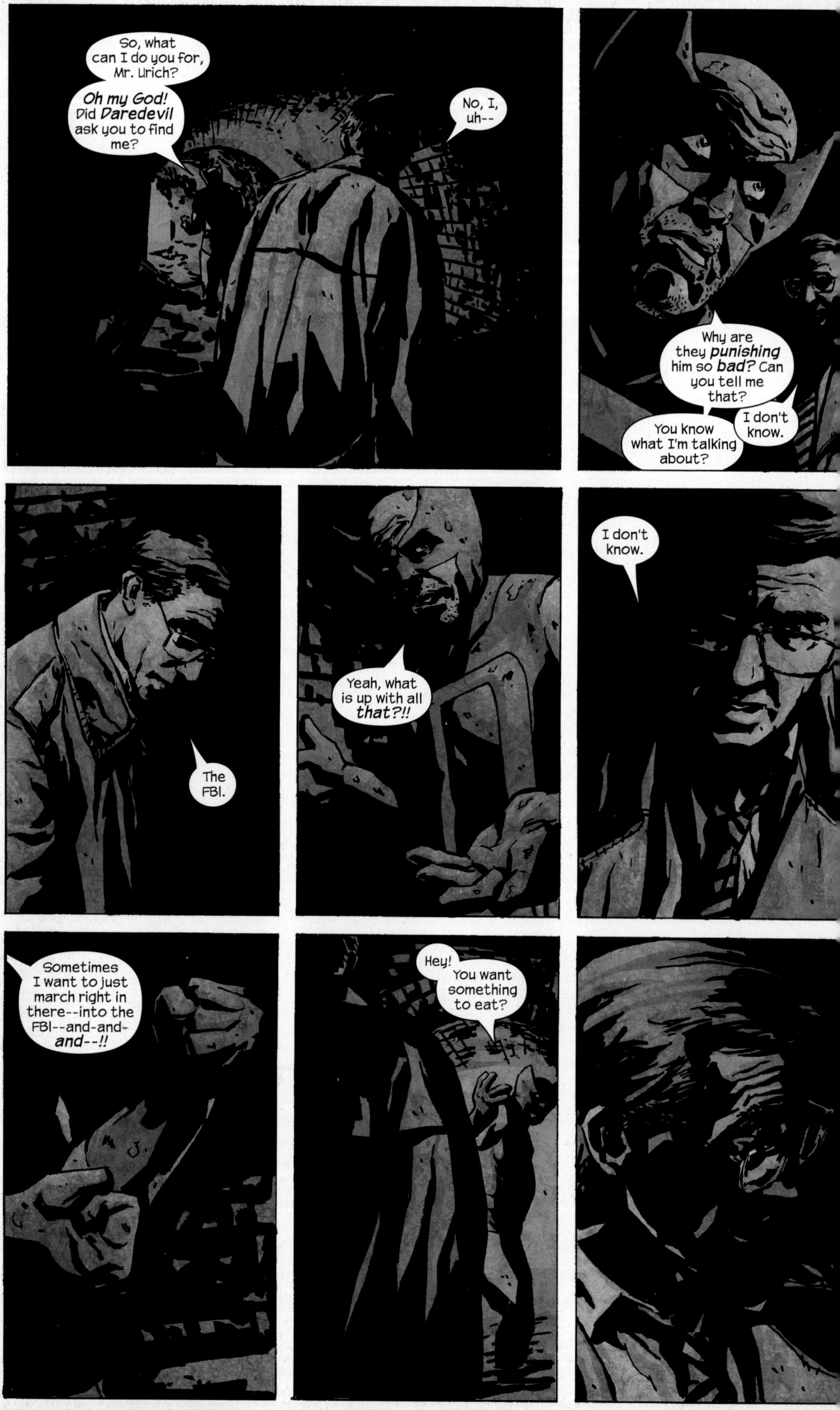
So, what can I do you for, Mr. Urich?
Oh my God! Did Daredevil ask you to find me?
No, I, uh--
Why are they punishing him so bad? Can you tell me that?
You know what I'm talking about?
I don't know.
The FBI.
Yeah, what is up with all that?!!
I don't know.
Sometimes I want to just march right in there--into the FBI--and-and-and--!!
Hey! You want something to eat?

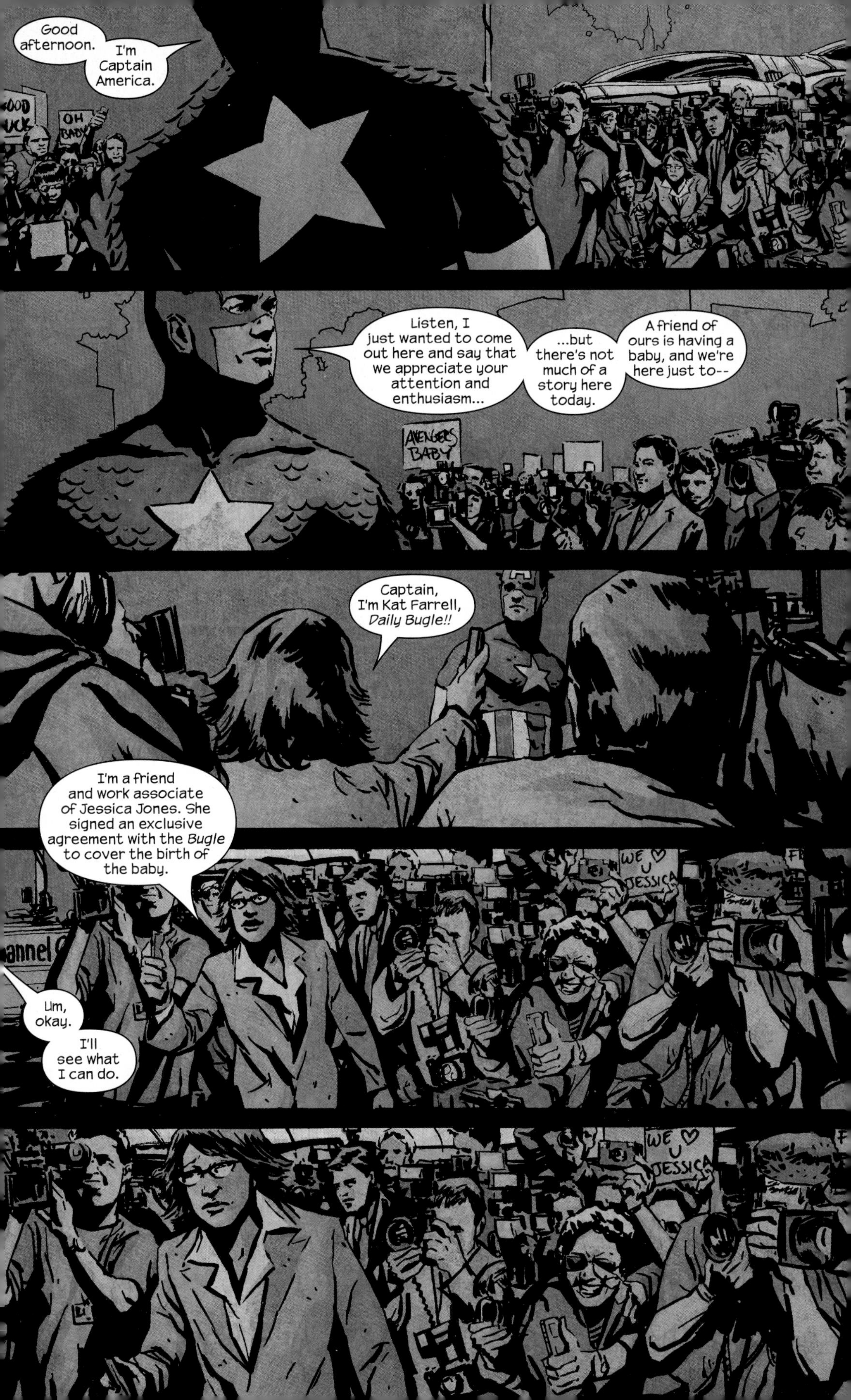

OOD
UCK
OH BABY
Good afternoon.
I'm Captain America.
AVENGERS BABY
Listen, I just wanted to come out here and say that we appreciate your attention and enthusiasm...
...but there's not much of a story here today.
A friend of ours is having a baby, and we're here just to--
Captain, I'm Kat Farrell, *Daily Bugle!!*
I'm a friend and work associate of Jessica Jones. She signed an exclusive agreement with the *Bugle* to cover the birth of the baby.
WE ♡ U JESSICA
Um, okay.
I'll see what I can do.
WE ♡ U JESSICA

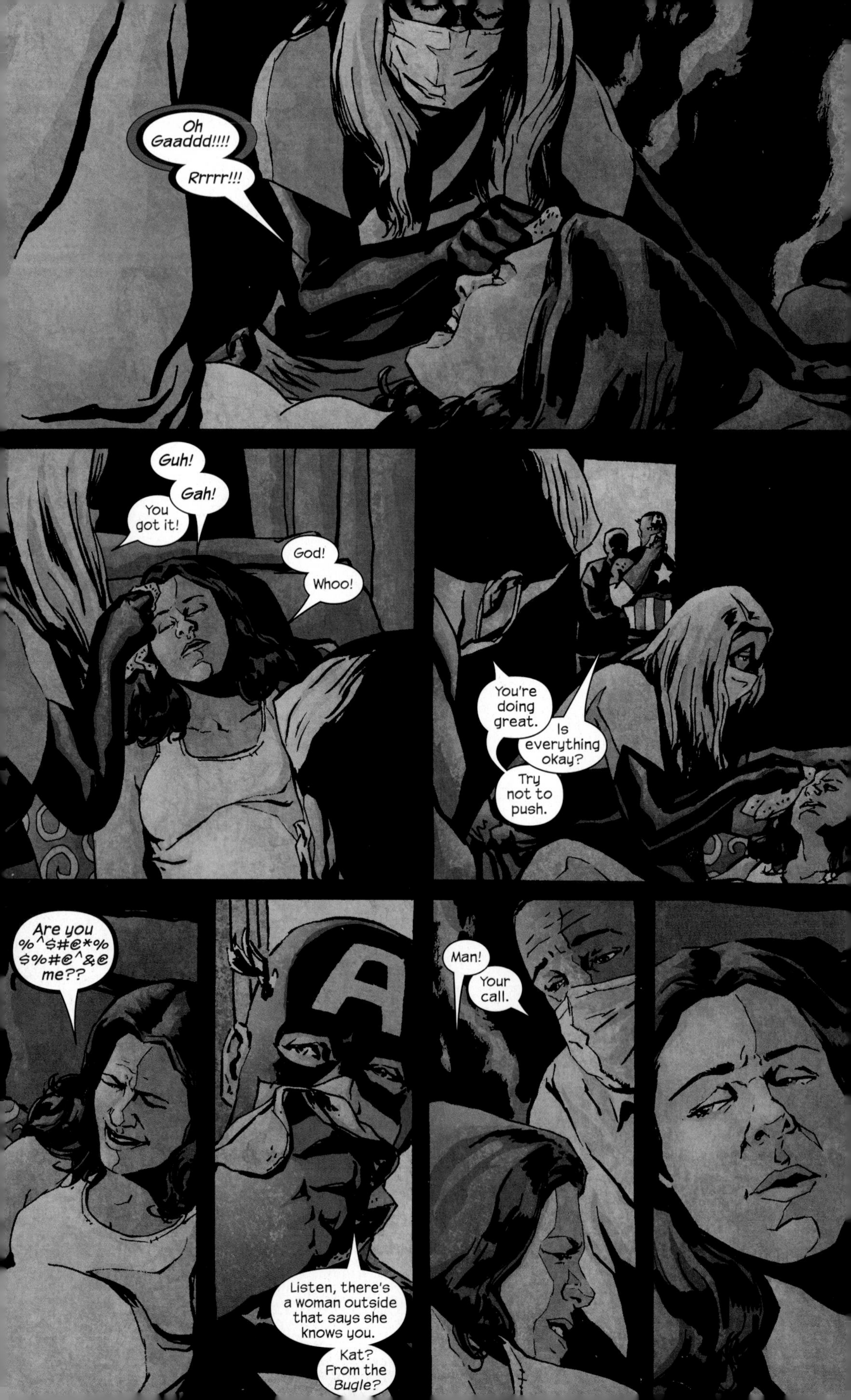
Oh Gaaddd!!!!
Rrrrr!!!
Guh!
Gah!
You got it!
God!
Whoo!
You're doing great.
Is everything okay?
Try not to push.
Are you %^$#@*% $%#@^&@ me??
Man!
Your call.
Listen, there's a woman outside that says she knows you.
Kat? From the *Bugle*?

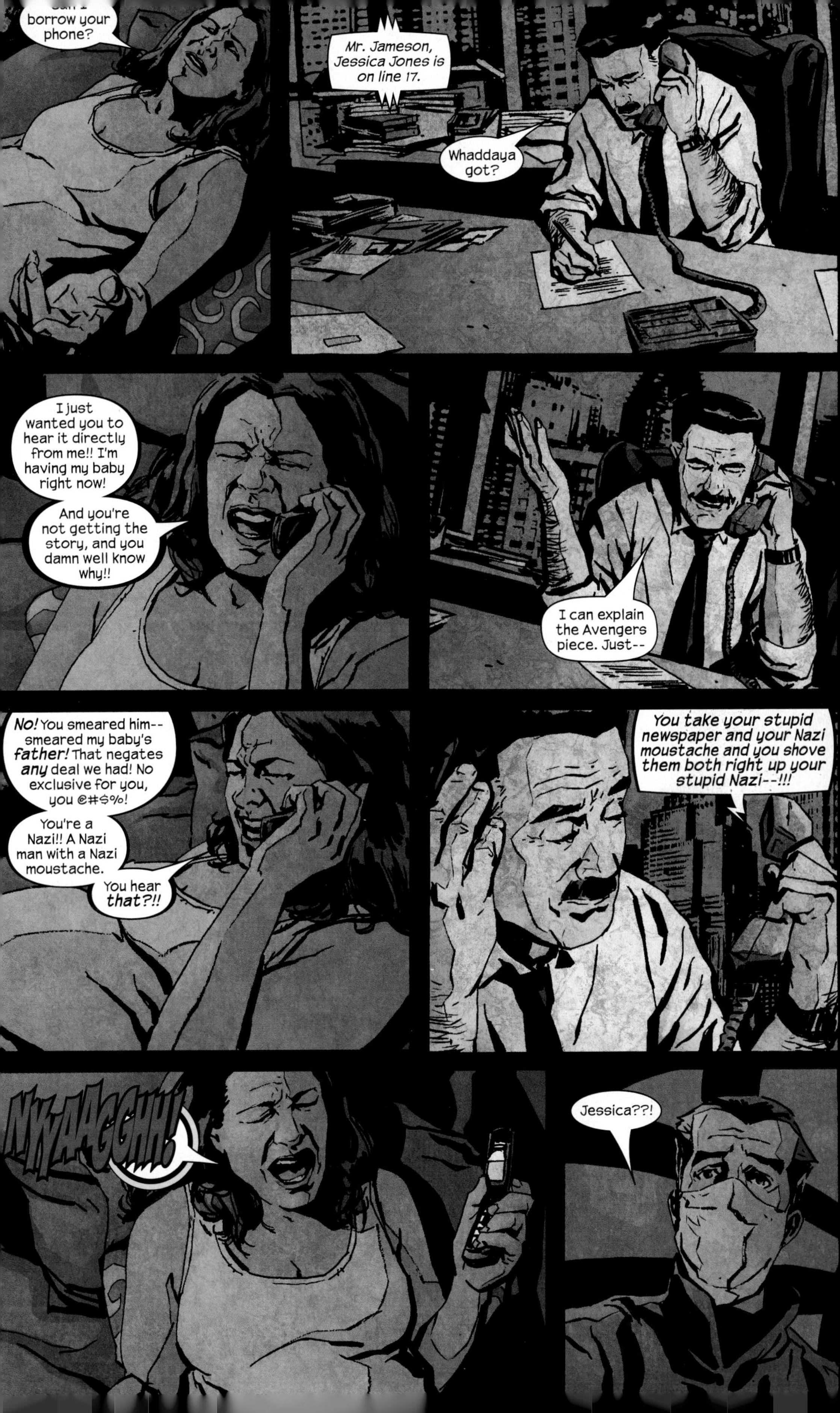

borrow your phone?
Mr. Jameson, Jessica Jones is on line 17.
Whaddaya got?
I just wanted you to hear it directly from me!! I'm having my baby right now!
And you're not getting the story, and you damn well know why!!
I can explain the Avengers piece. Just--
No! You smeared him--smeared my baby's father! That negates any deal we had! No exclusive for you, you @#$%!
You're a Nazi!! A Nazi man with a Nazi moustache.
You hear that?!!
You take your stupid newspaper and your Nazi moustache and you shove them both right up your stupid Nazi--!!!
NYAAGGHH!
Jessica??!

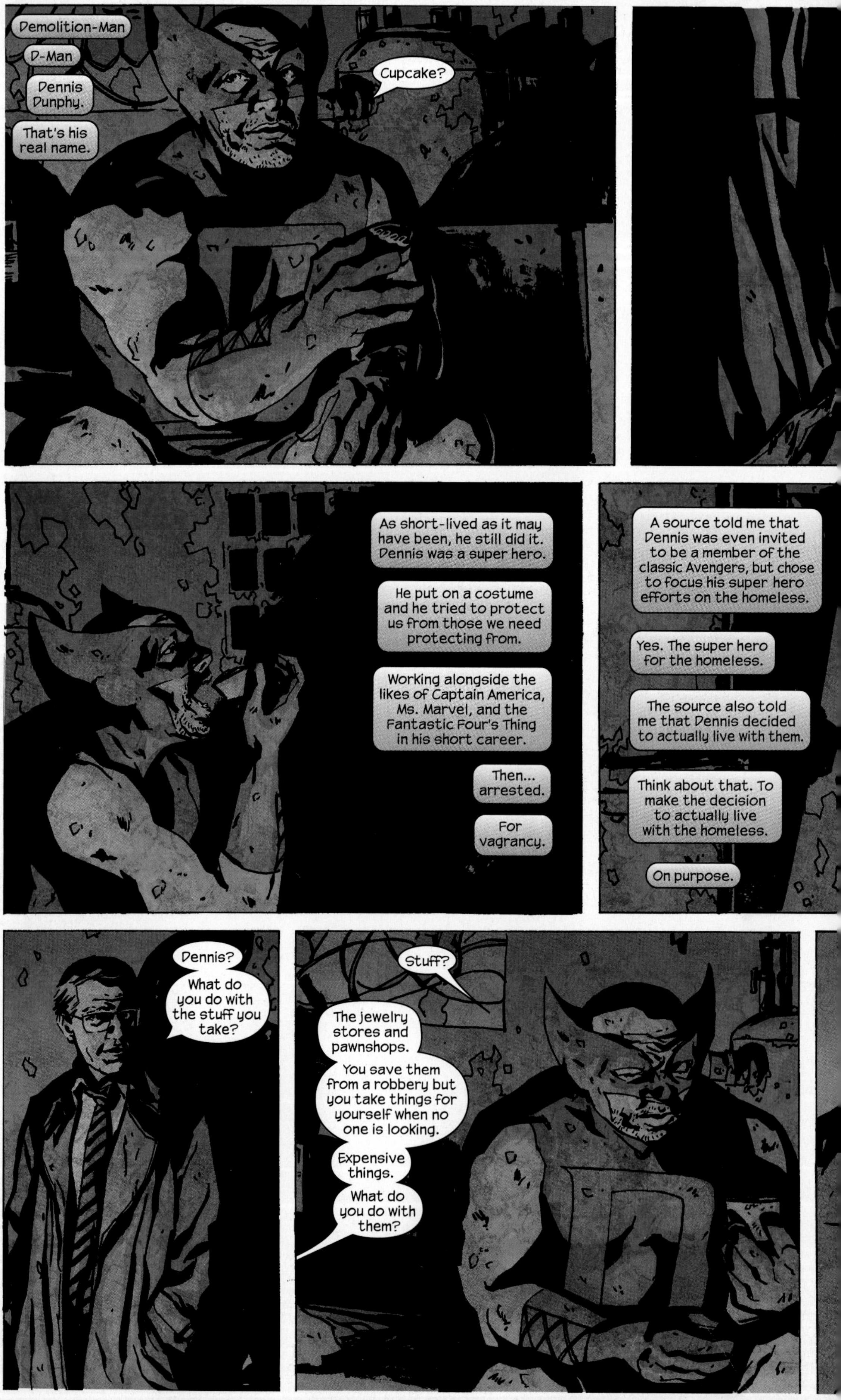
Demolition-Man
D-Man
Dennis Dunphy.
That's his real name.
Cupcake?
As short-lived as it may have been, he still did it. Dennis was a super hero.
He put on a costume and he tried to protect us from those we need protecting from.
Working alongside the likes of Captain America, Ms. Marvel, and the Fantastic Four's Thing in his short career.
Then... arrested.
For vagrancy.
A source told me that Dennis was even invited to be a member of the classic Avengers, but chose to focus his super hero efforts on the homeless.
Yes. The super hero for the homeless.
The source also told me that Dennis decided to actually live with them.
Think about that. To make the decision to actually live with the homeless.
On purpose.
Dennis?
What do you do with the stuff you take?
Stuff?
The jewelry stores and pawnshops.
You save them from a robbery but you take things for yourself when no one is looking.
Expensive things.
What do you do with them?

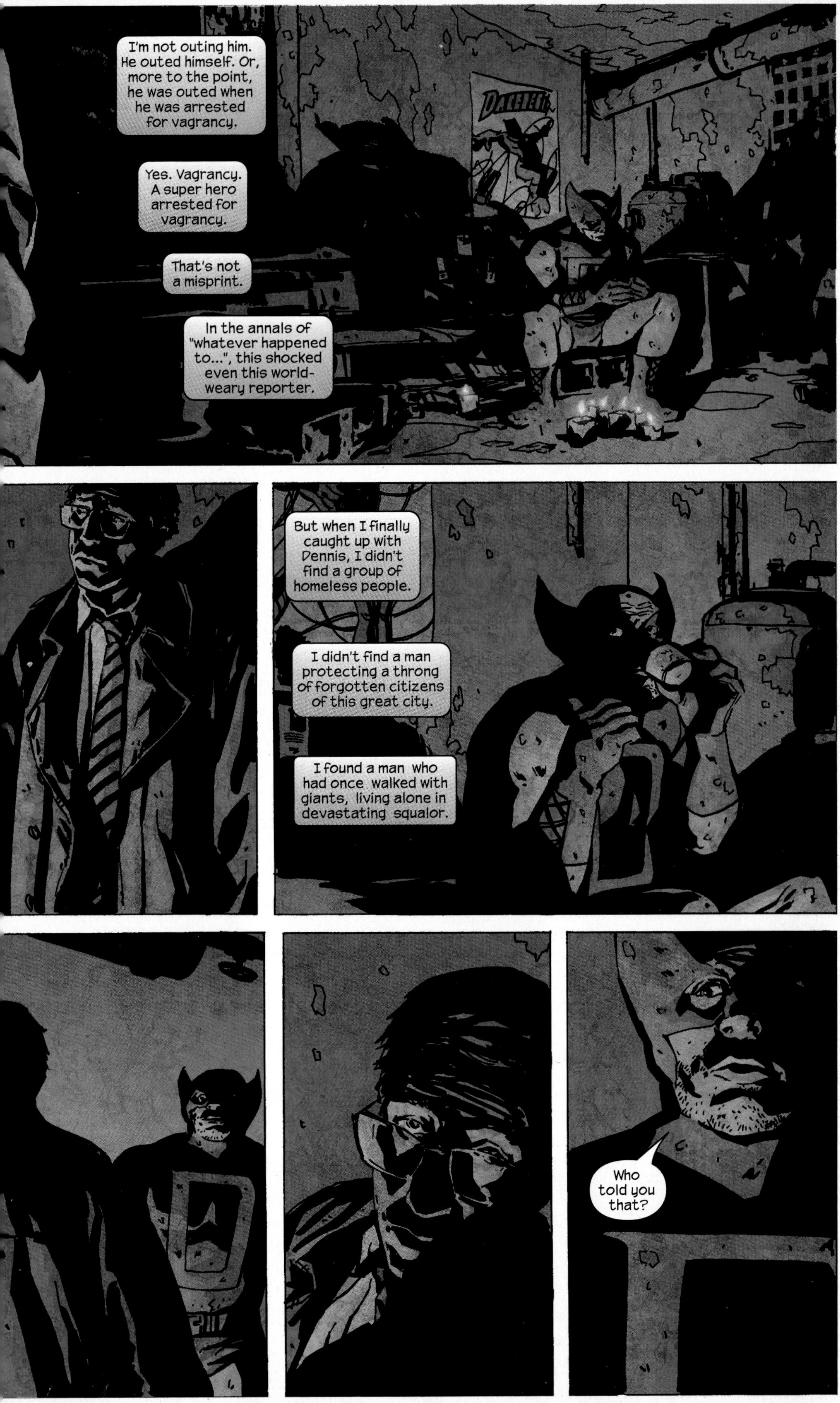
I'm not outing him. He outed himself. Or, more to the point, he was outed when he was arrested for vagrancy.
Yes. Vagrancy. A super hero arrested for vagrancy.
That's not a misprint.
In the annals of "whatever happened to...", this shocked even this world-weary reporter.
But when I finally caught up with Dennis, I didn't find a group of homeless people.
I didn't find a man protecting a throng of forgotten citizens of this great city.
I found a man who had once walked with giants, living alone in devastating squalor.
Who told you that?

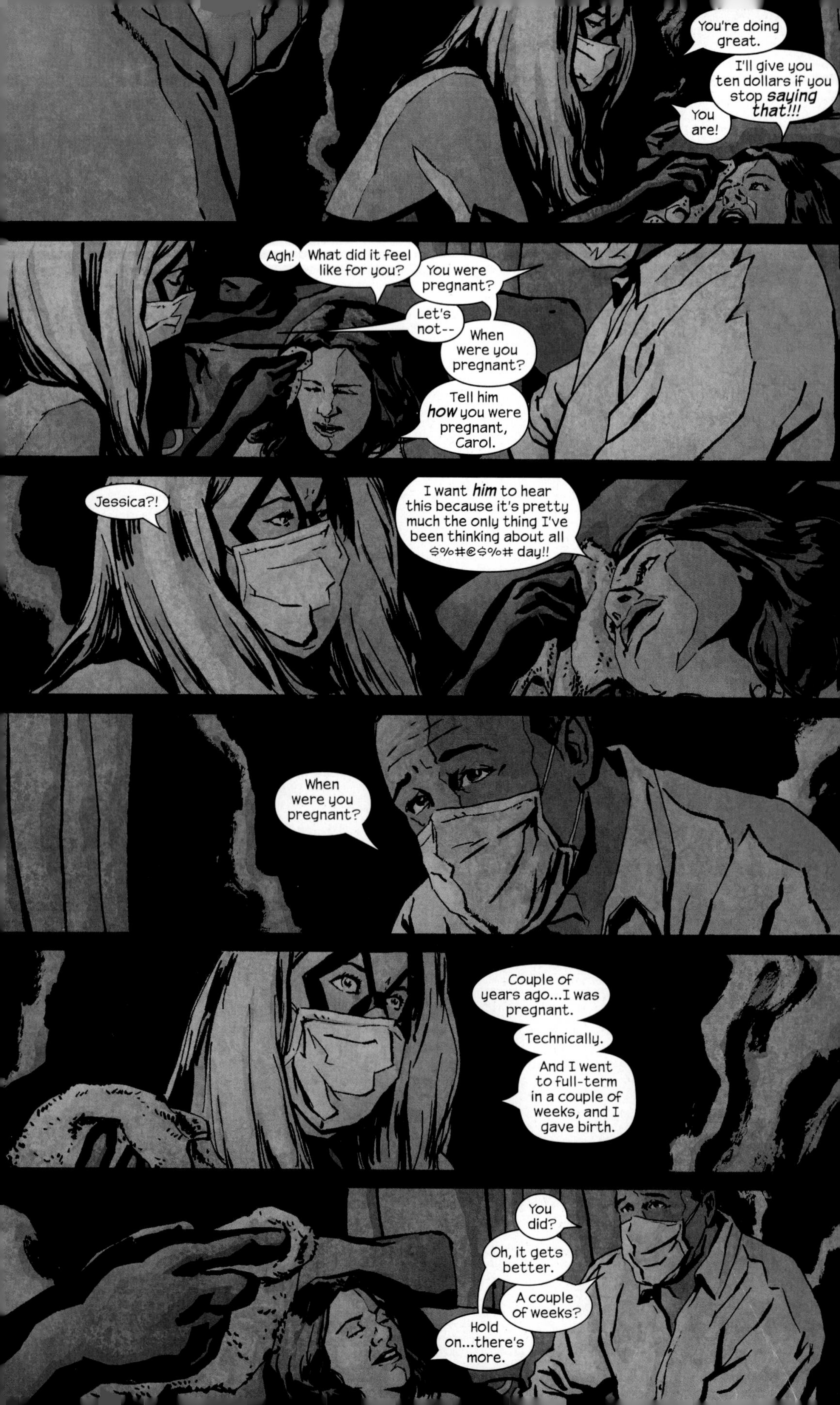
You're doing great.
I'll give you ten dollars if you stop *saying that!!!*
You are!
Agh!
What did it feel like for you?
You were pregnant?
Let's not--
When were you pregnant?
Tell him *how* you were pregnant, Carol.
Jessica?!
I want *him* to hear this because it's pretty much the only thing I've been thinking about all $%#@$%# day!!
When were you pregnant?
Couple of years ago...I was pregnant.
Technically.
And I went to full-term in a couple of weeks, and I gave birth.
You did?
Oh, it gets better.
A couple of weeks?
Hold on...there's more.

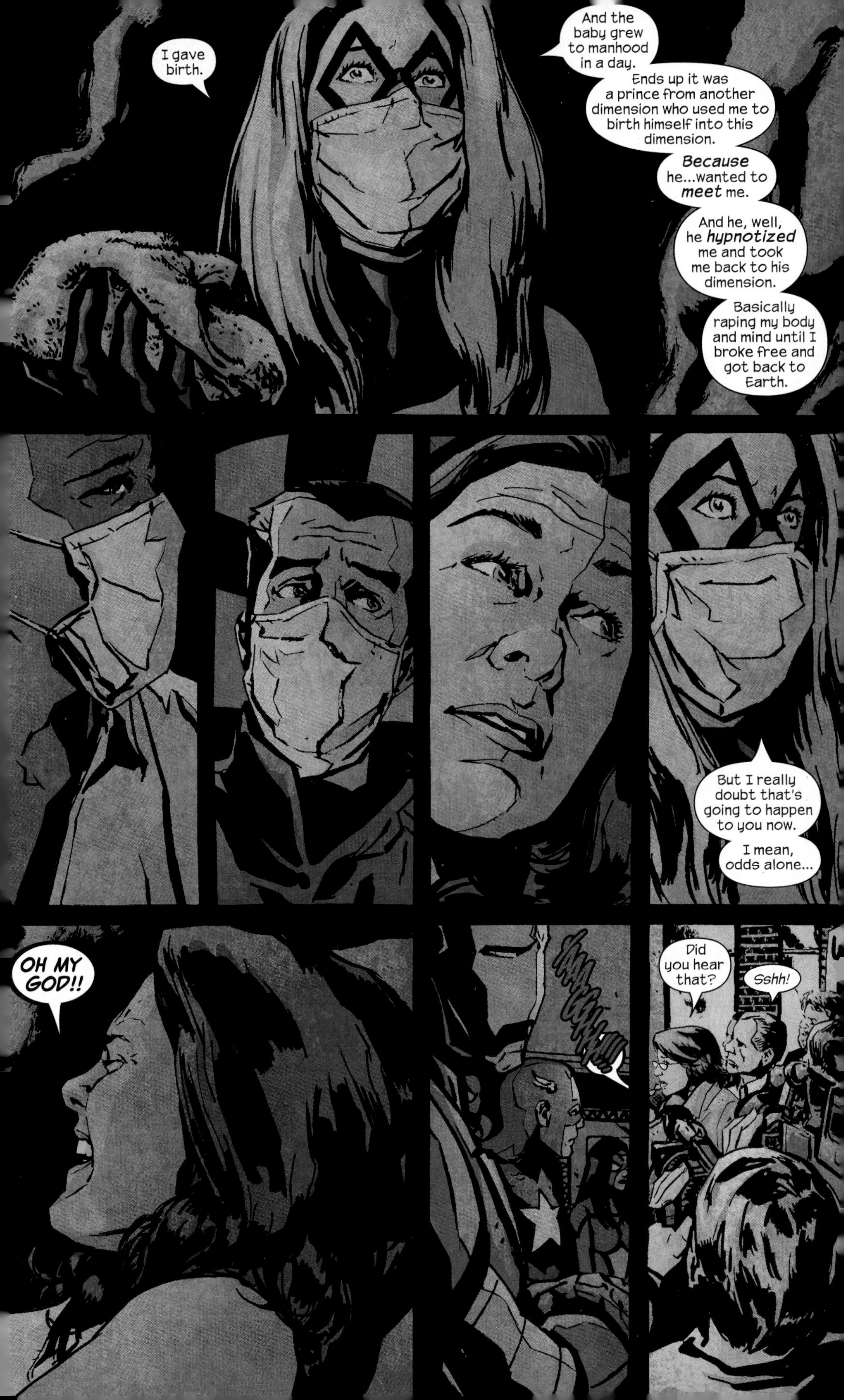
I gave birth.
And the baby grew to manhood in a day.
Ends up it was a prince from another dimension who used me to birth himself into this dimension.
Because he...wanted to *meet* me.
And he, well, he *hypnotized* me and took me back to his dimension.
Basically raping my body and mind until I broke free and got back to Earth.
But I really doubt that's going to happen to you now.
I mean, odds alone...
OH MY GOD!!
Did you hear that?
Sshh!

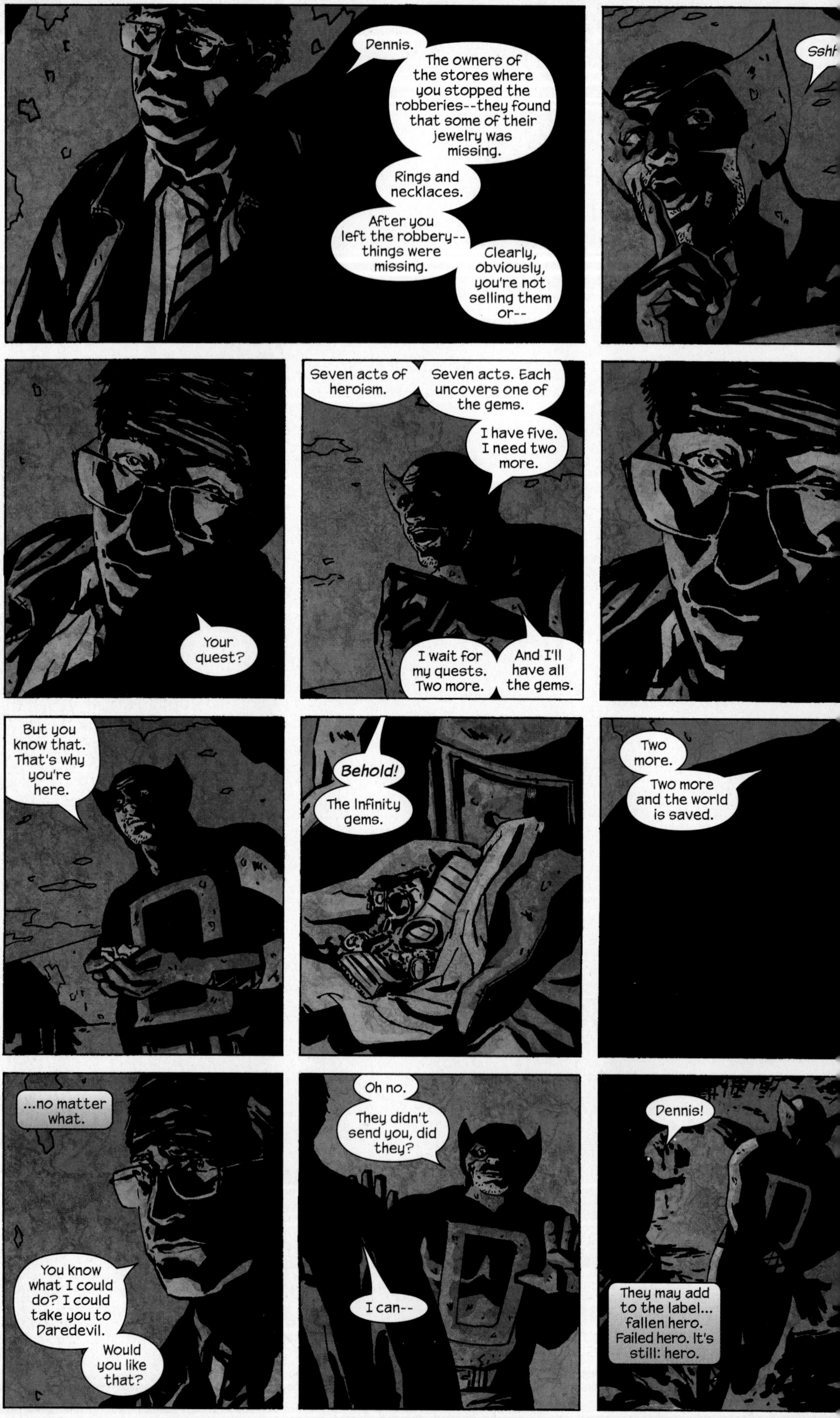
Dennis.
The owners of the stores where you stopped the robberies--they found that some of their jewelry was missing.
Rings and necklaces.
After you left the robbery--things were missing.
Clearly, obviously, you're not selling them or--
Sshh
Your quest?
Seven acts of heroism.
Seven acts. Each uncovers one of the gems.
I have five. I need two more.
I wait for my quests. Two more.
And I'll have all the gems.
But you know that. That's why you're here.
Behold!
The Infinity gems.
Two more.
Two more and the world is saved.
...no matter what.
You know what I could do? I could take you to Daredevil.
Would you like that?
Oh no.
They didn't send you, did they?
I can--
Dennis!
They may add to the label... fallen hero. Failed hero. It's still: hero.

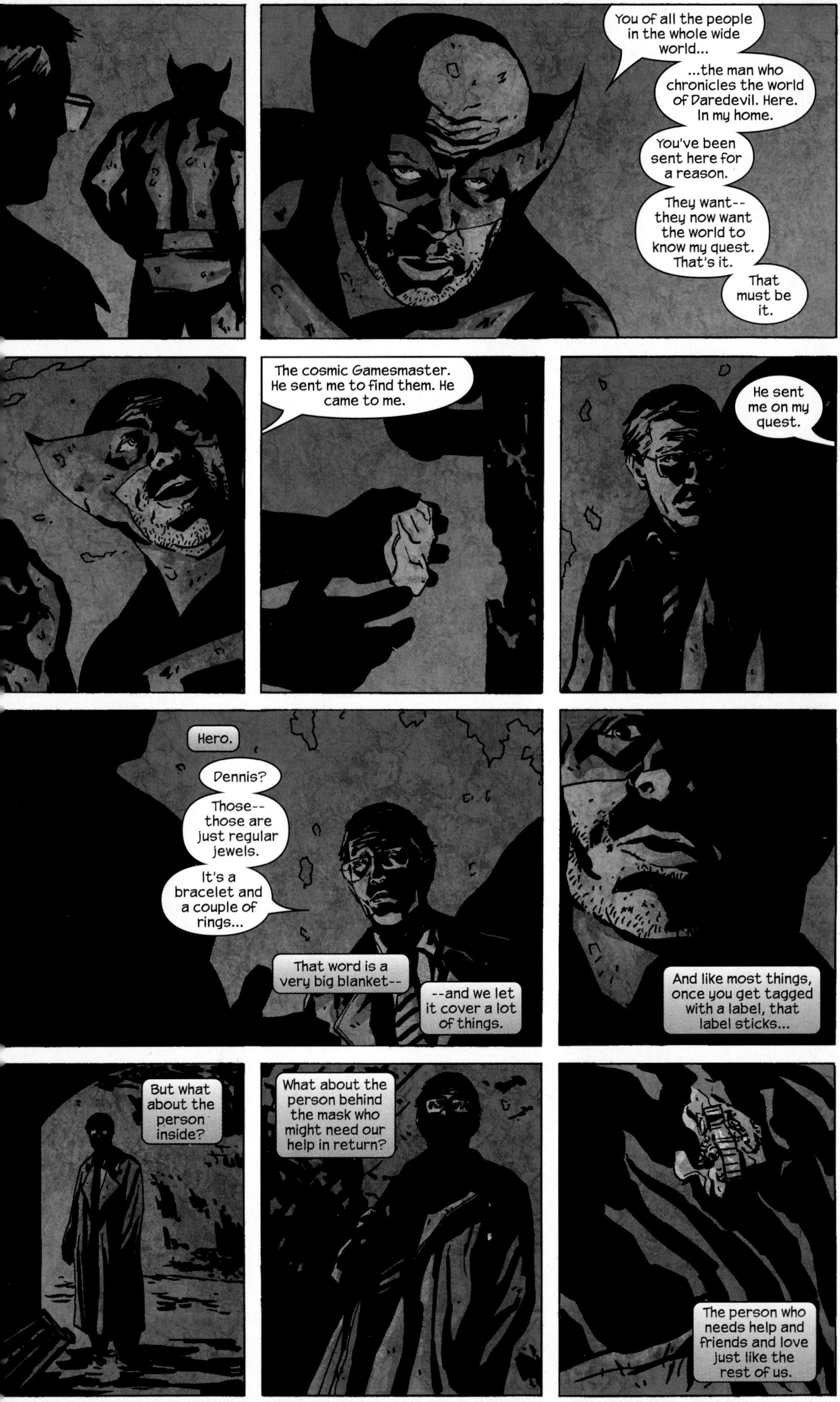
You of all the people in the whole wide world...
...the man who chronicles the world of Daredevil. Here. In my home.
You've been sent here for a reason.
They want-- they now want the world to know my quest. That's it.
That must be it.
The cosmic Gamesmaster. He sent me to find them. He came to me.
He sent me on my quest.
Hero.
Dennis?
Those-- those are just regular jewels.
It's a bracelet and a couple of rings...
That word is a very big blanket--
--and we let it cover a lot of things.
And like most things, once you get tagged with a label, that label sticks...
But what about the person inside?
What about the person behind the mask who might need our help in return?
The person who needs help and friends and love just like the rest of us.

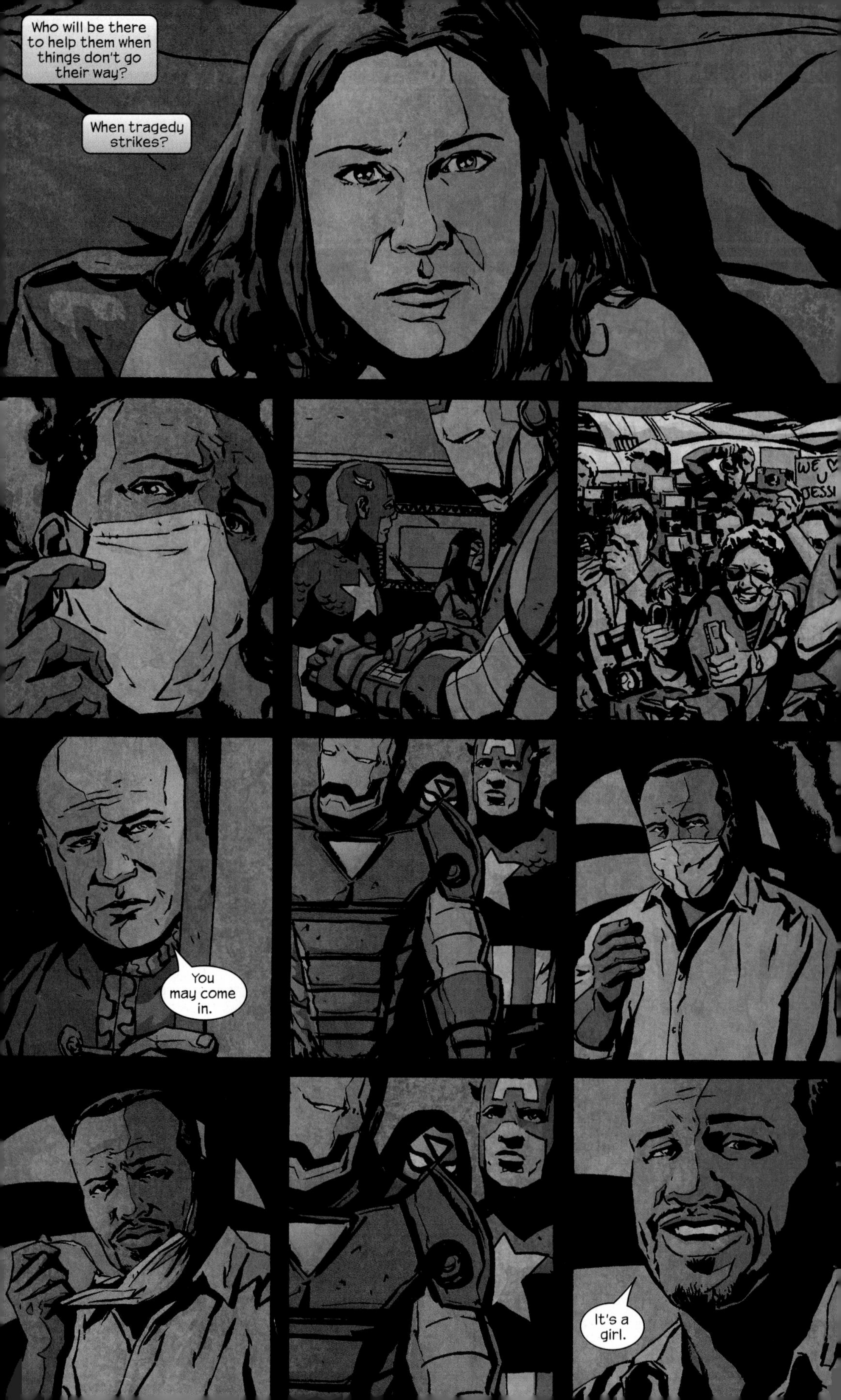

Who will be there to help them when things don't go their way?
When tragedy strikes?
You may come in.
It's a girl.

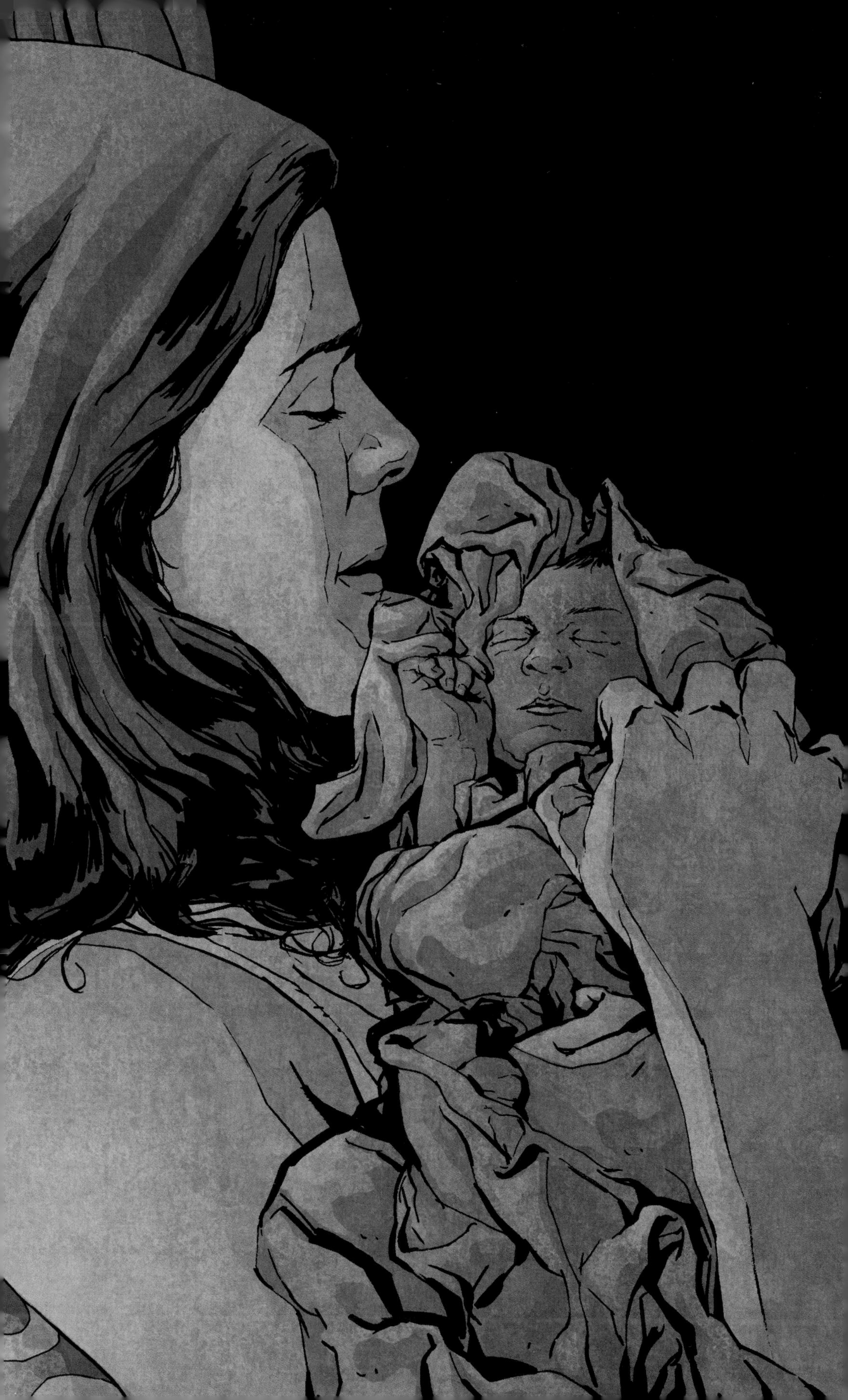

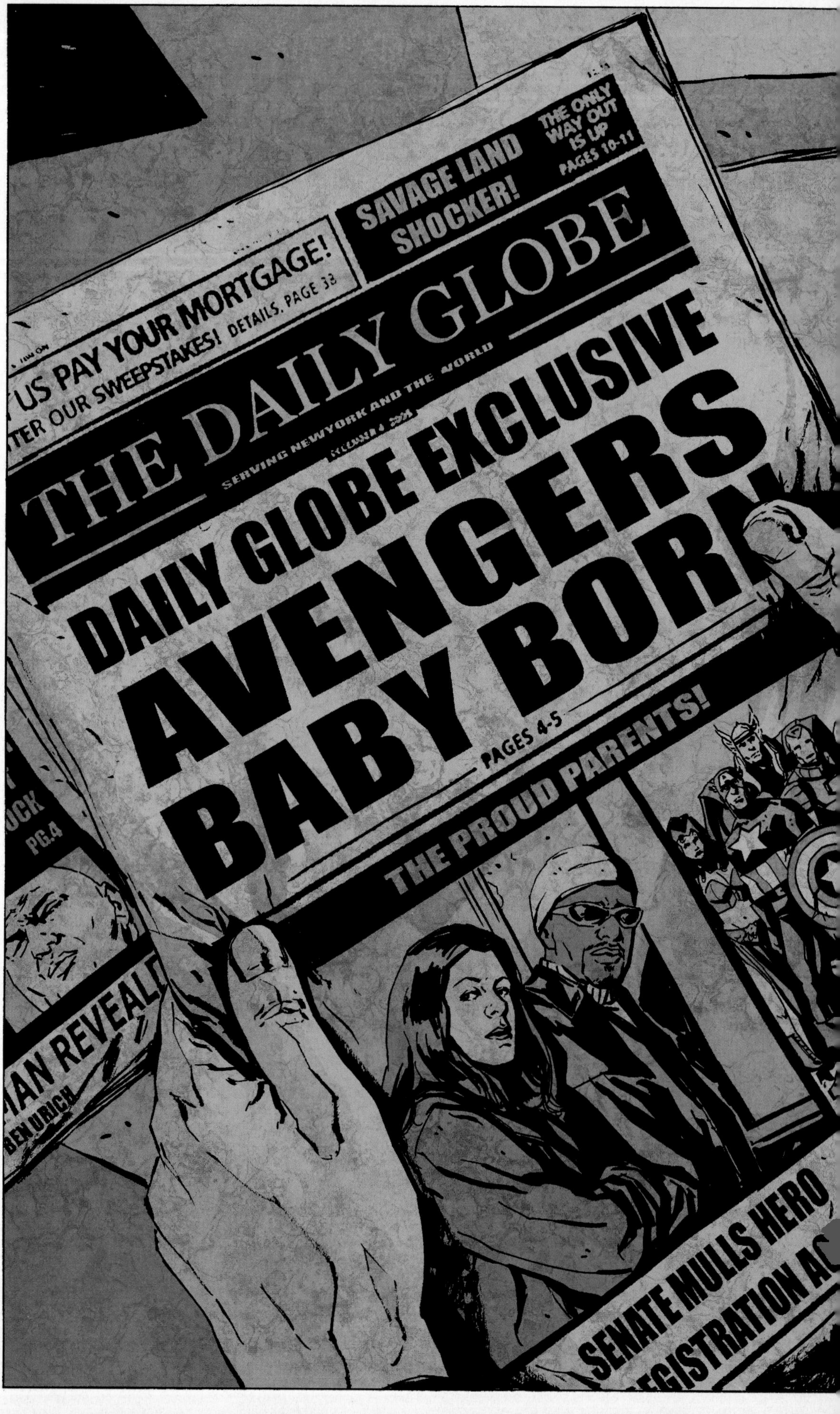
US PAY YOUR MORTGAGE!
TER OUR SWEEPSTAKES! DETAILS, PAGE 38
SAVAGE LAND SHOCKER!
THE ONLY WAY OUT IS UP PAGES 10-11
THE DAILY GLOBE
SERVING NEW YORK AND THE WORLD
DAILY GLOBE EXCLUSIVE
AVENGERS BABY BOR
PAGES 4-5
THE PROUD PARENTS!
OCK
PG.4
MAN REVEALE
BEN URICH
SENATE MULLS HERO
EGISTRATION AC

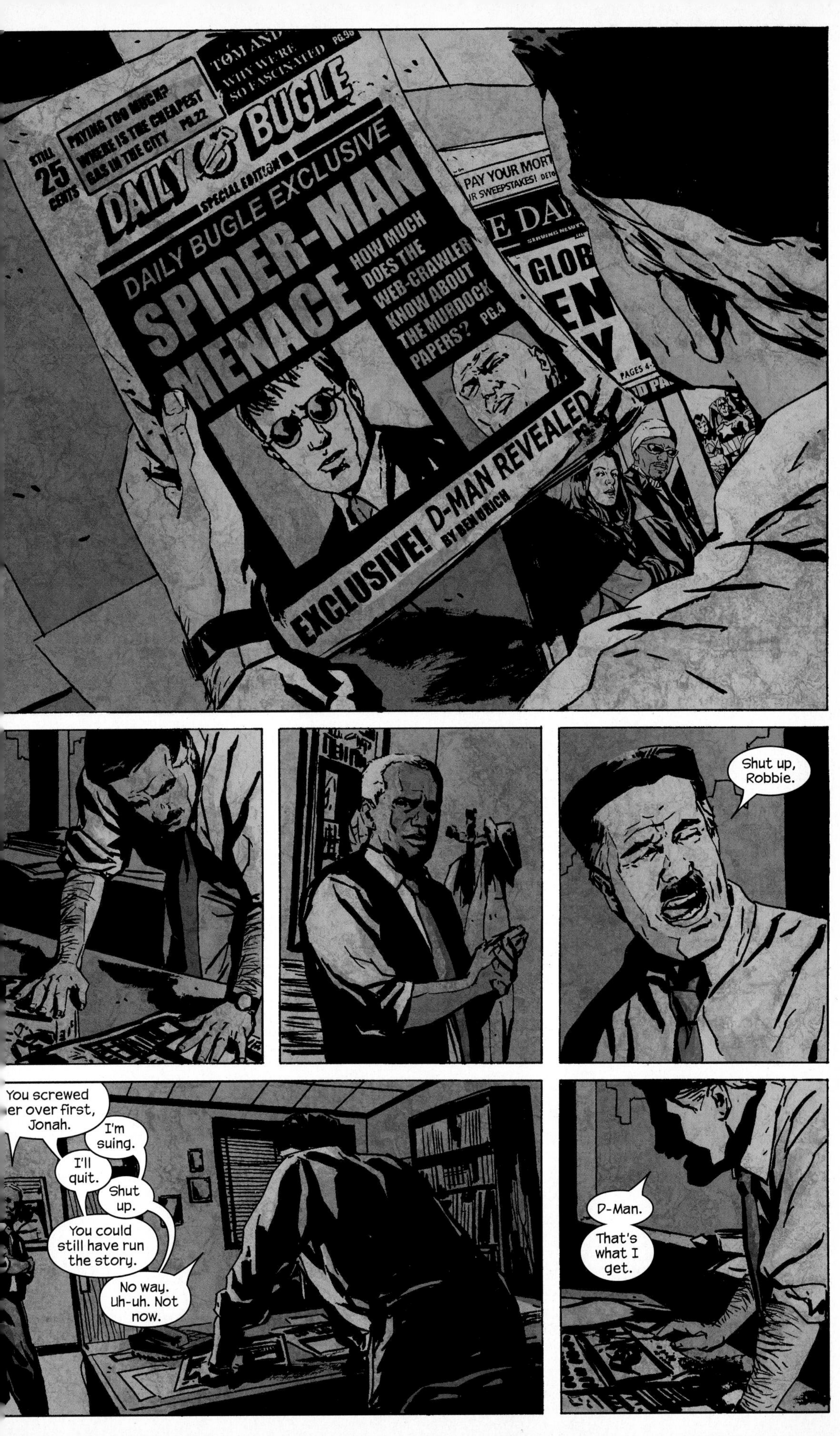
WHY WE'RE SO FASCINATED PG.9D
PAYING TOO MUCH? WHERE IS THE CHEAPEST GAS IN THE CITY PG.22
STILL 25 CENTS
DAILY BUGLE
SPECIAL EDITION
DAILY BUGLE EXCLUSIVE
SPIDER-MAN MENACE
HOW MUCH DOES THE WEB-CRAWLER KNOW ABOUT THE MURDOCK PAPERS? PG.4
EXCLUSIVE! D-MAN REVEALED
BY BEN URICH
Shut up, Robbie.
You screwed er over first, Jonah.
I'm suing.
I'll quit.
Shut up.
You could still have run the story.
No way. Uh-uh. Not now.
D-Man.
That's what I get.

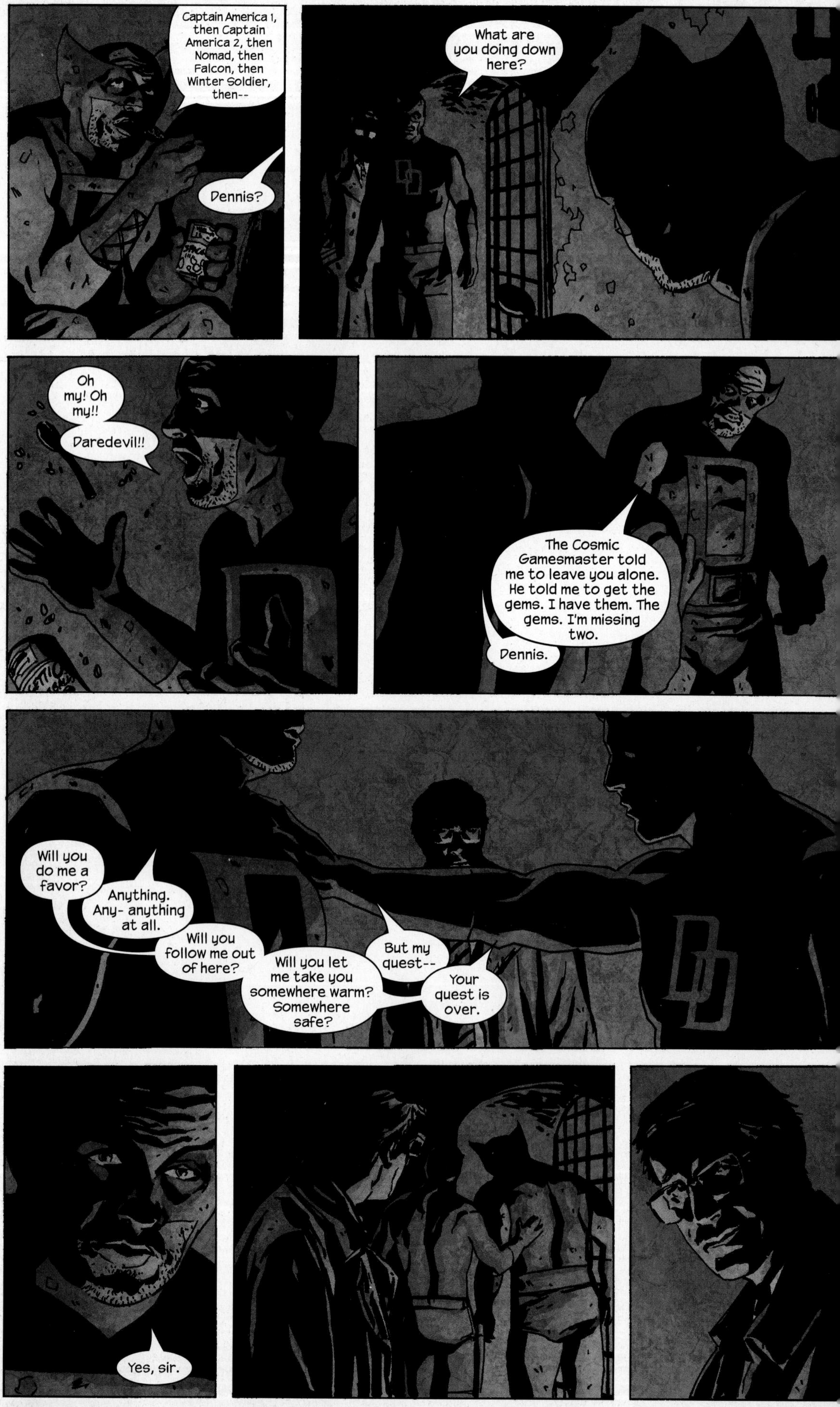
Captain America 1, then Captain America 2, then Nomad, then Falcon, then Winter Soldier, then--
Dennis?
What are you doing down here?
Oh my! Oh my!!
Daredevil!!
The Cosmic Gamesmaster told me to leave you alone. He told me to get the gems. I have them. The gems. I'm missing two.
Dennis.
Will you do me a favor?
Anything. Any- anything at all.
Will you follow me out of here?
Will you let me take you somewhere warm? Somewhere safe?
But my quest--
Your quest is over.
Yes, sir.

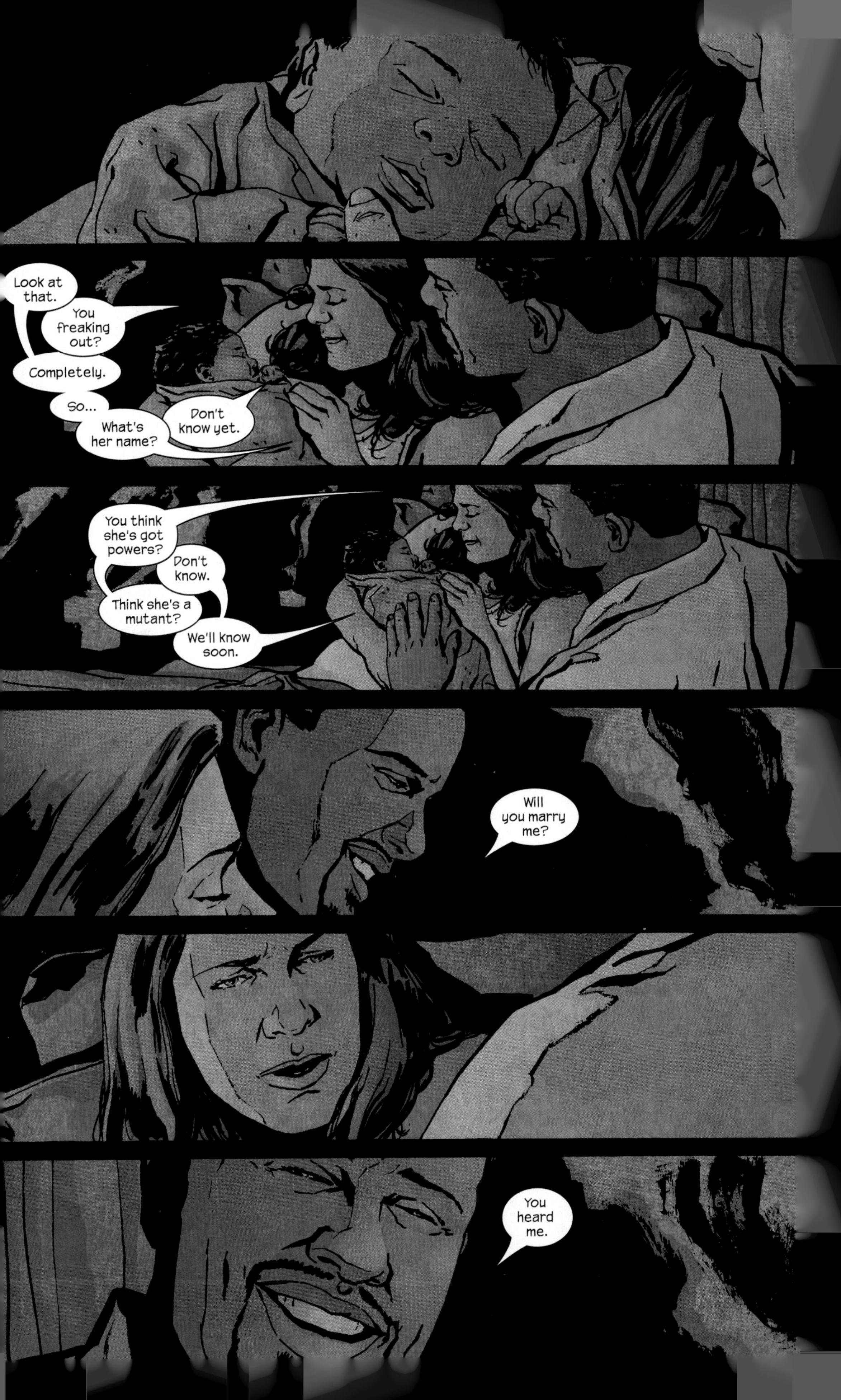
Look at that.
You freaking out?
Completely.
So...
What's her name?
Don't know yet.
You think she's got powers?
Don't know.
Think she's a mutant?
We'll know soon.
Will you marry me?
You heard me.

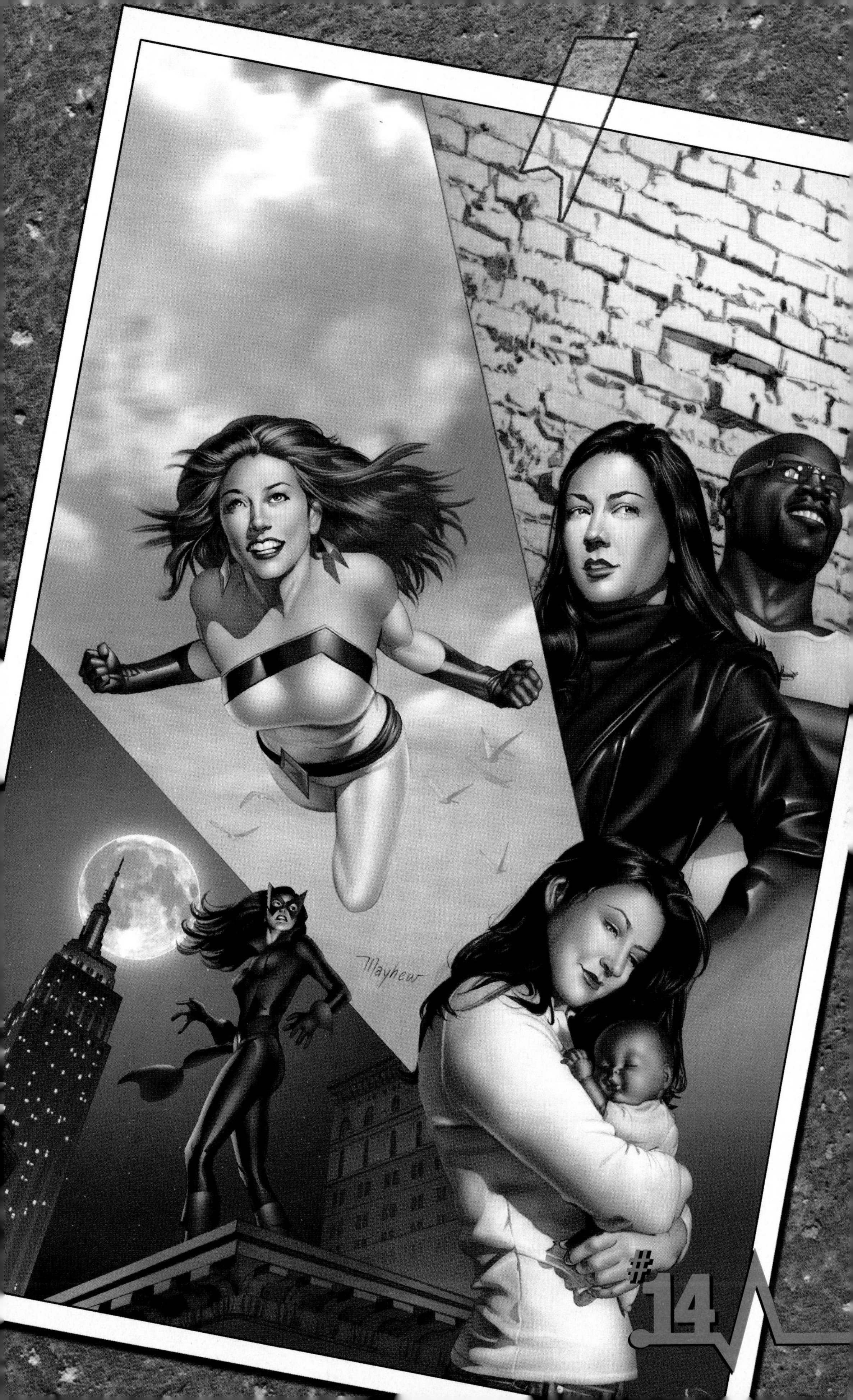
Mayhew
#14

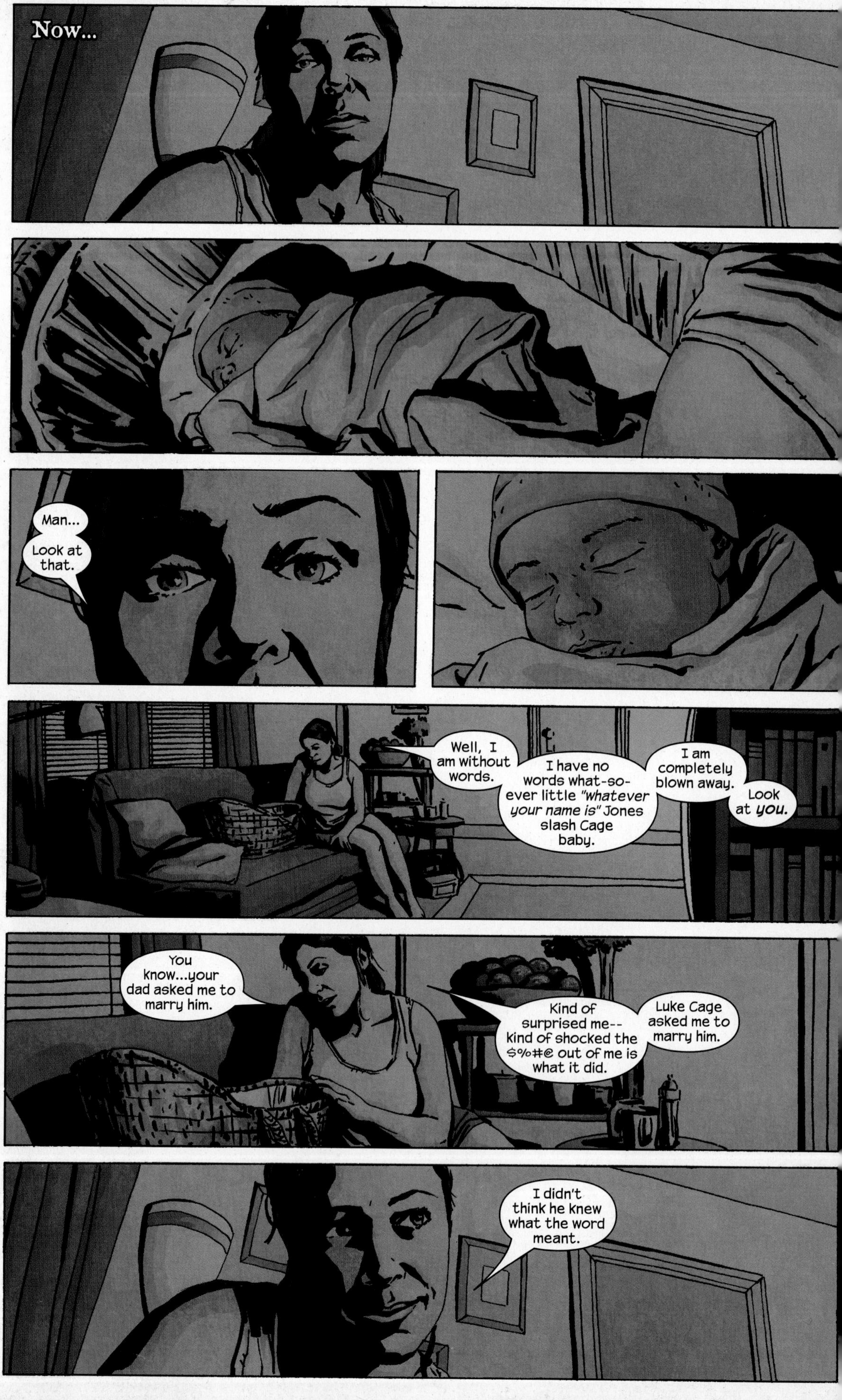
Now...
Man...
Look at that.
Well, I am without words.
I have no words what-so-ever little "whatever your name is" Jones slash Cage baby.
I am completely blown away.
Look at you.
You know...your dad asked me to marry him.
Kind of surprised me-- kind of shocked the $%#@ out of me is what it did.
Luke Cage asked me to marry him.
I didn't think he knew what the word meant.

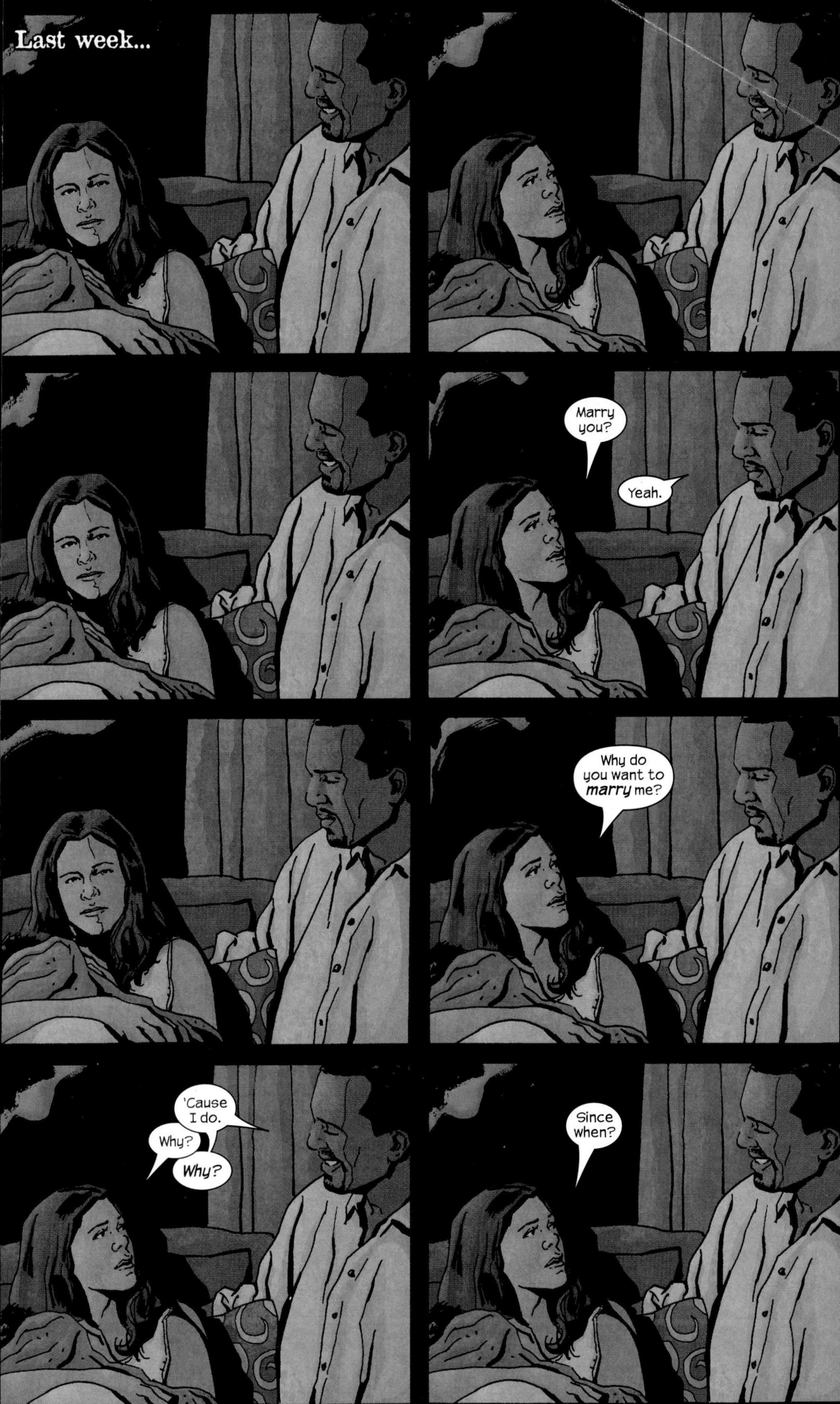
Last week...
Marry you?
Yeah.
Why do you want to *marry* me?
'Cause I do.
Why?
Why?
Since when?

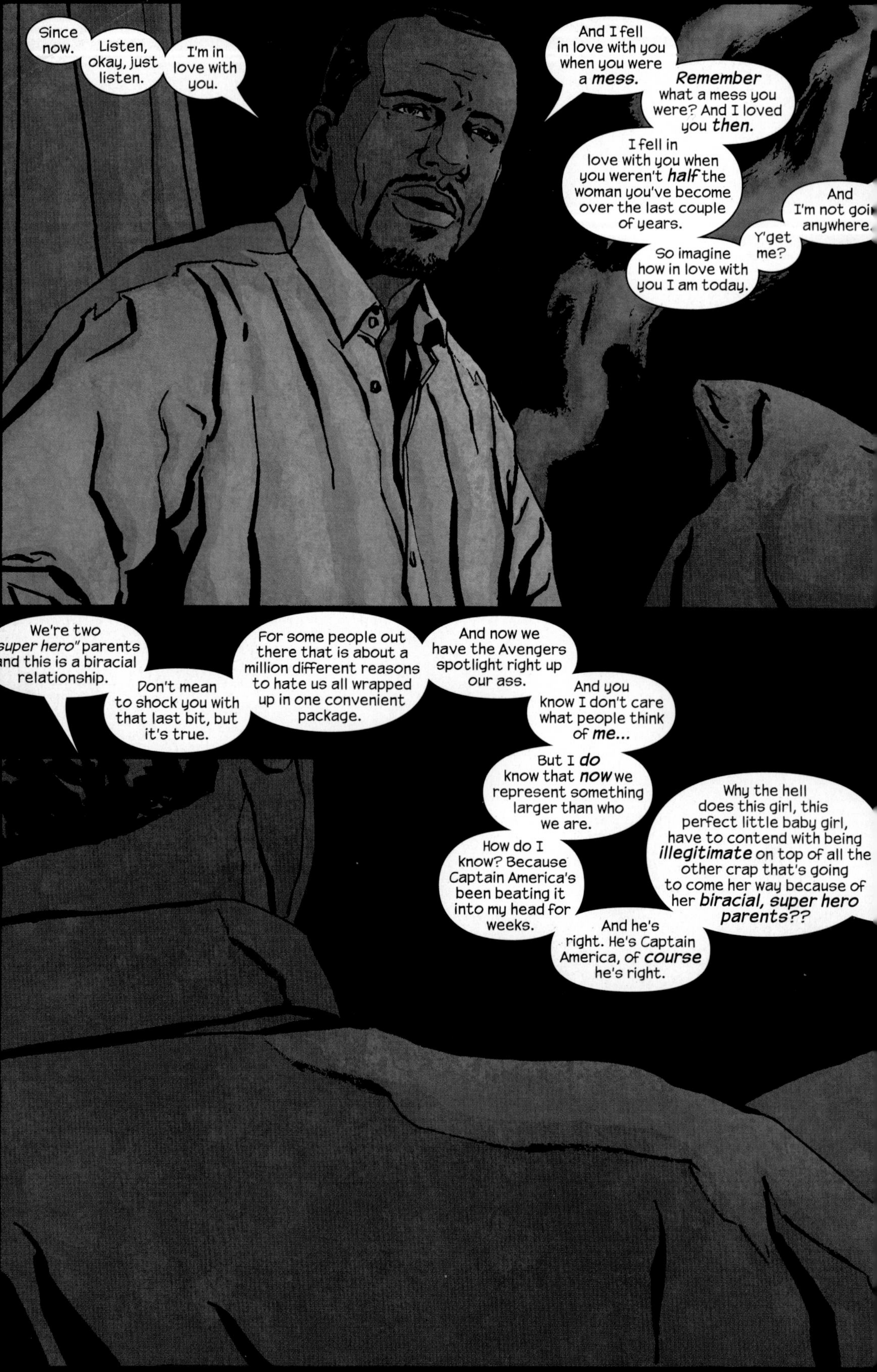

Since now.
Listen, okay, just listen.
I'm in love with you.
And I fell in love with you when you were a *mess.*
Remember what a mess you were? And I loved you *then.*
I fell in love with you when you weren't *half* the woman you've become over the last couple of years.
So imagine how in love with you I am today.
Y'get me?
And I'm not goi anywhere.
We're two *"super hero"* parents and this is a biracial relationship.
Don't mean to shock you with that last bit, but it's true.
For some people out there that is about a million different reasons to hate us all wrapped up in one convenient package.
And now we have the Avengers spotlight right up our ass.
And you know I don't care what people think of *me...*
But I *do* know that *now* we represent something larger than who we are.
How do I know? Because Captain America's been beating it into my head for weeks.
And he's right. He's Captain America, of *course* he's right.
Why the hell does this girl, this perfect little baby girl, have to contend with being *illegitimate* on top of all the other crap that's going to come her way because of her *biracial, super hero parents??*

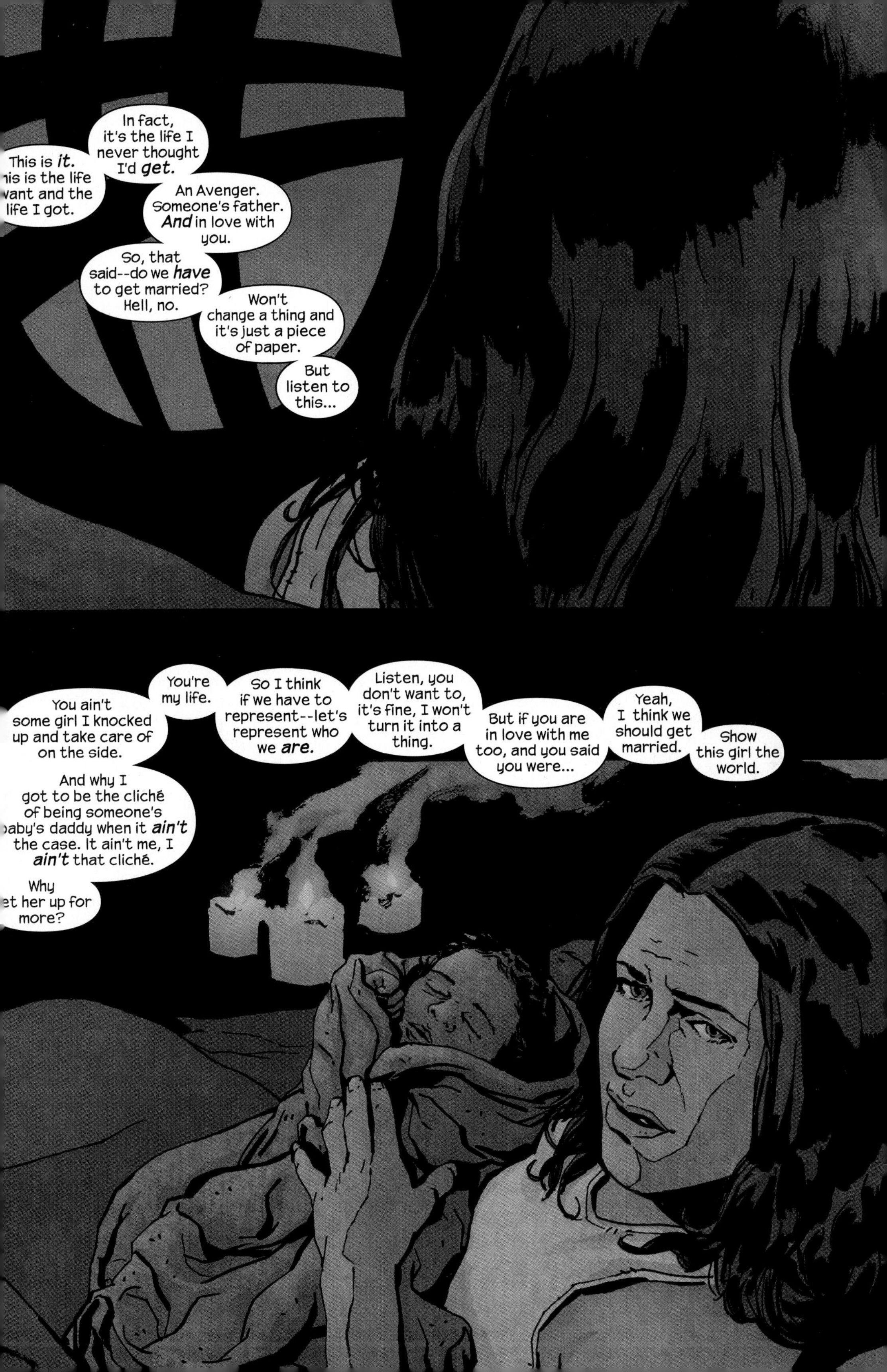

This is it.
his is the life
want and the
life I got.
In fact, it's the life I never thought I'd get.
An Avenger. Someone's father. And in love with you.
So, that said--do we have to get married? Hell, no.
Won't change a thing and it's just a piece of paper.
But listen to this...
You ain't some girl I knocked up and take care of on the side.
And why I got to be the cliché of being someone's
baby's daddy when it ain't the case. It ain't me, I ain't that cliché.
Why
et her up for more?
You're my life.
So I think if we have to represent--let's represent who we are.
Listen, you don't want to, it's fine, I won't turn it into a thing.
But if you are in love with me too, and you said you were...
Yeah, I think we should get married.
Show this girl the world.

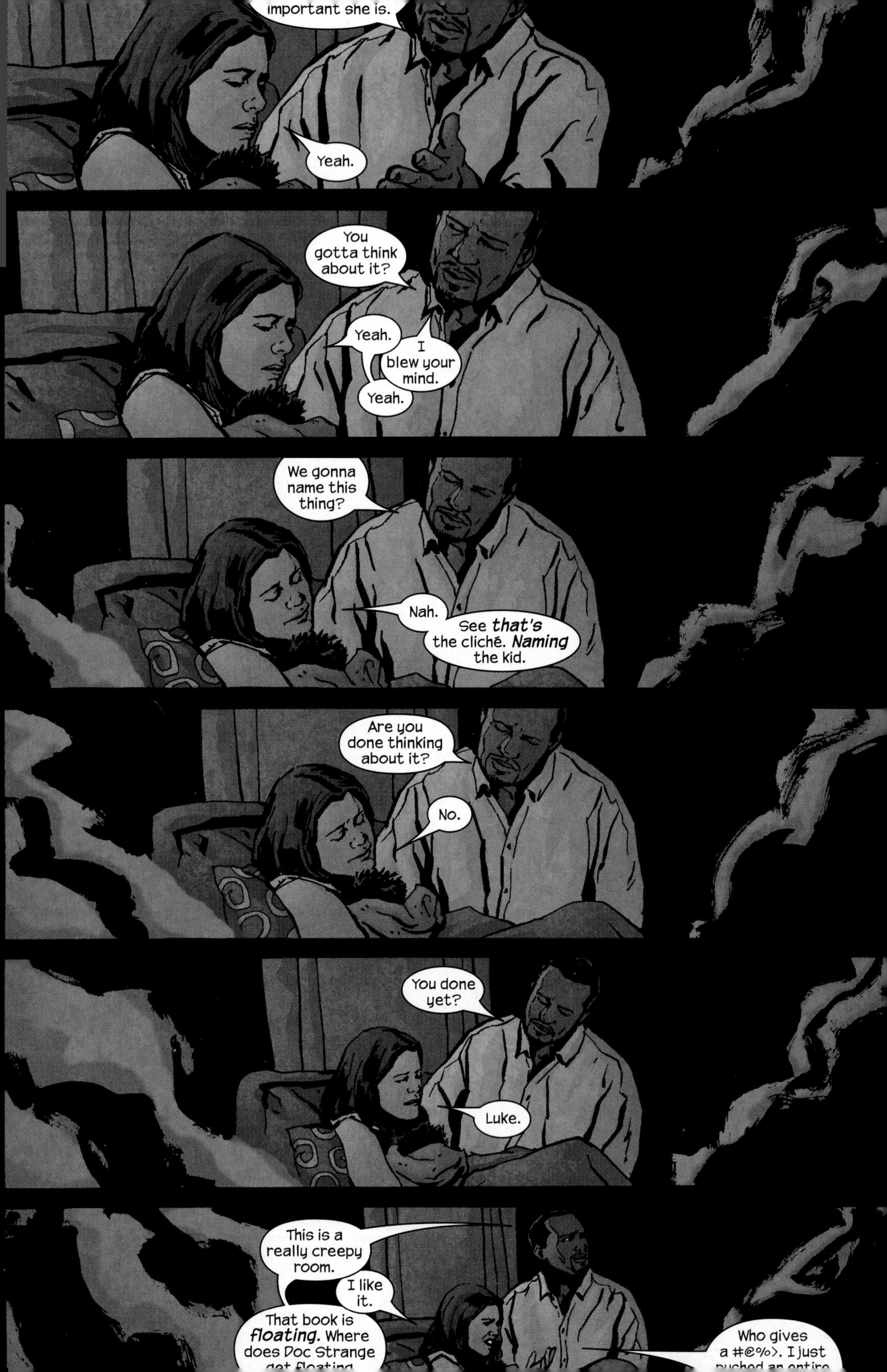
important she is.
Yeah.
You gotta think about it?
Yeah.
I blew your mind.
Yeah.
We gonna name this thing?
Nah.
See *that's* the cliché. *Naming* the kid.
Are you done thinking about it?
No.
You done yet?
Luke.
This is a really creepy room.
I like it.
That book is *floating.* Where does Doc Strange
Who gives a #@%>. I just

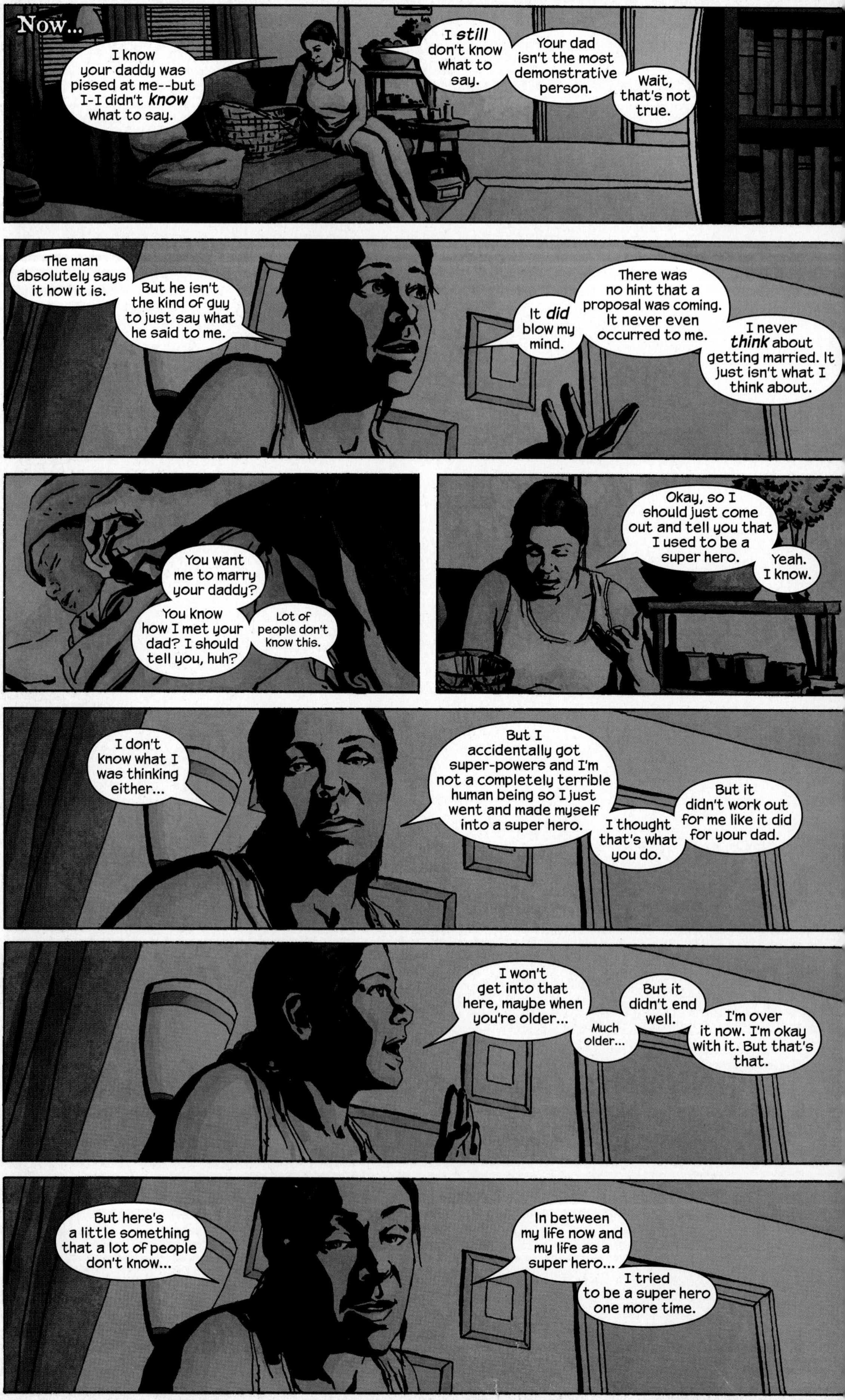

Now...
I know your daddy was pissed at me--but I-I didn't *know* what to say.
I *still* don't know what to say.
Your dad isn't the most demonstrative person.
Wait, that's not true.
The man absolutely says it how it is.
But he isn't the kind of guy to just say what he said to me.
It *did* blow my mind.
There was no hint that a proposal was coming. It never even occurred to me.
I never *think* about getting married. It just isn't what I think about.
You want me to marry your daddy?
You know how I met your dad? I should tell you, huh?
Lot of people don't know this.
Okay, so I should just come out and tell you that I used to be a super hero.
Yeah. I know.
I don't know what I was thinking either...
But I accidentally got super-powers and I'm not a completely terrible human being so I just went and made myself into a super hero.
I thought that's what you do.
But it didn't work out for me like it did for your dad.
I won't get into that here, maybe when you're older...
Much older...
But it didn't end well.
I'm over it now. I'm okay with it. But that's that.
But here's a little something that a lot of people don't know...
In between my life now and my life as a super hero...
I tried to be a super hero one more time.

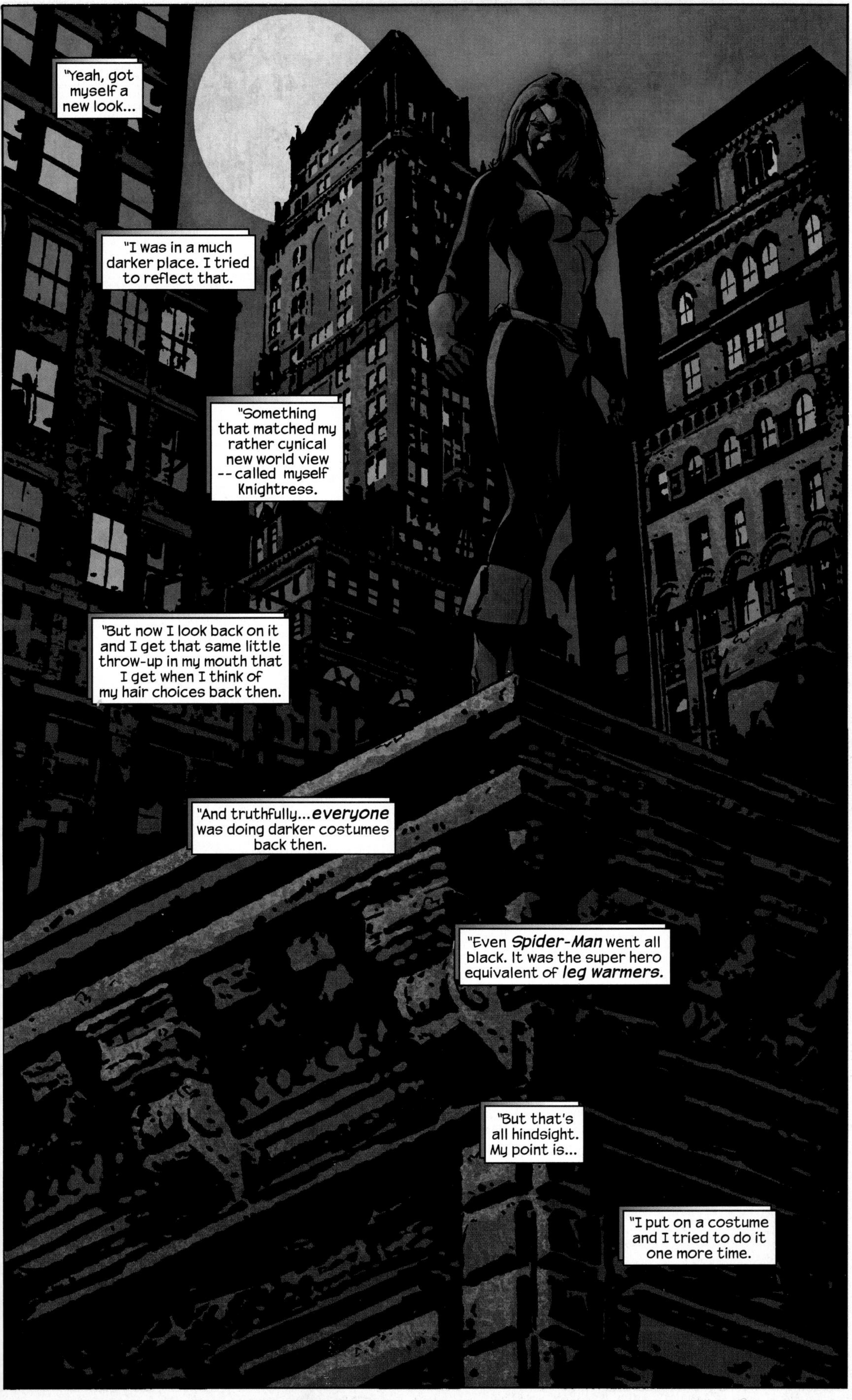
"Yeah, got myself a new look...
"I was in a much darker place. I tried to reflect that.
"Something that matched my rather cynical new world view -- called myself Knightress.
"But now I look back on it and I get that same little throw-up in my mouth that I get when I think of my hair choices back then.
"And truthfully... *everyone* was doing darker costumes back then.
"Even *Spider-Man* went all black. It was the super hero equivalent of *leg warmers.*
"But that's all hindsight. My point is...
"I put on a costume and I tried to do it one more time.

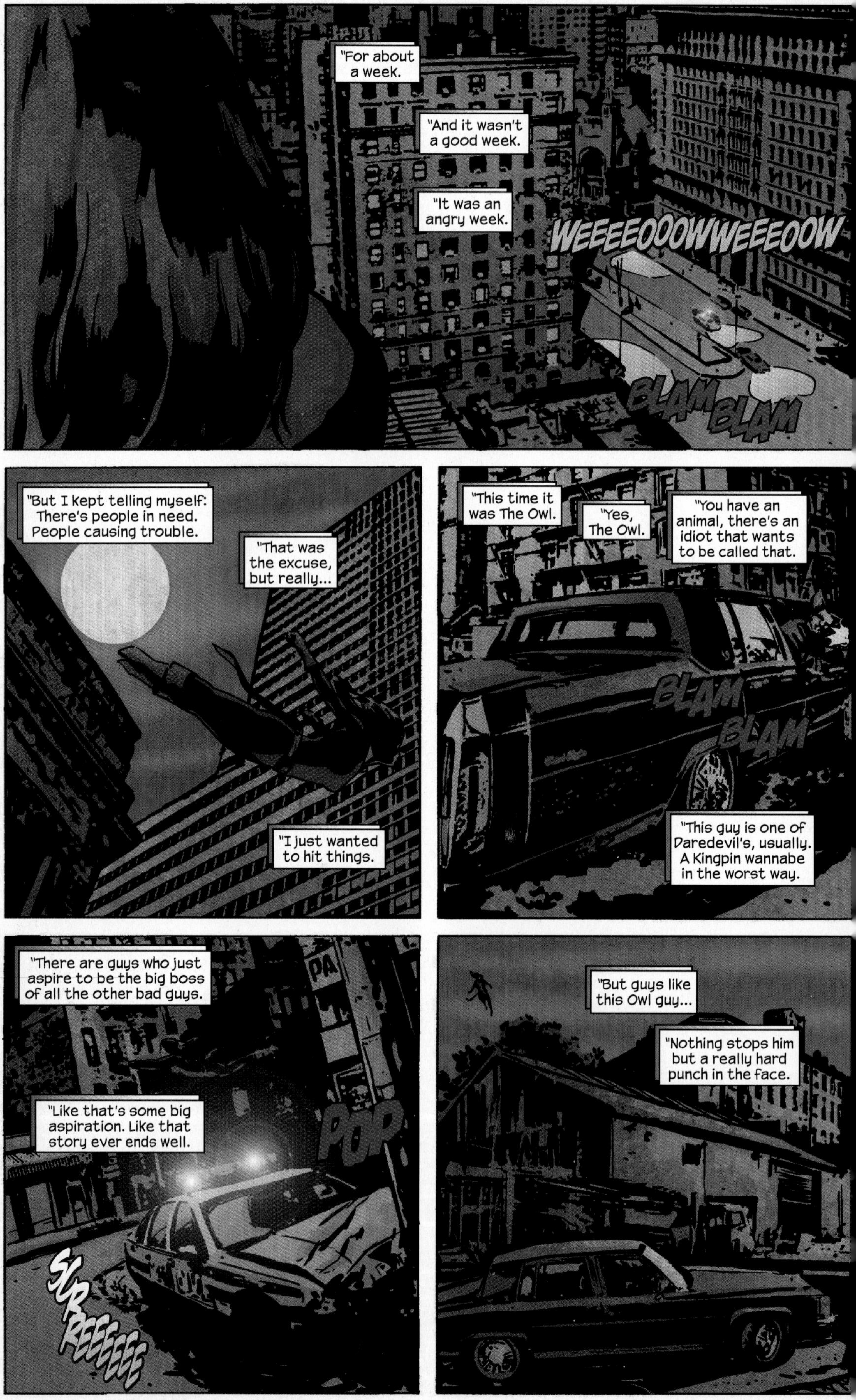
"For about a week.
"And it wasn't a good week.
"It was an angry week.
WEEEEOOOWWEEEOOW
BLAM BLAM
"But I kept telling myself: There's people in need. People causing trouble.
"That was the excuse, but really...
"I just wanted to hit things.
"This time it was The Owl.
"Yes, The Owl.
"You have an animal, there's an idiot that wants to be called that.
BLAM
BLAM
"This guy is one of Daredevil's, usually. A Kingpin wannabe in the worst way.
"There are guys who just aspire to be the big boss of all the other bad guys.
"Like that's some big aspiration. Like that story ever ends well.
POP
SCREEEEEE
"But guys like this Owl guy...
"Nothing stops him but a really hard punch in the face.

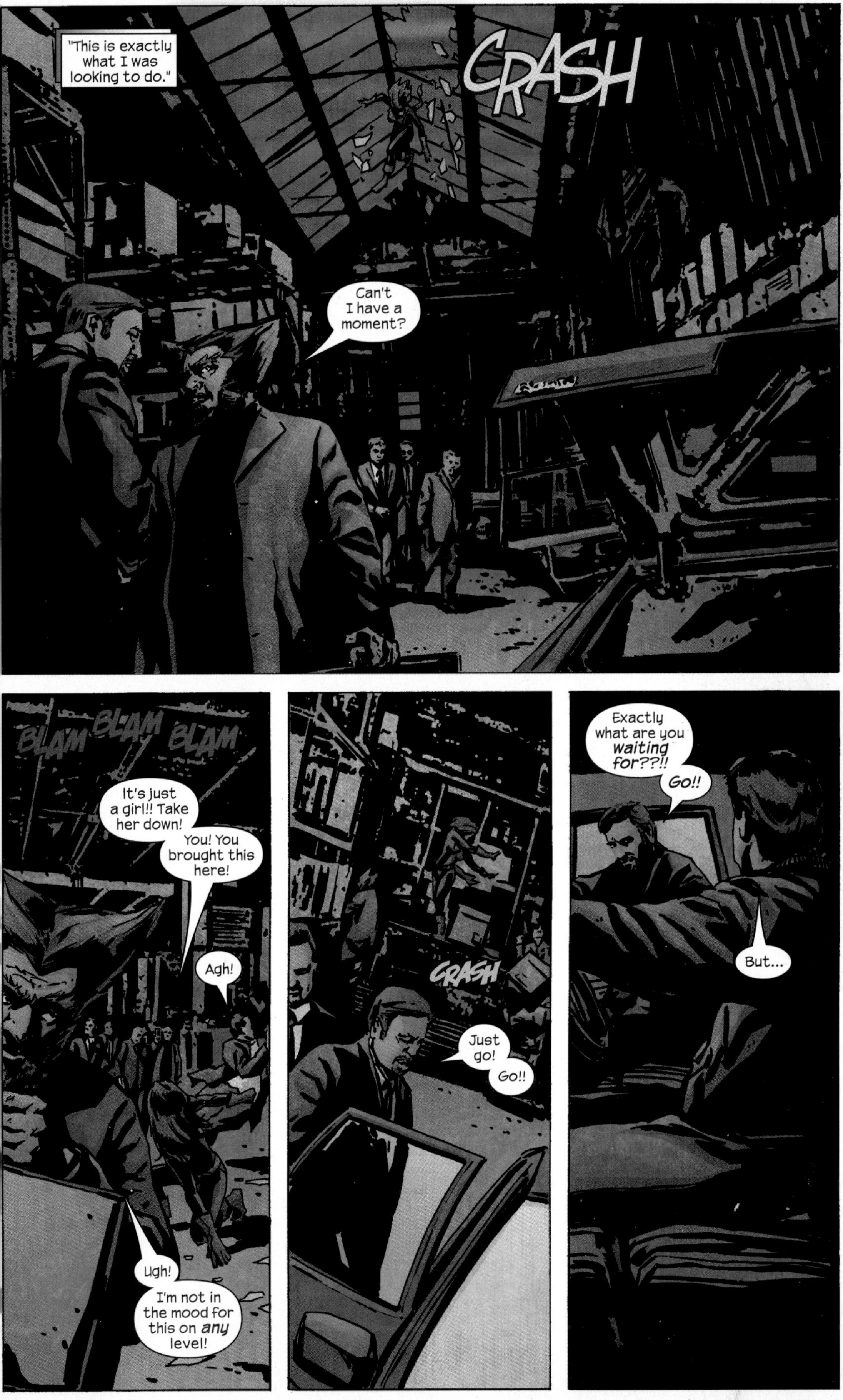

"This is exactly what I was looking to do."
CRASH
Can't I have a moment?
BLAM BLAM BLAM
It's just a girl!! Take her down!
You! You brought this here!
Agh!
Ugh!
I'm not in the mood for this on *any* level!
CRASH
Just go!
Go!!
Exactly what are you *waiting for??!!*
Go!!
But...

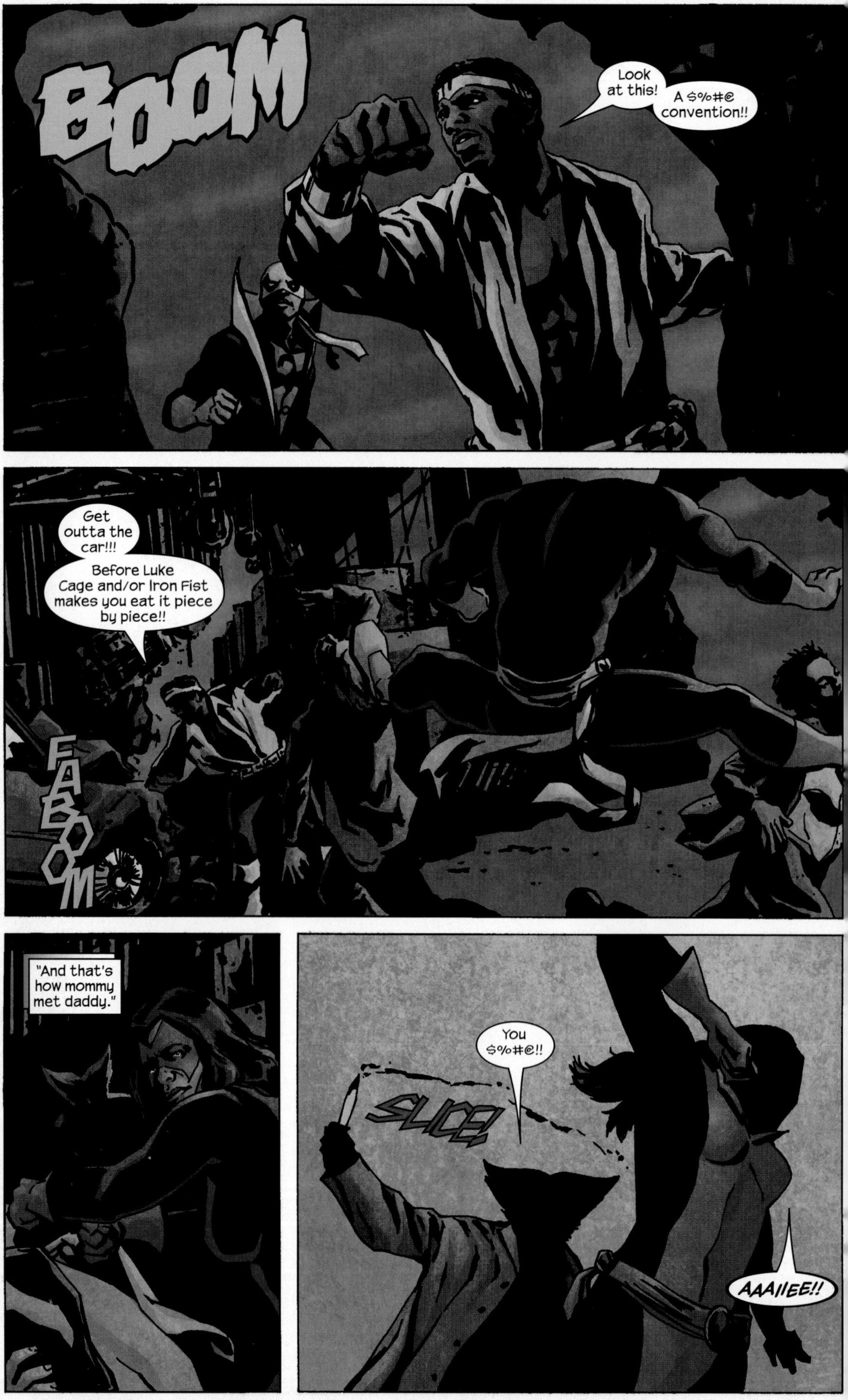
BOOM
Look at this!
A $%#@ convention!!
Get outta the car!!!
Before Luke Cage and/or Iron Fist makes you eat it piece by piece!!
FABOOM
"And that's how mommy met daddy."
You $%#@!!
SLICE!
AAAIIEE!!

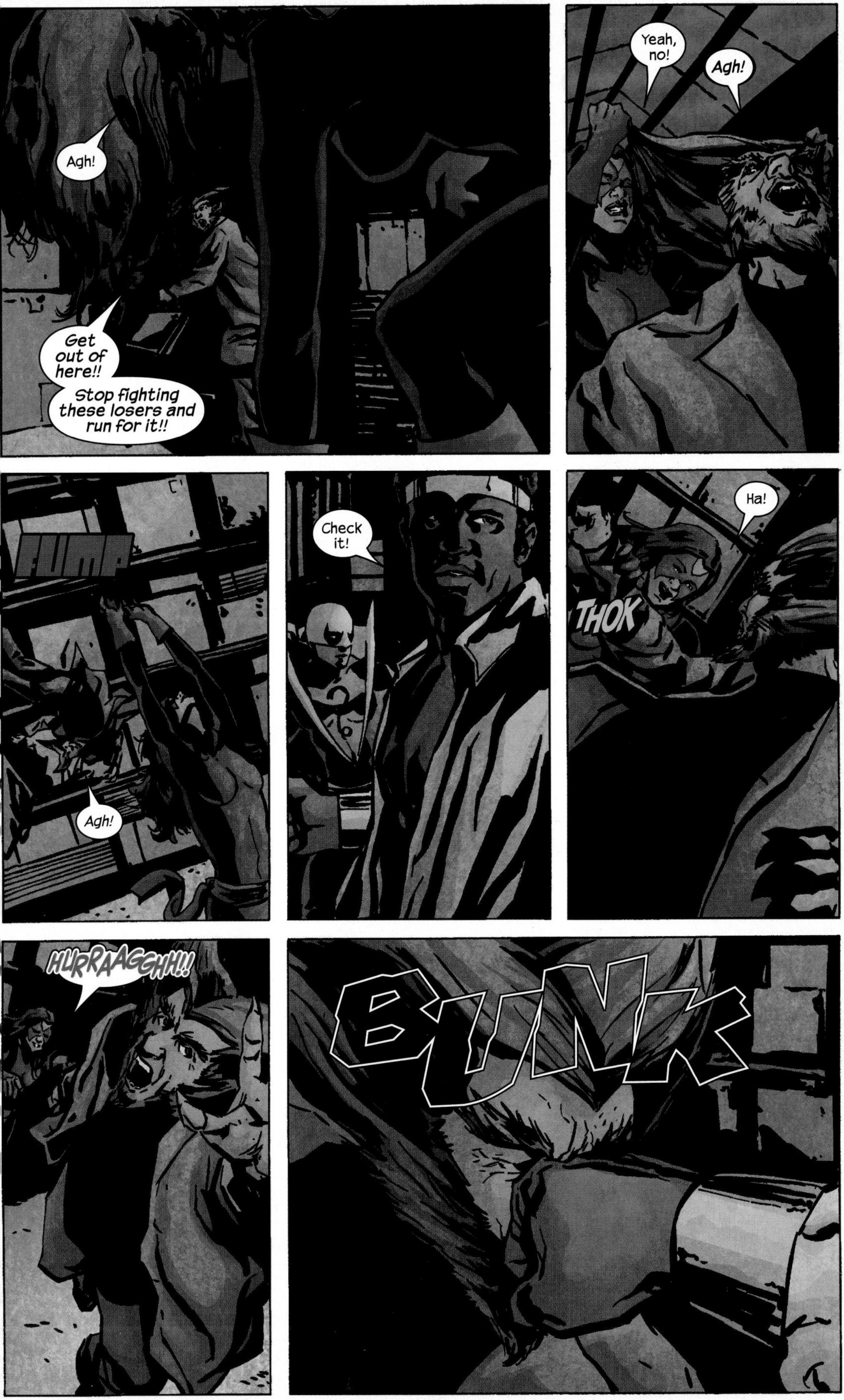
Agh!
Get out of here!!
Stop fighting these losers and run for it!!
Yeah, no!
Agh!
FUMP
Agh!
Check it!
Ha!
THOK
HURRAAGGHH!!
BUNK

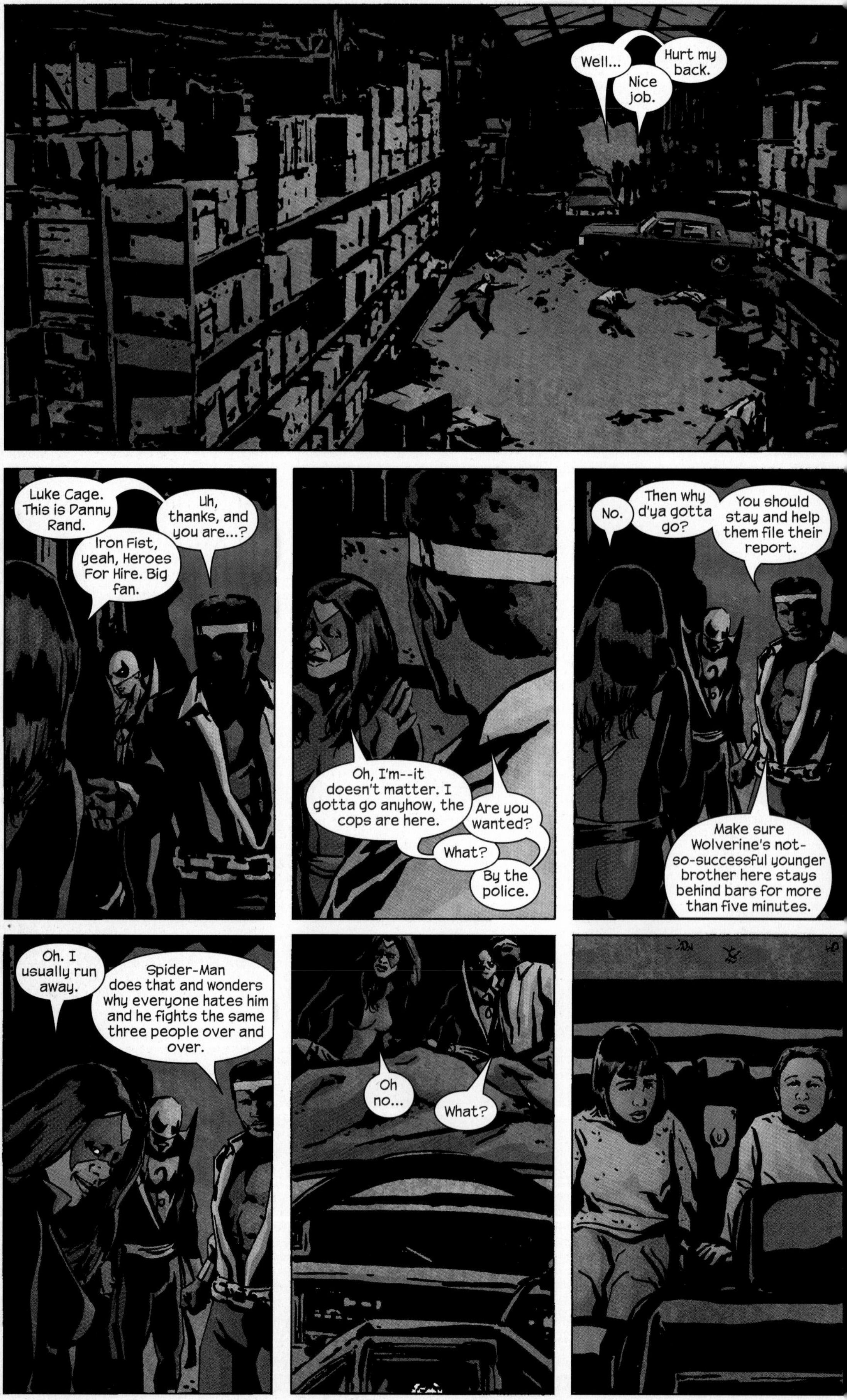
Well...
Nice job.
Hurt my back.
Luke Cage. This is Danny Rand.
Uh, thanks, and you are...?
Iron Fist, yeah, Heroes For Hire. Big fan.
Oh, I'm--it doesn't matter. I gotta go anyhow, the cops are here.
Are you wanted?
What?
By the police.
No.
Then why d'ya gotta go?
You should stay and help them file their report.
Make sure Wolverine's not-so-successful younger brother here stays behind bars for more than five minutes.
Oh. I usually run away.
Spider-Man does that and wonders why everyone hates him and he fights the same three people over and over.
Oh no...
What?

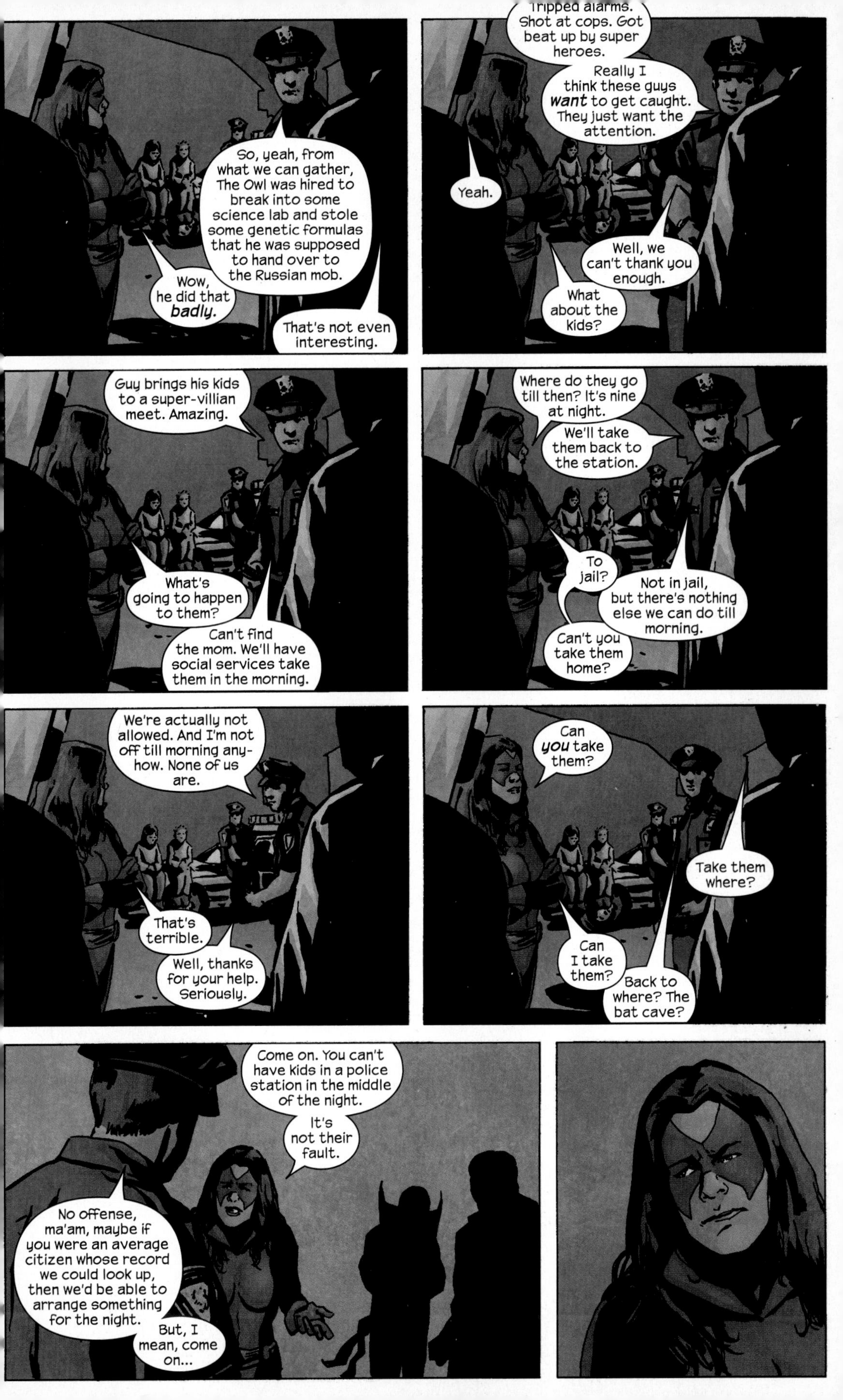
So, yeah, from what we can gather, The Owl was hired to break into some science lab and stole some genetic formulas that he was supposed to hand over to the Russian mob.
Wow, he did that *badly*.
That's not even interesting.
Tripped alarms. Shot at cops. Got beat up by super heroes.
Really I think these guys *want* to get caught. They just want the attention.
Yeah.
Well, we can't thank you enough.
What about the kids?
Guy brings his kids to a super-villian meet. Amazing.
What's going to happen to them?
Can't find the mom. We'll have social services take them in the morning.
Where do they go till then? It's nine at night.
We'll take them back to the station.
To jail?
Not in jail, but there's nothing else we can do till morning.
Can't you take them home?
We're actually not allowed. And I'm not off till morning any-how. None of us are.
That's terrible.
Well, thanks for your help. Seriously.
Can *you* take them?
Take them where?
Can I take them?
Back to where? The bat cave?
Come on. You can't have kids in a police station in the middle of the night.
It's not their fault.
No offense, ma'am, maybe if you were an average citizen whose record we could look up, then we'd be able to arrange something for the night.
But, I mean, come on...

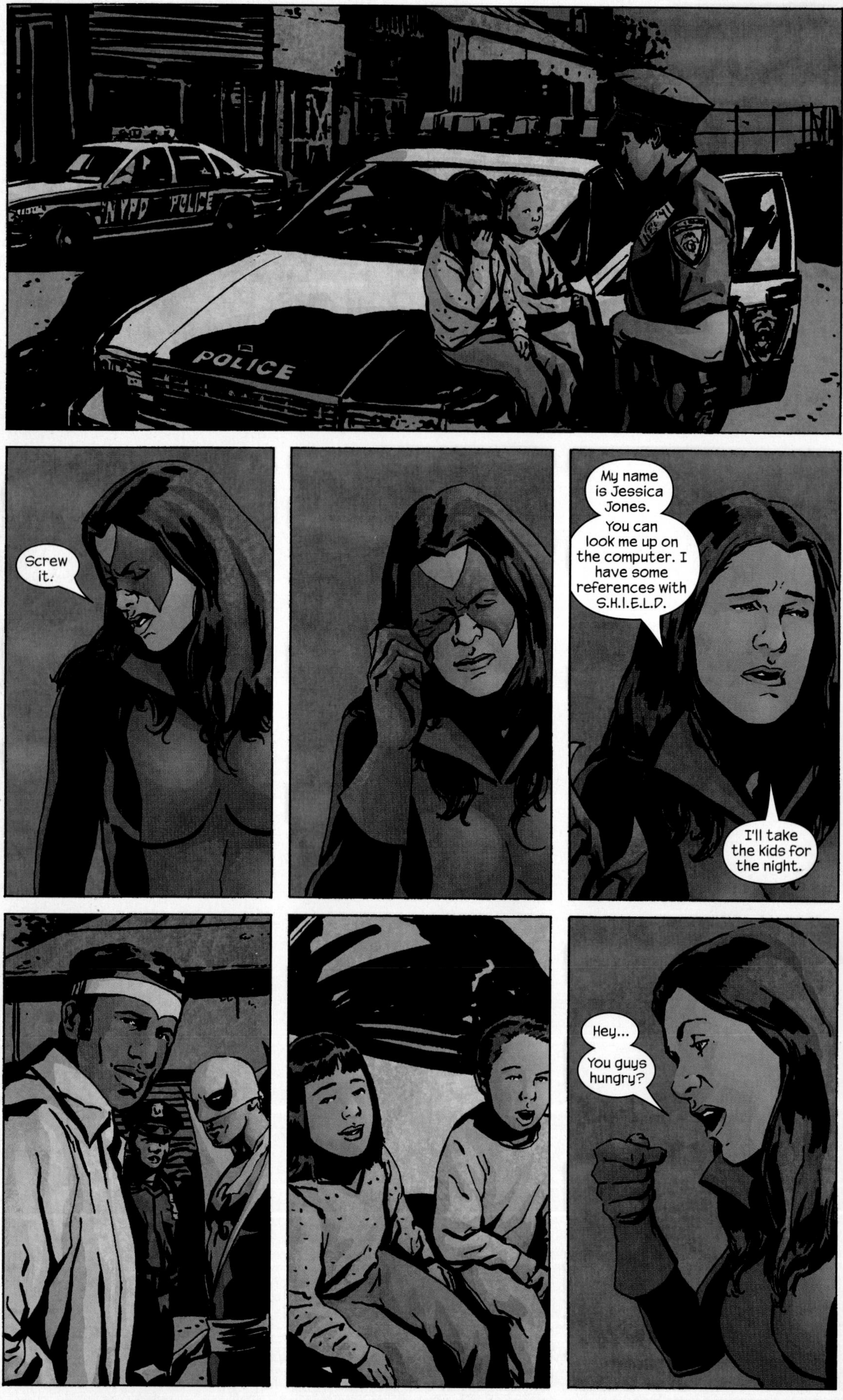

NYPD POLICE
POLICE
Screw it.
My name is Jessica Jones.
You can look me up on the computer. I have some references with S.H.I.E.L.D.
I'll take the kids for the night.
Hey...
You guys hungry?

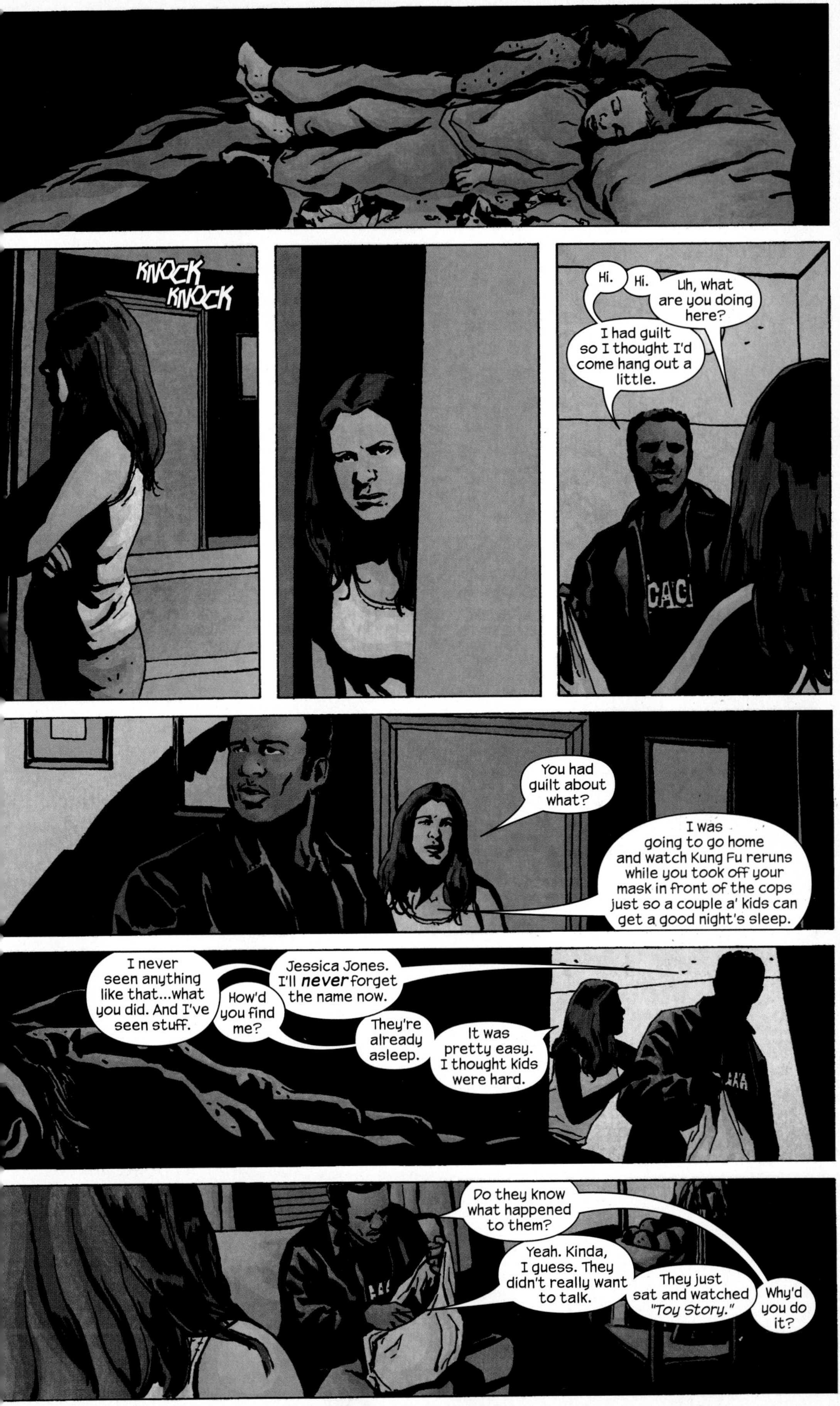
KNOCK KNOCK
Hi.
Hi.
Uh, what are you doing here?
I had guilt so I thought I'd come hang out a little.
You had guilt about what?
I was going to go home and watch Kung Fu reruns while you took off your mask in front of the cops just so a couple a' kids can get a good night's sleep.
I never seen anything like that...what you did. And I've seen stuff.
Jessica Jones. I'll *never* forget the name now.
How'd you find me?
They're already asleep.
It was pretty easy. I thought kids were hard.
Do they know what happened to them?
Yeah. Kinda, I guess. They didn't really want to talk.
They just sat and watched *"Toy Story."*
Why'd you do it?

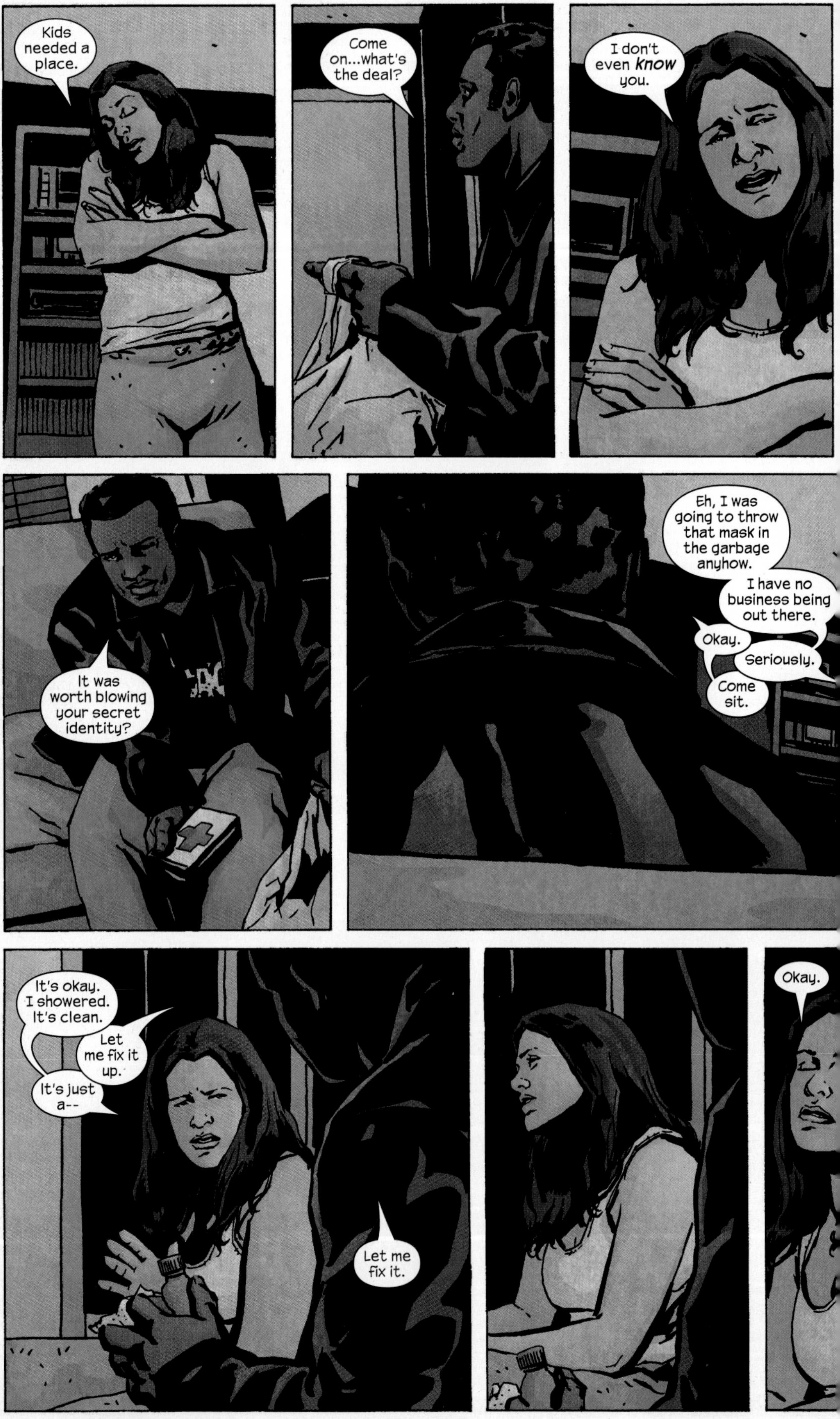
Kids needed a place.
Come on...what's the deal?
I don't even KNOW you.
It was worth blowing your secret identity?
Eh, I was going to throw that mask in the garbage anyhow.
I have no business being out there.
Okay.
Seriously.
Come sit.
It's okay. I showered. It's clean.
Let me fix it up.
It's just a--
Let me fix it.
Okay.

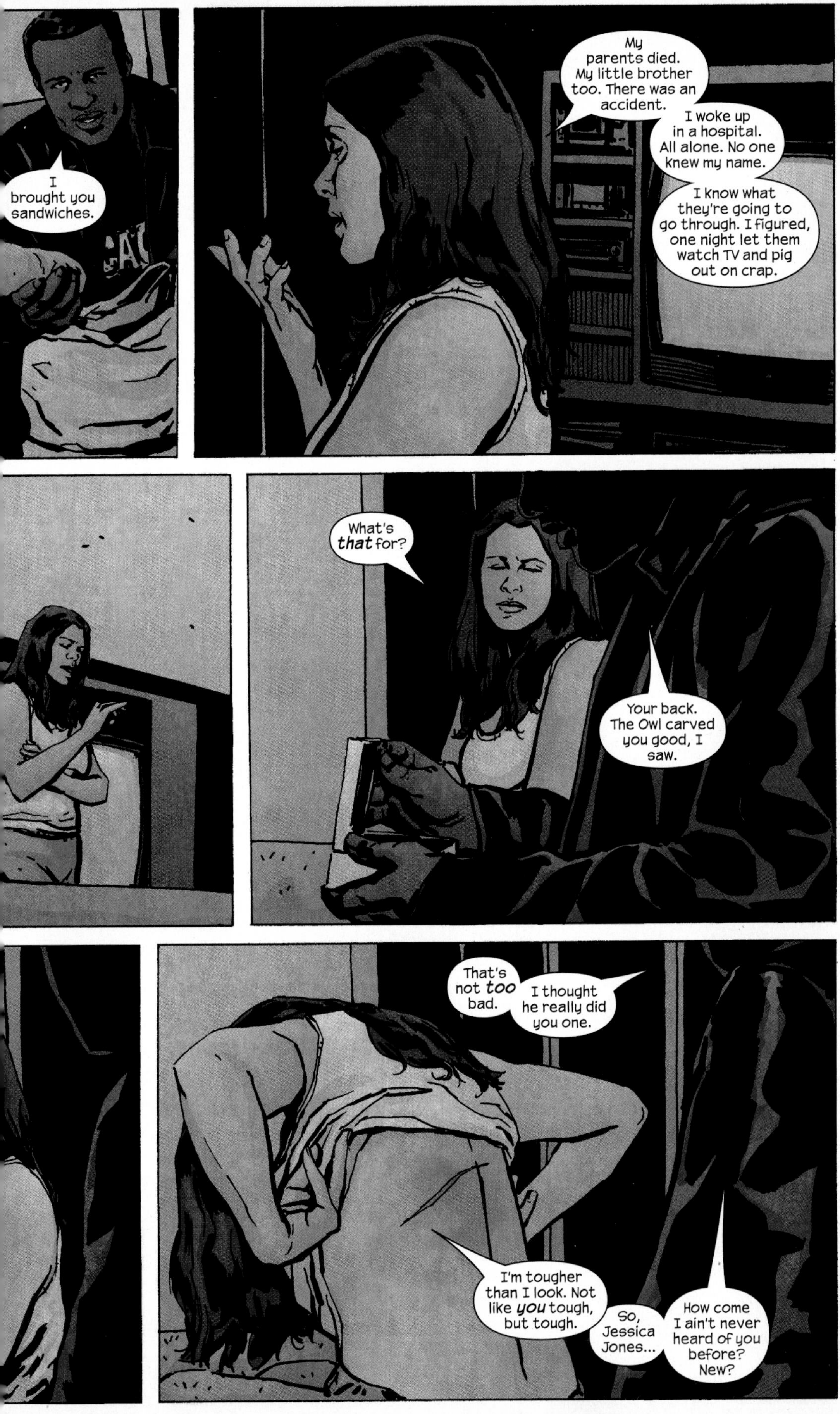
I brought you sandwiches.
My parents died. My little brother too. There was an accident.
I woke up in a hospital. All alone. No one knew my name.
I know what they're going to go through. I figured, one night let them watch TV and pig out on crap.
What's *that* for?
Your back. The Owl carved you good, I saw.
That's not *too* bad.
I thought he really did you one.
I'm tougher than I look. Not like *you* tough, but tough.
So, Jessica Jones...
How come I ain't never heard of you before? New?

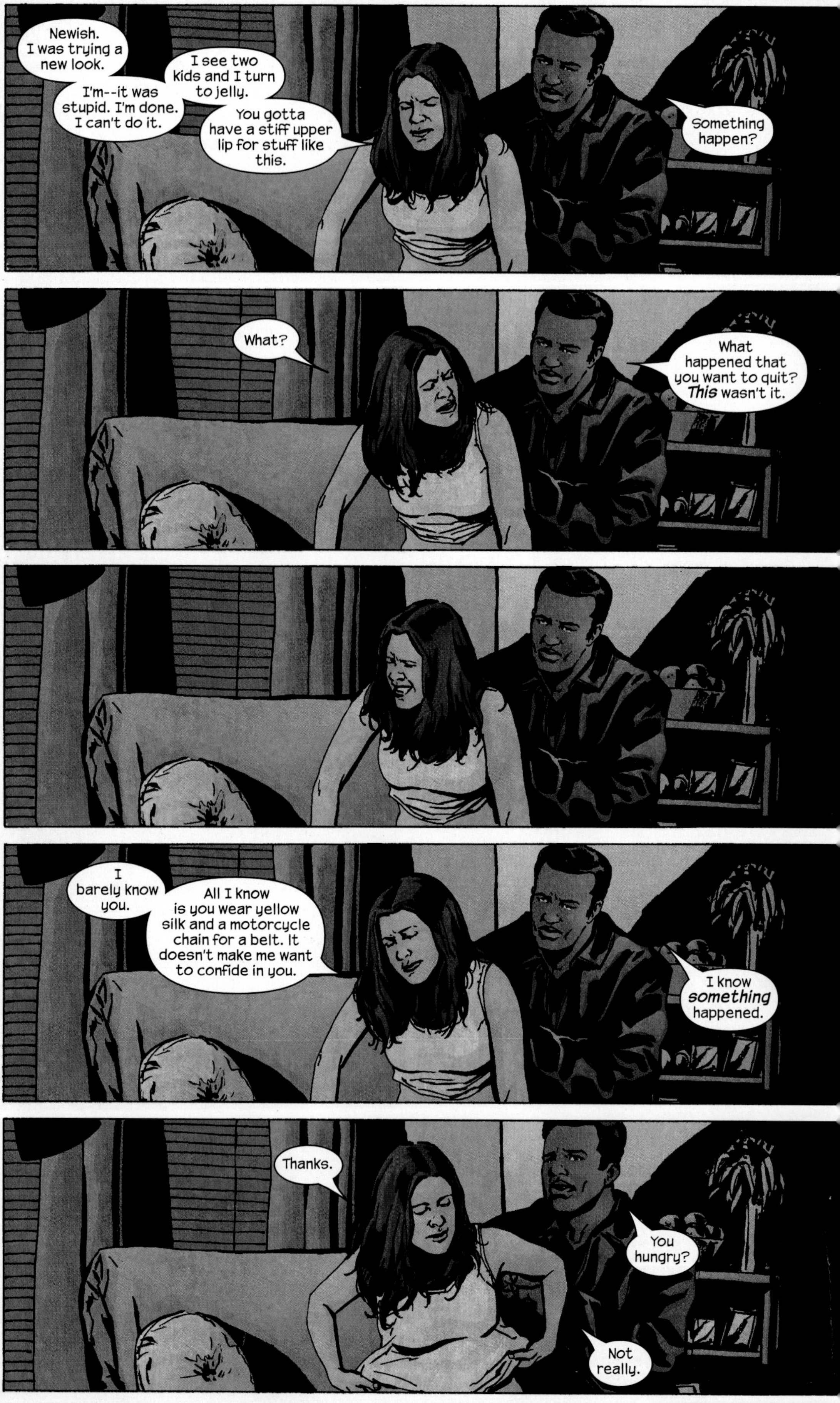

Newish. I was trying a new look.
I'm--it was stupid. I'm done. I can't do it.
I see two kids and I turn to jelly.
You gotta have a stiff upper lip for stuff like this.
Something happen?
What?
What happened that you want to quit? *This* wasn't it.
I barely know you.
All I know is you wear yellow silk and a motorcycle chain for a belt. It doesn't make me want to confide in you.
I know *something* happened.
Thanks.
You hungry?
Not really.

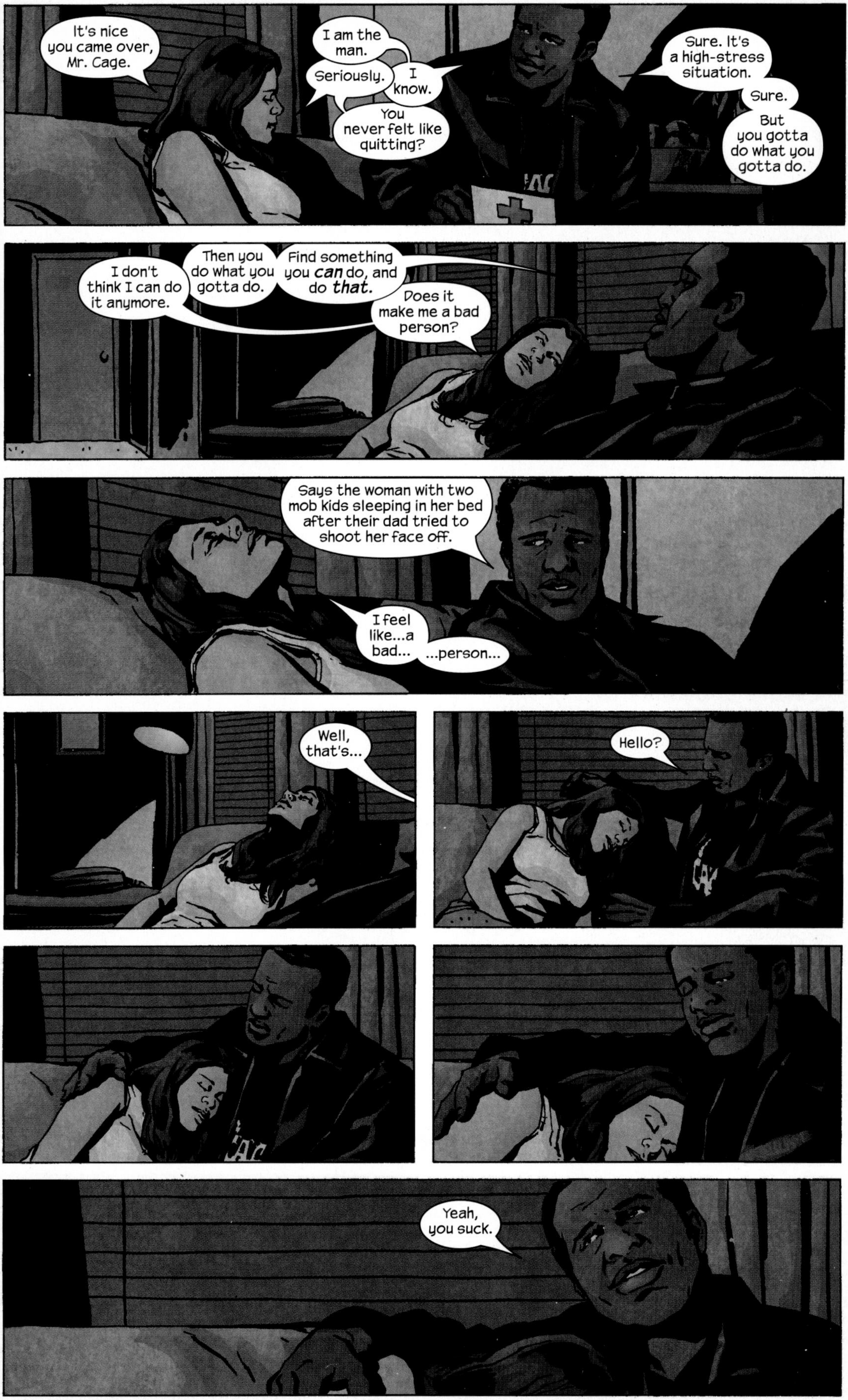
It's nice you came over, Mr. Cage.
I am the man.
Seriously.
I know.
You never felt like quitting?
Sure. It's a high-stress situation.
Sure.
But you gotta do what you gotta do.
I don't think I can do it anymore.
Then you do what you gotta do.
Find something you *can* do, and do *that.*
Does it make me a bad person?
Says the woman with two mob kids sleeping in her bed after their dad tried to shoot her face off.
I feel like...a bad...
...person...
Well, that's...
Hello?
Yeah, you suck.

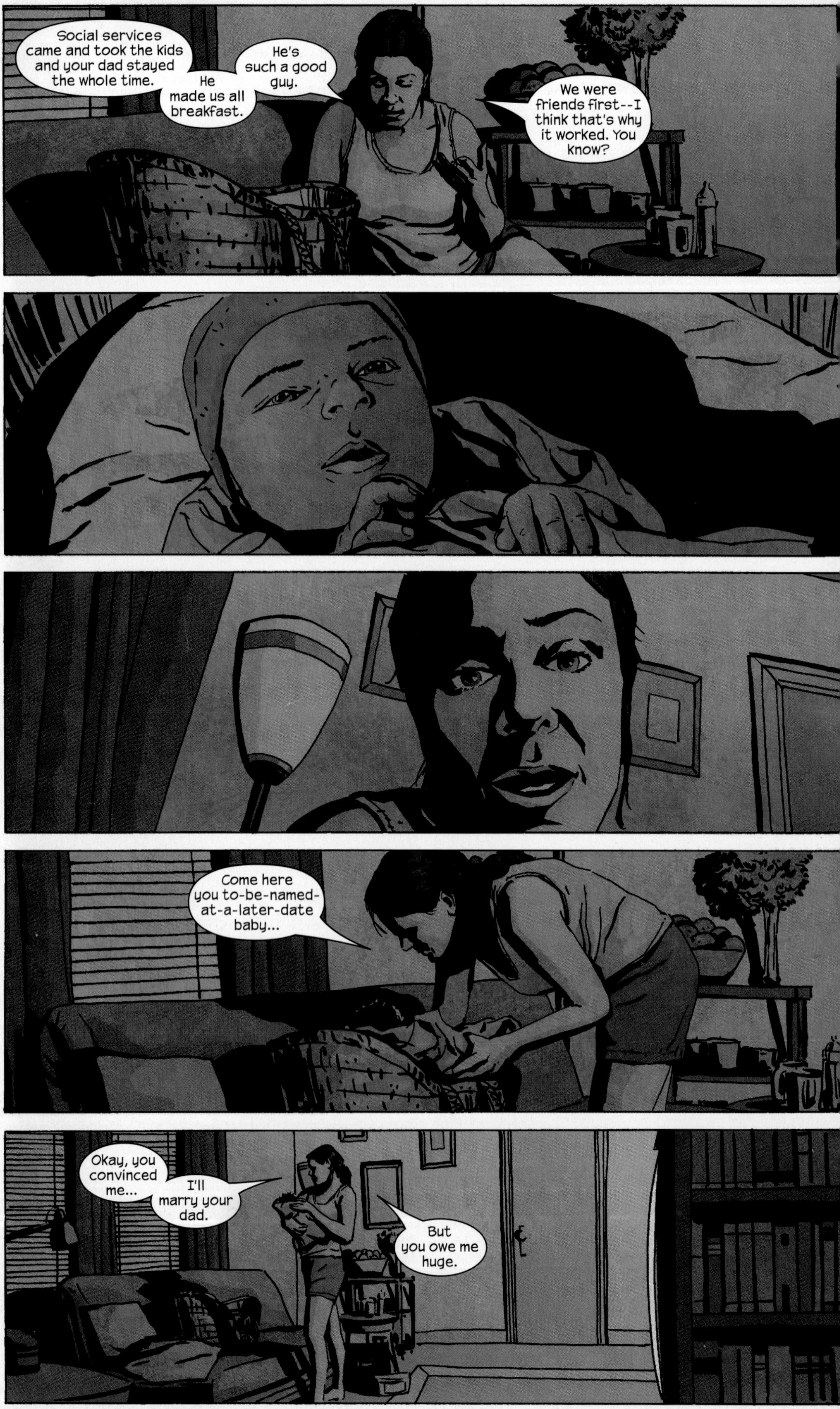
Social services came and took the kids and your dad stayed the whole time.
He made us all breakfast.
He's such a good guy.
We were friends first--I think that's why it worked. You know?
Come here you to-be-named-at-a-later-date baby...
Okay, you convinced me...
I'll marry your dad.
But you owe me huge.

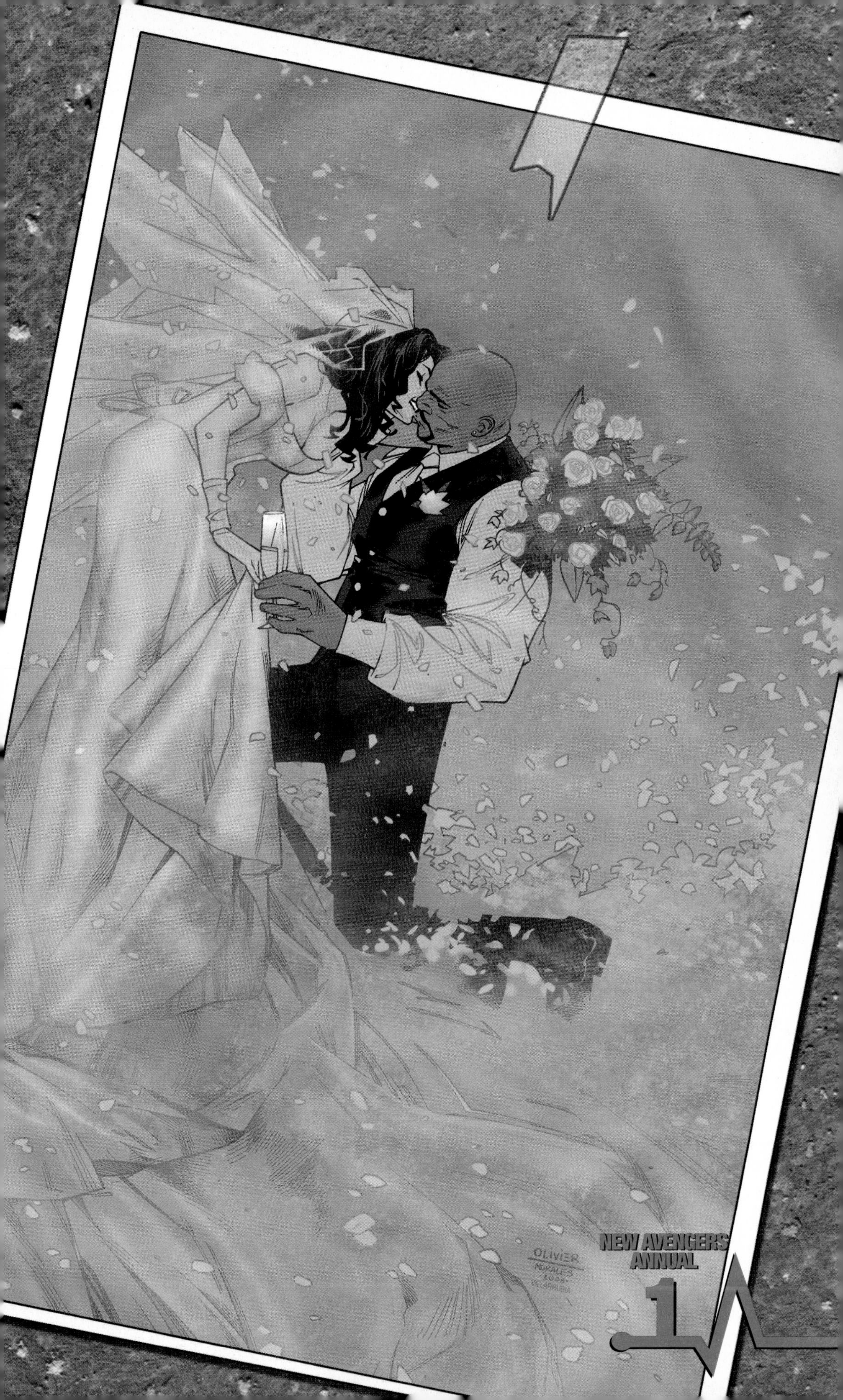

OLIVIER
MORALES
2005
VILLARRUBIA
NEW AVENGERS
ANNUAL
1

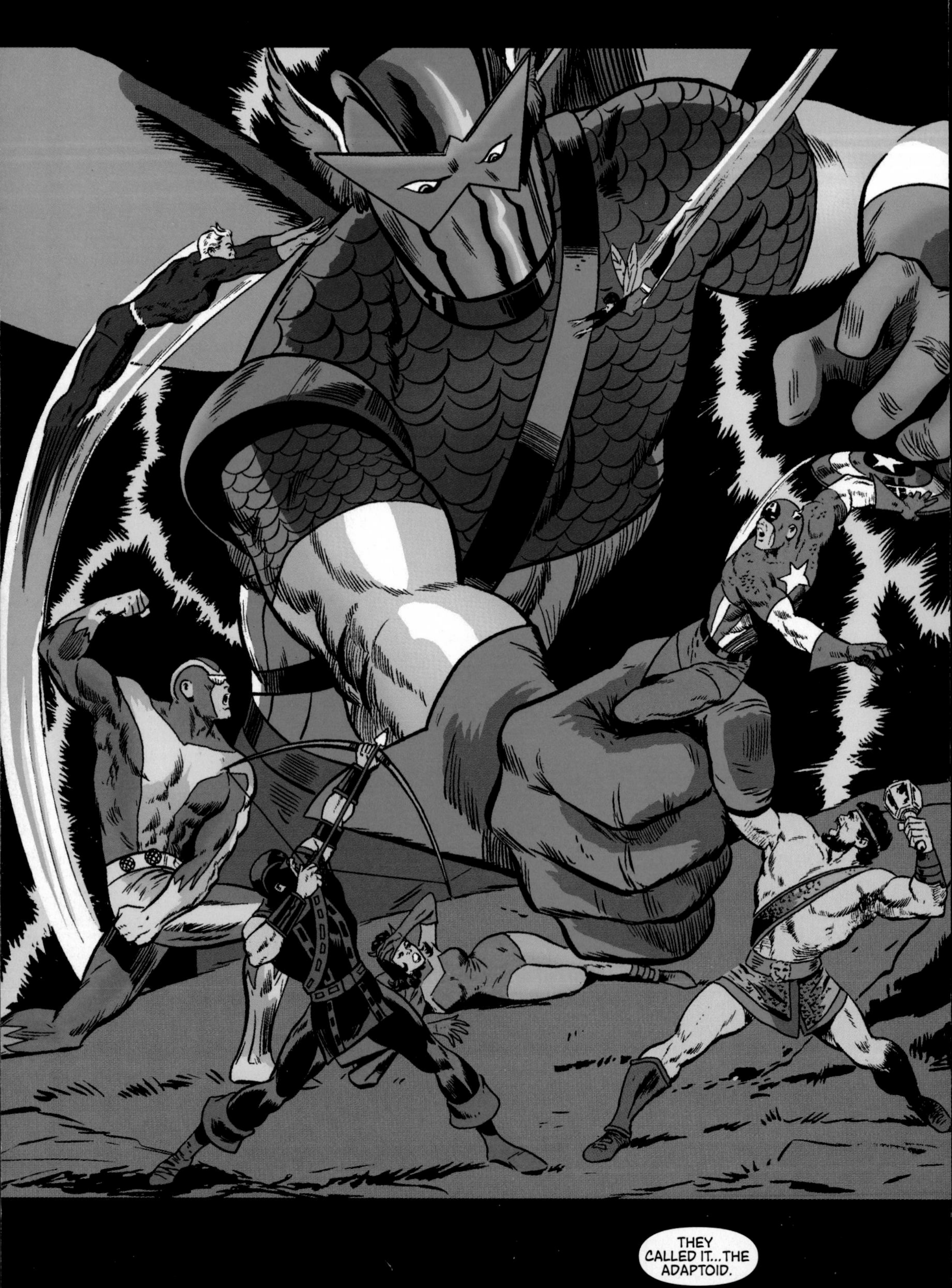
THEY CALLED IT... THE ADAPTOID.

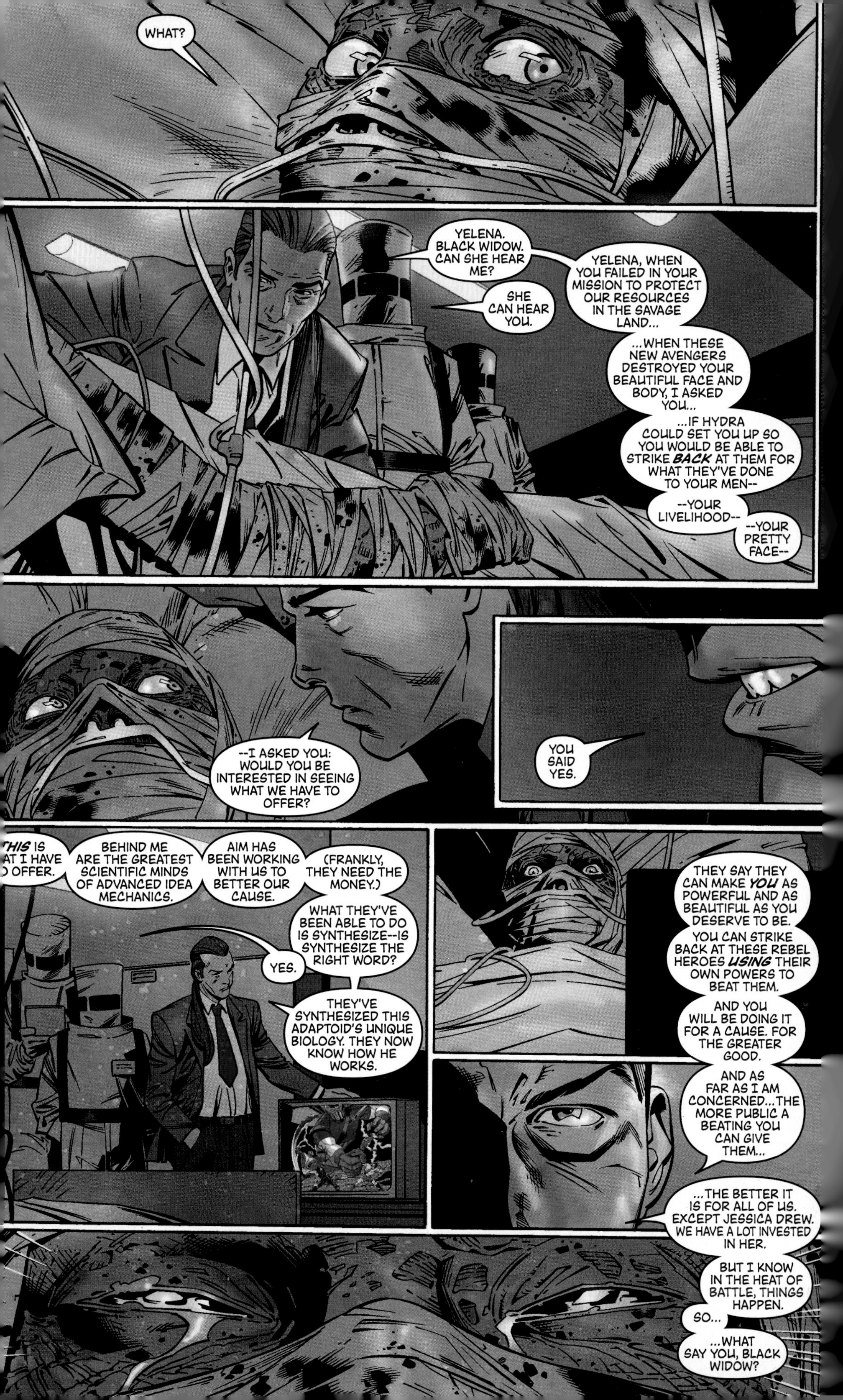
WHAT?
YELENA. BLACK WIDOW. CAN SHE HEAR ME?
SHE CAN HEAR YOU.
YELENA, WHEN YOU FAILED IN YOUR MISSION TO PROTECT OUR RESOURCES IN THE SAVAGE LAND...
...WHEN THESE NEW AVENGERS DESTROYED YOUR BEAUTIFUL FACE AND BODY, I ASKED YOU...
...IF HYDRA COULD SET YOU UP SO YOU WOULD BE ABLE TO STRIKE BACK AT THEM FOR WHAT THEY'VE DONE TO YOUR MEN--
--YOUR LIVELIHOOD--
--YOUR PRETTY FACE--
--I ASKED YOU: WOULD YOU BE INTERESTED IN SEEING WHAT WE HAVE TO OFFER?
YOU SAID YES.
THIS IS AT I HAVE OFFER.
BEHIND ME ARE THE GREATEST SCIENTIFIC MINDS OF ADVANCED IDEA MECHANICS.
AIM HAS BEEN WORKING WITH US TO BETTER OUR CAUSE.
(FRANKLY, THEY NEED THE MONEY.)
WHAT THEY'VE BEEN ABLE TO DO IS SYNTHESIZE--IS SYNTHESIZE THE RIGHT WORD?
YES.
THEY'VE SYNTHESIZED THIS ADAPTOID'S UNIQUE BIOLOGY. THEY NOW KNOW HOW HE WORKS.
THEY SAY THEY CAN MAKE YOU AS POWERFUL AND AS BEAUTIFUL AS YOU DESERVE TO BE.
YOU CAN STRIKE BACK AT THESE REBEL HEROES USING THEIR OWN POWERS TO BEAT THEM.
AND YOU WILL BE DOING IT FOR A CAUSE. FOR THE GREATER GOOD.
AND AS FAR AS I AM CONCERNED...THE MORE PUBLIC A BEATING YOU CAN GIVE THEM...
...THE BETTER IT IS FOR ALL OF US. EXCEPT JESSICA DREW. WE HAVE A LOT INVESTED IN HER.
BUT I KNOW IN THE HEAT OF BATTLE, THINGS HAPPEN.
SO...
...WHAT SAY YOU, BLACK WIDOW?

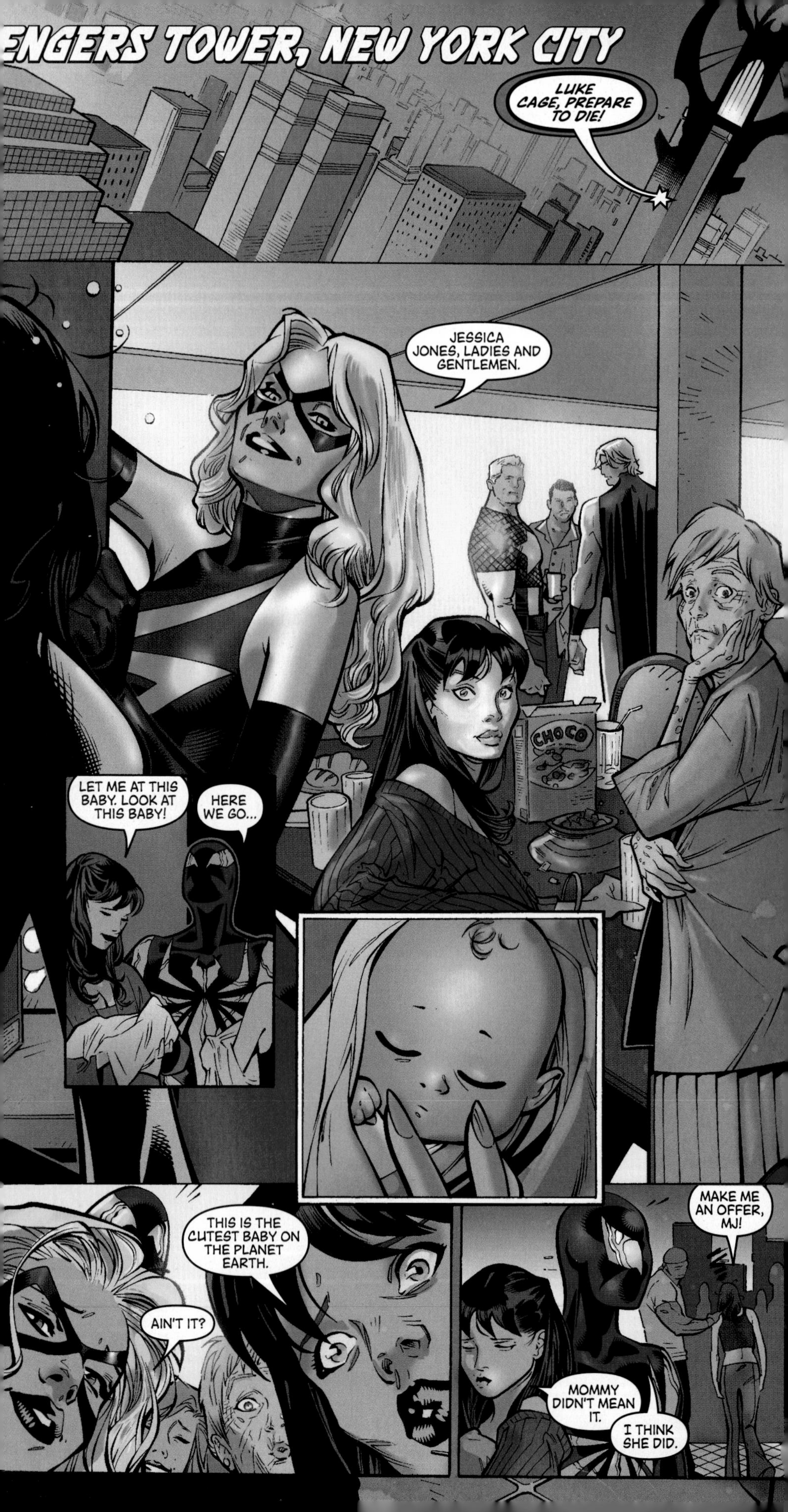

ENGERS TOWER, NEW YORK CITY
LUKE CAGE, PREPARE TO DIE!
JESSICA JONES, LADIES AND GENTLEMEN.
LET ME AT THIS BABY. LOOK AT THIS BABY!
HERE WE GO...
CHOCO
THIS IS THE CUTEST BABY ON THE PLANET EARTH.
AIN'T IT?
MAKE ME AN OFFER, MJ!
MOMMY DIDN'T MEAN IT.
I THINK SHE DID.

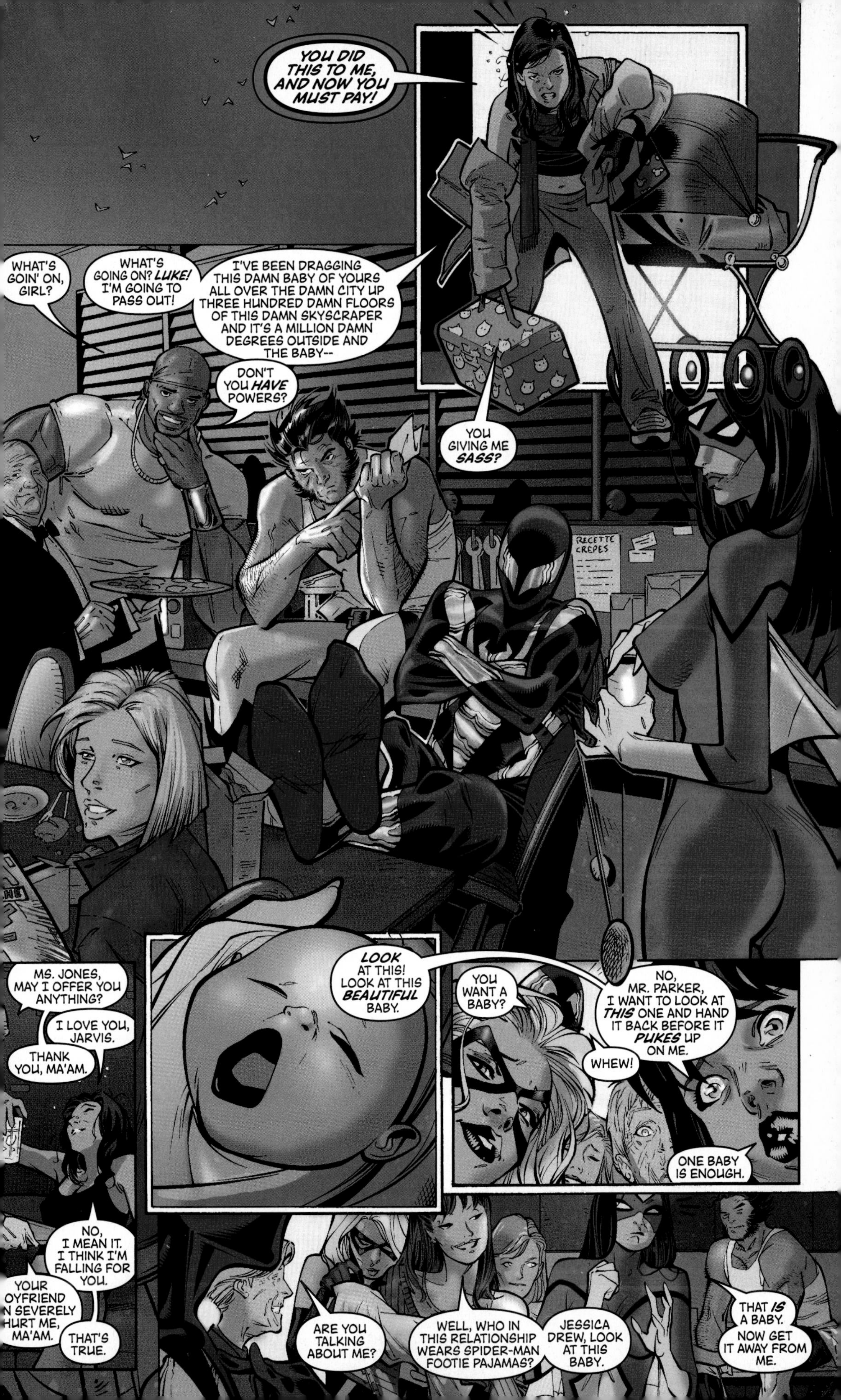
YOU DID THIS TO ME, AND NOW YOU MUST PAY!
WHAT'S GOIN' ON, GIRL?
WHAT'S GOING ON? LUKE! I'M GOING TO PASS OUT!
I'VE BEEN DRAGGING THIS DAMN BABY OF YOURS ALL OVER THE DAMN CITY UP THREE HUNDRED DAMN FLOORS OF THIS DAMN SKYSCRAPER AND IT'S A MILLION DAMN DEGREES OUTSIDE AND THE BABY--
DON'T YOU HAVE POWERS?
YOU GIVING ME SASS?
RECETTE CREPES
MS. JONES, MAY I OFFER YOU ANYTHING?
I LOVE YOU, JARVIS.
THANK YOU, MA'AM.
LOOK AT THIS! LOOK AT THIS BEAUTIFUL BABY.
YOU WANT A BABY?
NO, MR. PARKER, I WANT TO LOOK AT THIS ONE AND HAND IT BACK BEFORE IT PUKES UP ON ME.
WHEW!
ONE BABY IS ENOUGH.
NO, I MEAN IT. I THINK I'M FALLING FOR YOU.
YOUR OYFRIEND N SEVERELY HURT ME, MA'AM.
THAT'S TRUE.
ARE YOU TALKING ABOUT ME?
WELL, WHO IN THIS RELATIONSHIP WEARS SPIDER-MAN FOOTIE PAJAMAS?
JESSICA DREW, LOOK AT THIS BABY.
THAT IS A BABY. NOW GET IT AWAY FROM ME.

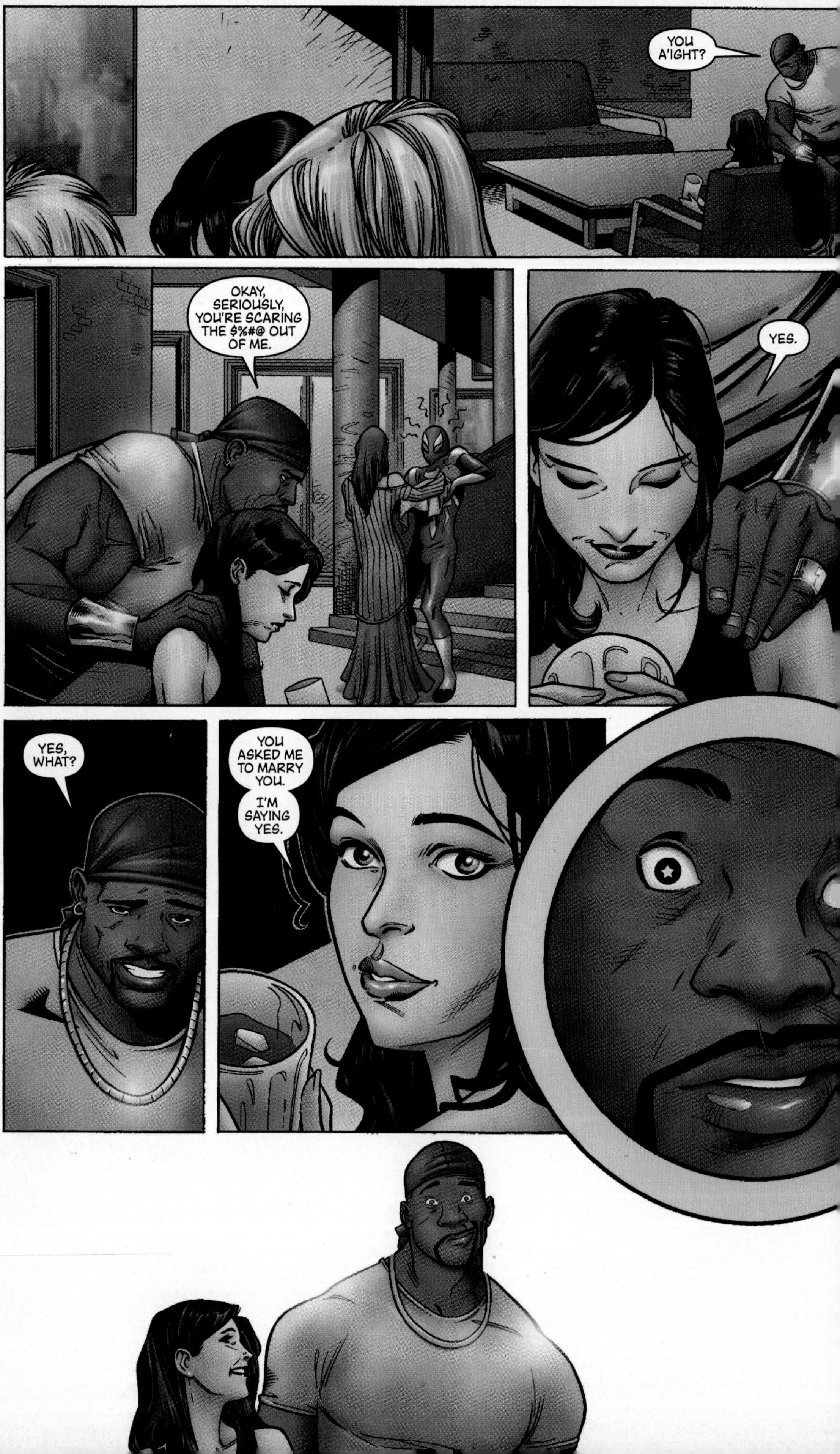
YOU A'IGHT?
OKAY, SERIOUSLY, YOU'RE SCARING THE $%#@ OUT OF ME.
YES.
YES, WHAT?
YOU ASKED ME TO MARRY YOU.
I'M SAYING YES.

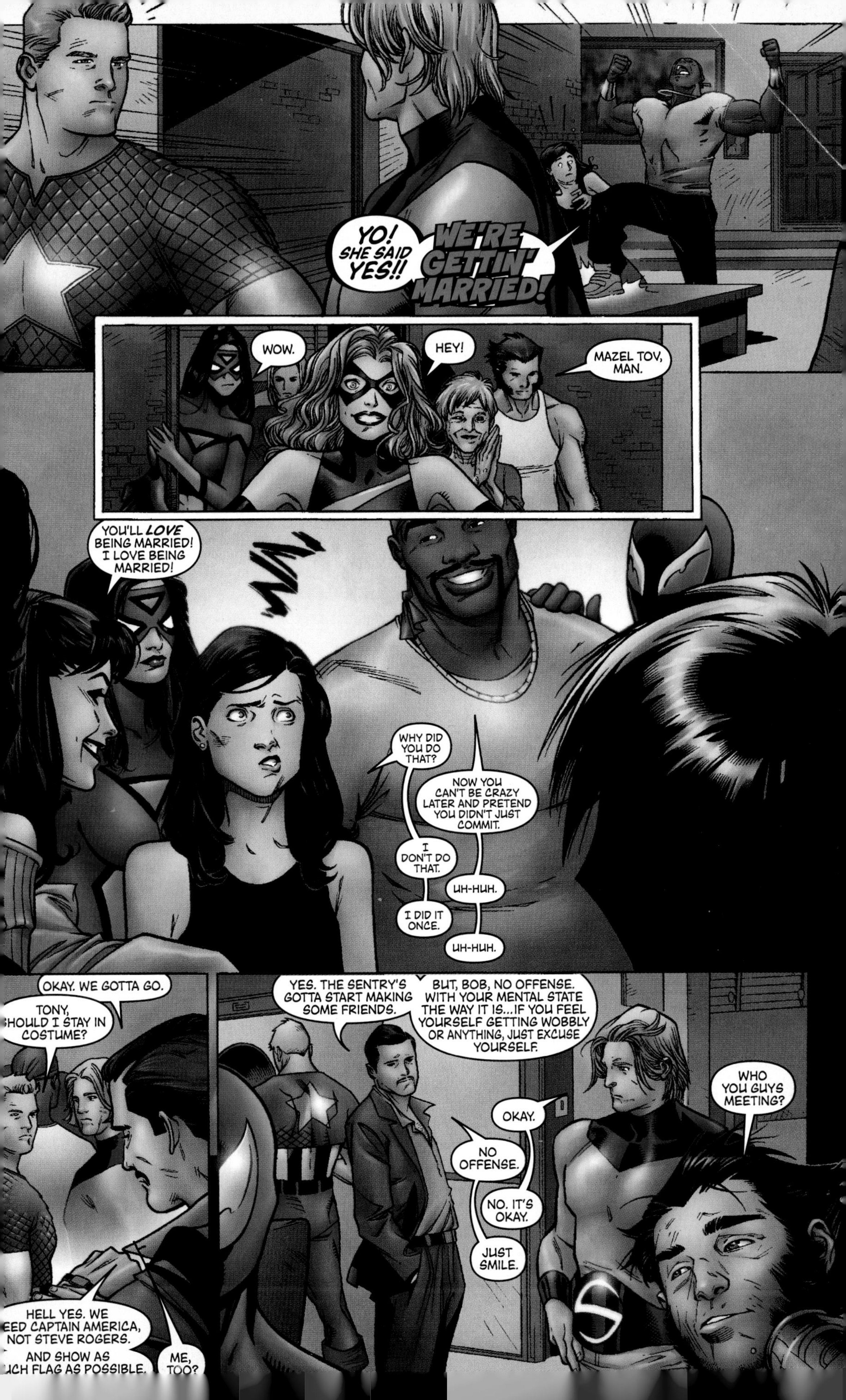

YO! SHE SAID YES!!
WE'RE GETTIN' MARRIED!
WOW.
HEY!
MAZEL TOV, MAN.
YOU'LL LOVE BEING MARRIED! I LOVE BEING MARRIED!
WHY DID YOU DO THAT?
NOW YOU CAN'T BE CRAZY LATER AND PRETEND YOU DIDN'T JUST COMMIT.
I DON'T DO THAT.
UH-HUH.
I DID IT ONCE.
UH-HUH.
OKAY. WE GOTTA GO.
TONY, SHOULD I STAY IN COSTUME?
HELL YES. WE NEED CAPTAIN AMERICA, NOT STEVE ROGERS.
AND SHOW AS MUCH FLAG AS POSSIBLE.
ME, TOO?
YES. THE SENTRY'S GOTTA START MAKING SOME FRIENDS.
BUT, BOB, NO OFFENSE. WITH YOUR MENTAL STATE THE WAY IT IS...IF YOU FEEL YOURSELF GETTING WOBBLY OR ANYTHING, JUST EXCUSE YOURSELF.
OKAY.
NO OFFENSE.
NO. IT'S OKAY.
JUST SMILE.
WHO YOU GUYS MEETING?

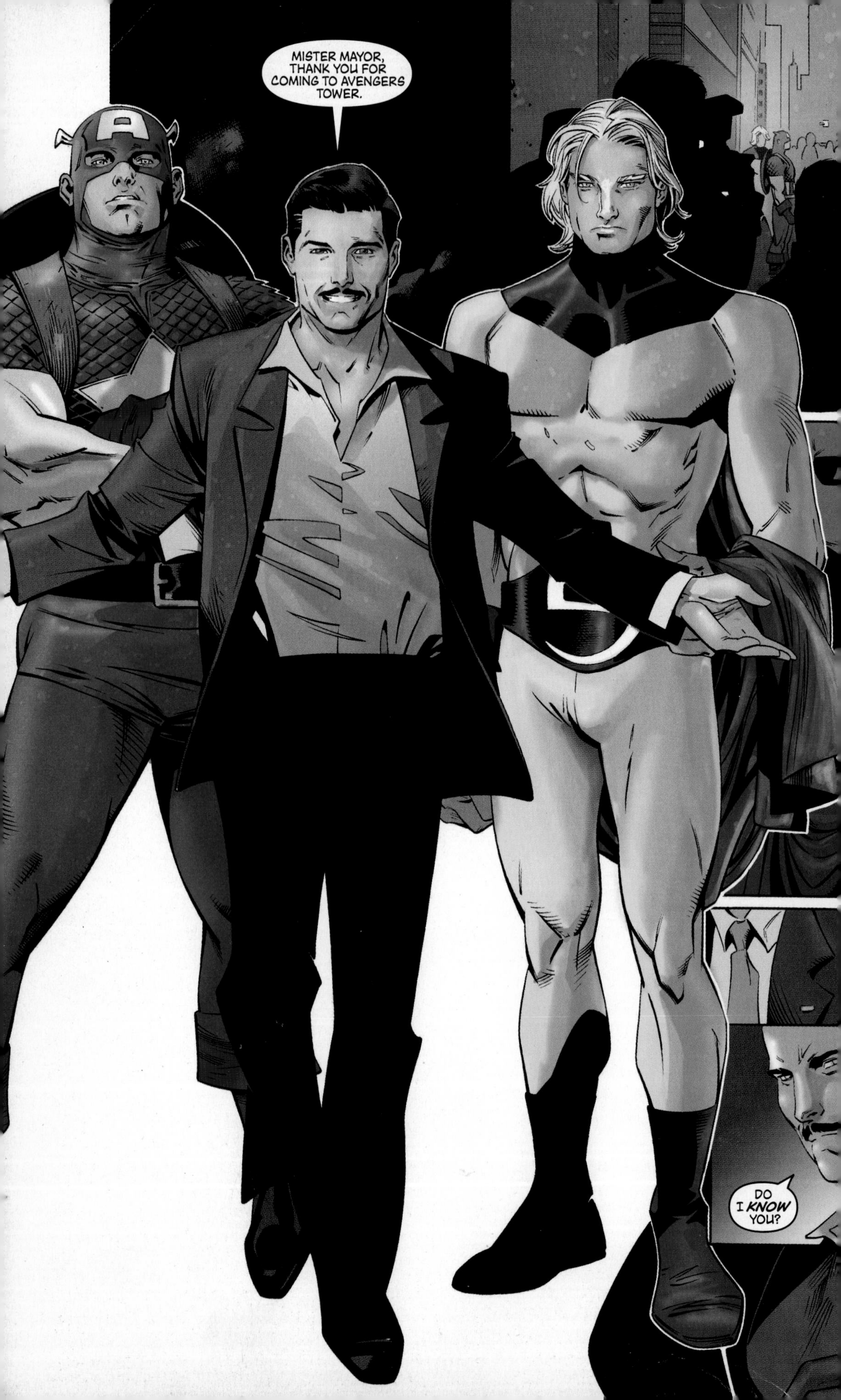
MISTER MAYOR, THANK YOU FOR COMING TO AVENGERS TOWER.
DO I KNOW YOU?

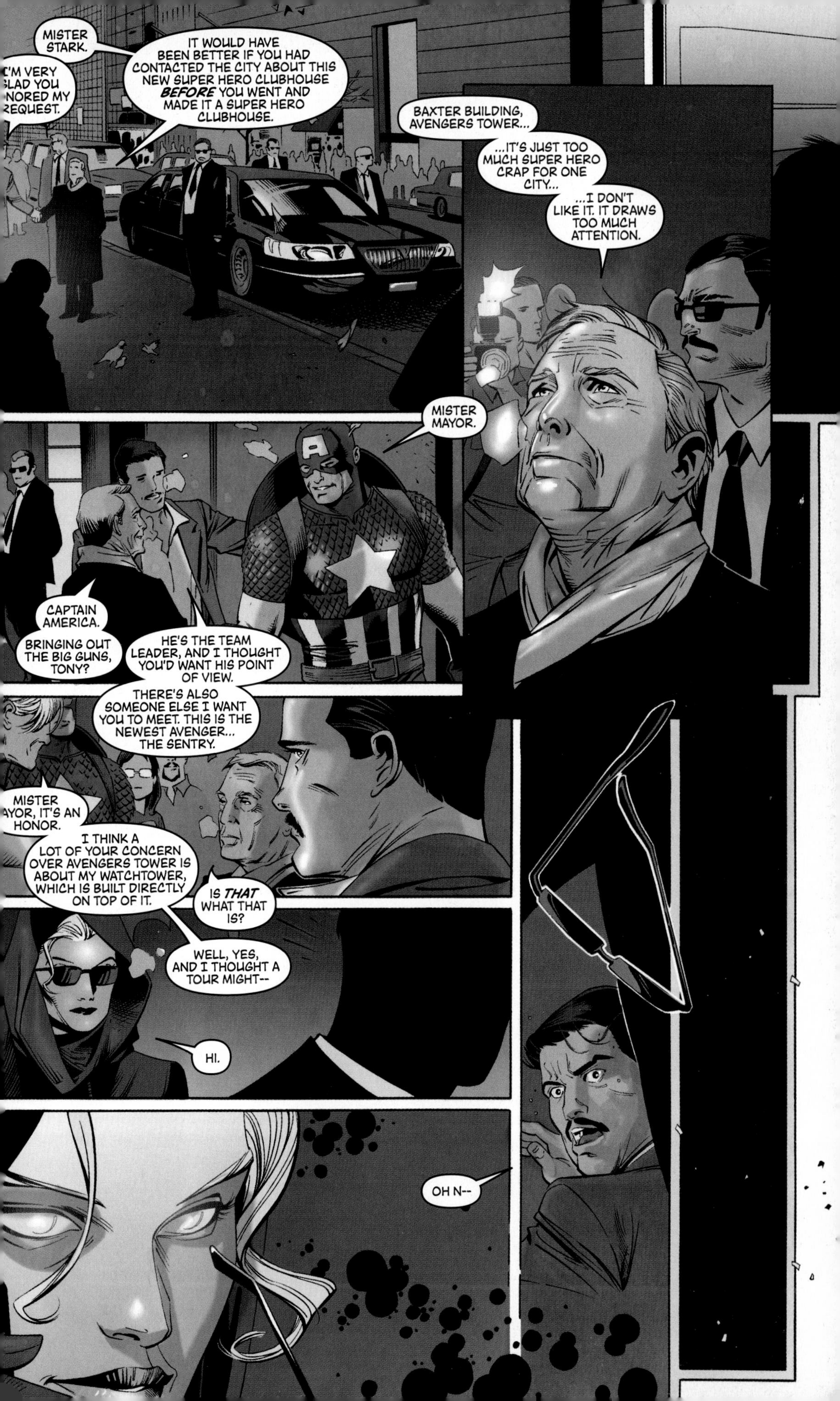

MISTER STARK.
I'M VERY GLAD YOU HONORED MY REQUEST.
IT WOULD HAVE BEEN BETTER IF YOU HAD CONTACTED THE CITY ABOUT THIS NEW SUPER HERO CLUBHOUSE *BEFORE* YOU WENT AND MADE IT A SUPER HERO CLUBHOUSE.
BAXTER BUILDING, AVENGERS TOWER...
...IT'S JUST TOO MUCH SUPER HERO CRAP FOR ONE CITY...
...I DON'T LIKE IT. IT DRAWS TOO MUCH ATTENTION.
MISTER MAYOR.
CAPTAIN AMERICA.
BRINGING OUT THE BIG GUNS, TONY?
HE'S THE TEAM LEADER, AND I THOUGHT YOU'D WANT HIS POINT OF VIEW.
THERE'S ALSO SOMEONE ELSE I WANT YOU TO MEET. THIS IS THE NEWEST AVENGER... THE SENTRY.
MISTER MAYOR, IT'S AN HONOR.
I THINK A LOT OF YOUR CONCERN OVER AVENGERS TOWER IS ABOUT MY WATCHTOWER, WHICH IS BUILT DIRECTLY ON TOP OF IT.
IS *THAT* WHAT THAT IS?
WELL, YES, AND I THOUGHT A TOUR MIGHT--
HI.
OH N--

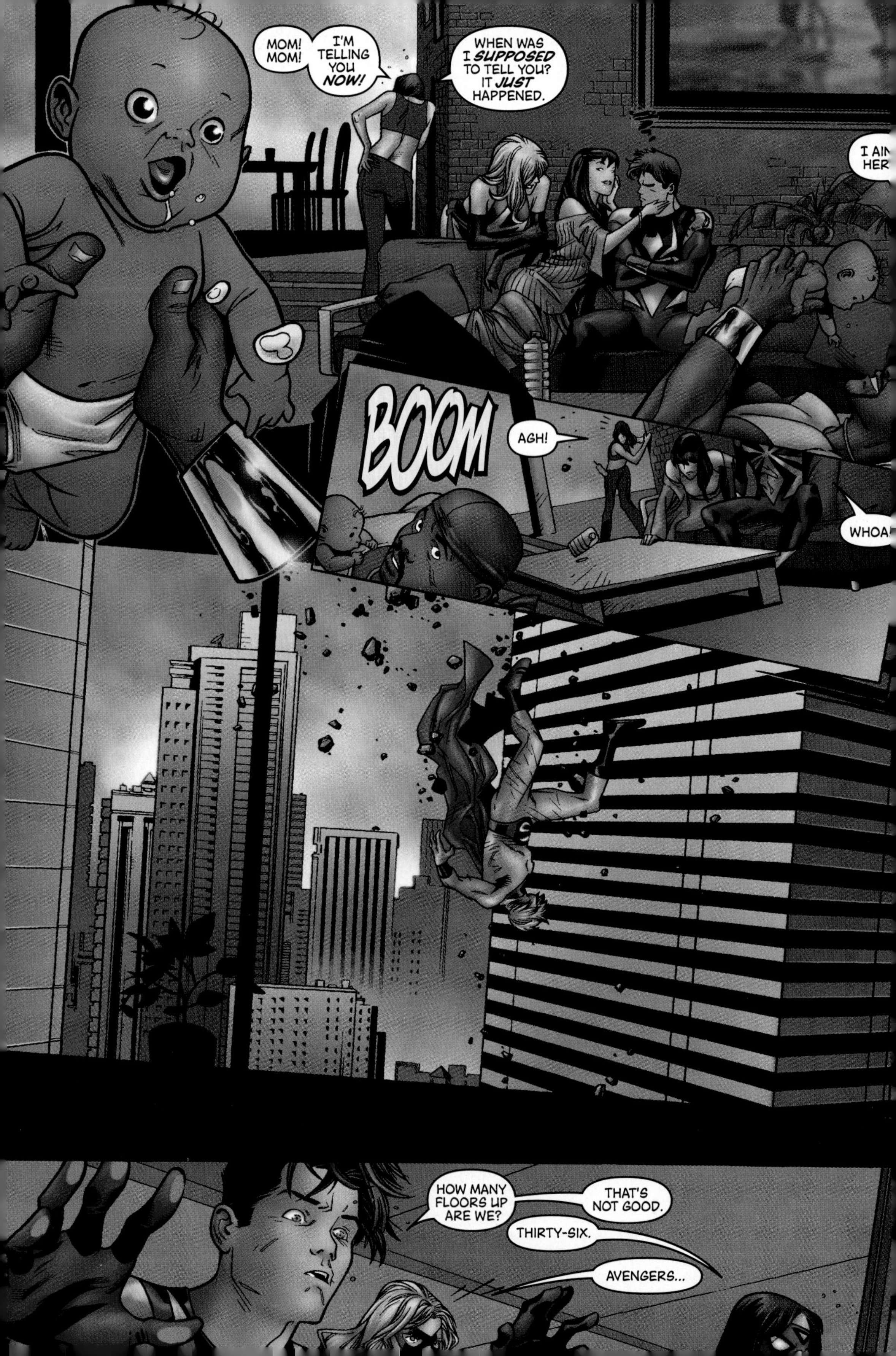

MOM! MOM!
I'M TELLING YOU NOW!
WHEN WAS I SUPPOSED TO TELL YOU? IT JUST HAPPENED.
I AIN HER
BOOM
AGH!
WHOA
HOW MANY FLOORS UP ARE WE?
THAT'S NOT GOOD.
THIRTY-SIX.
AVENGERS...

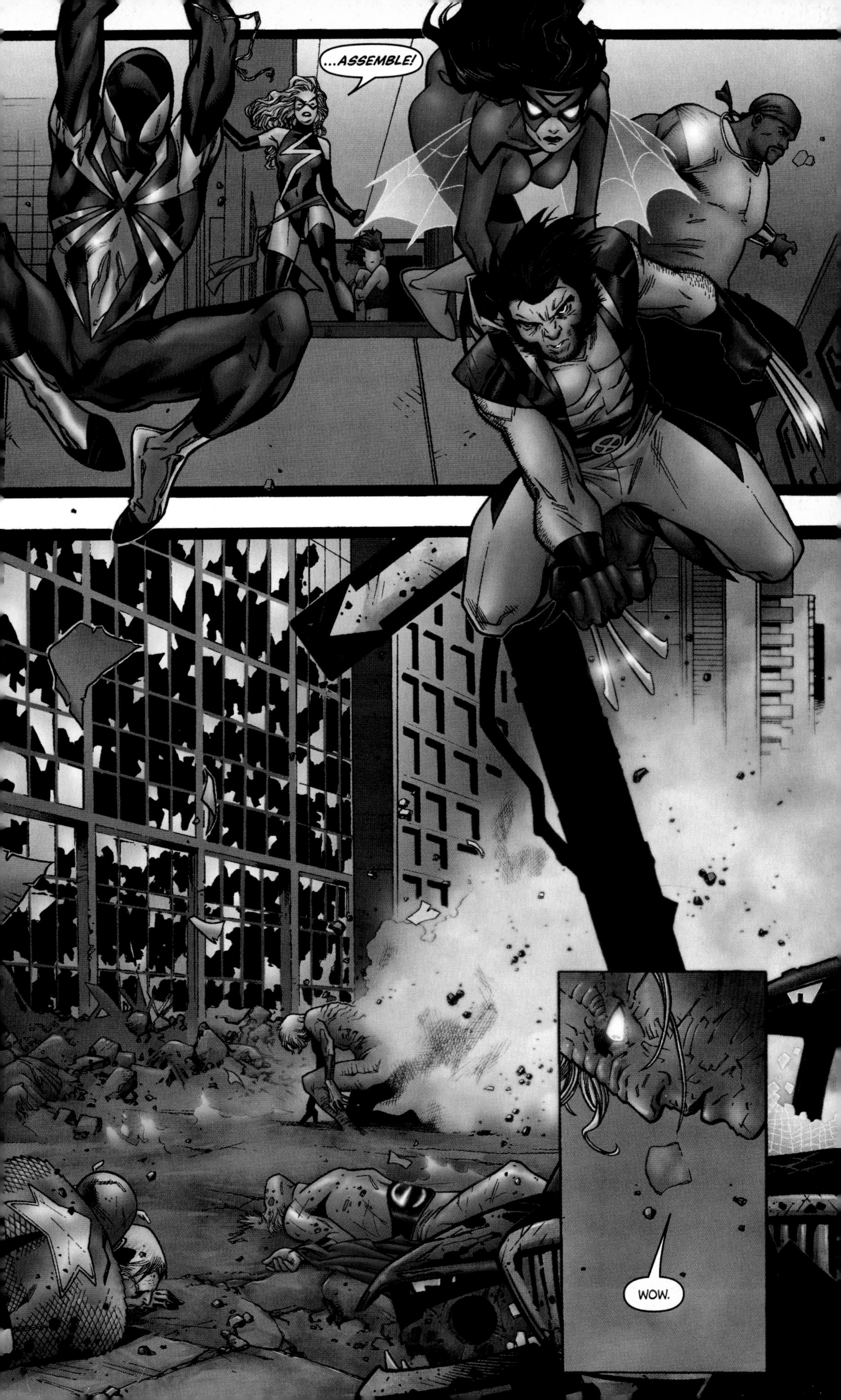
...ASSEMBLE!
WOW.

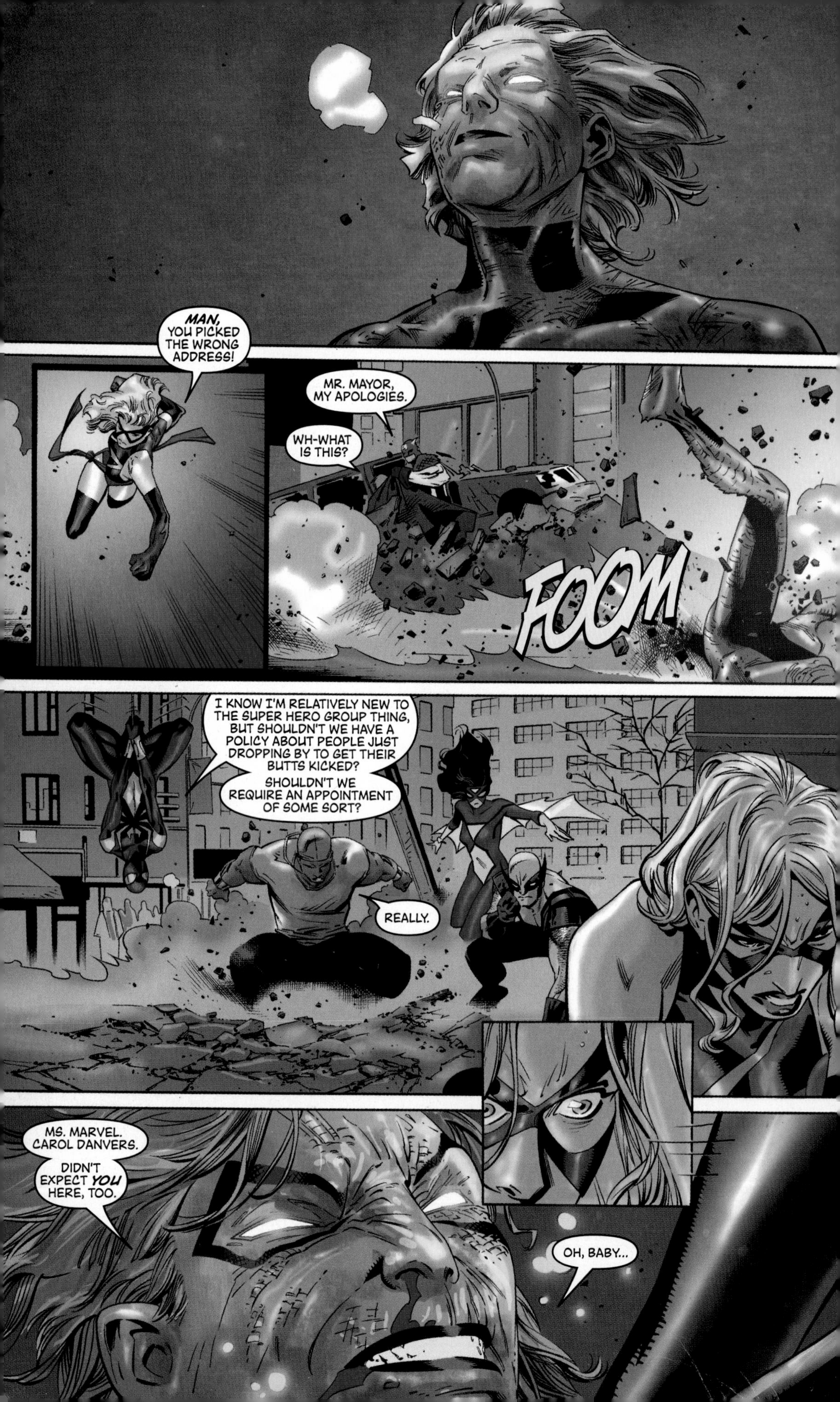
MAN, YOU PICKED THE WRONG ADDRESS!
MR. MAYOR, MY APOLOGIES.
WH-WHAT IS THIS?
FOOM
I KNOW I'M RELATIVELY NEW TO THE SUPER HERO GROUP THING, BUT SHOULDN'T WE HAVE A POLICY ABOUT PEOPLE JUST DROPPING BY TO GET THEIR BUTTS KICKED?
SHOULDN'T WE REQUIRE AN APPOINTMENT OF SOME SORT?
REALLY.
MS. MARVEL. CAROL DANVERS.
DIDN'T EXPECT YOU HERE, TOO.
OH, BABY...

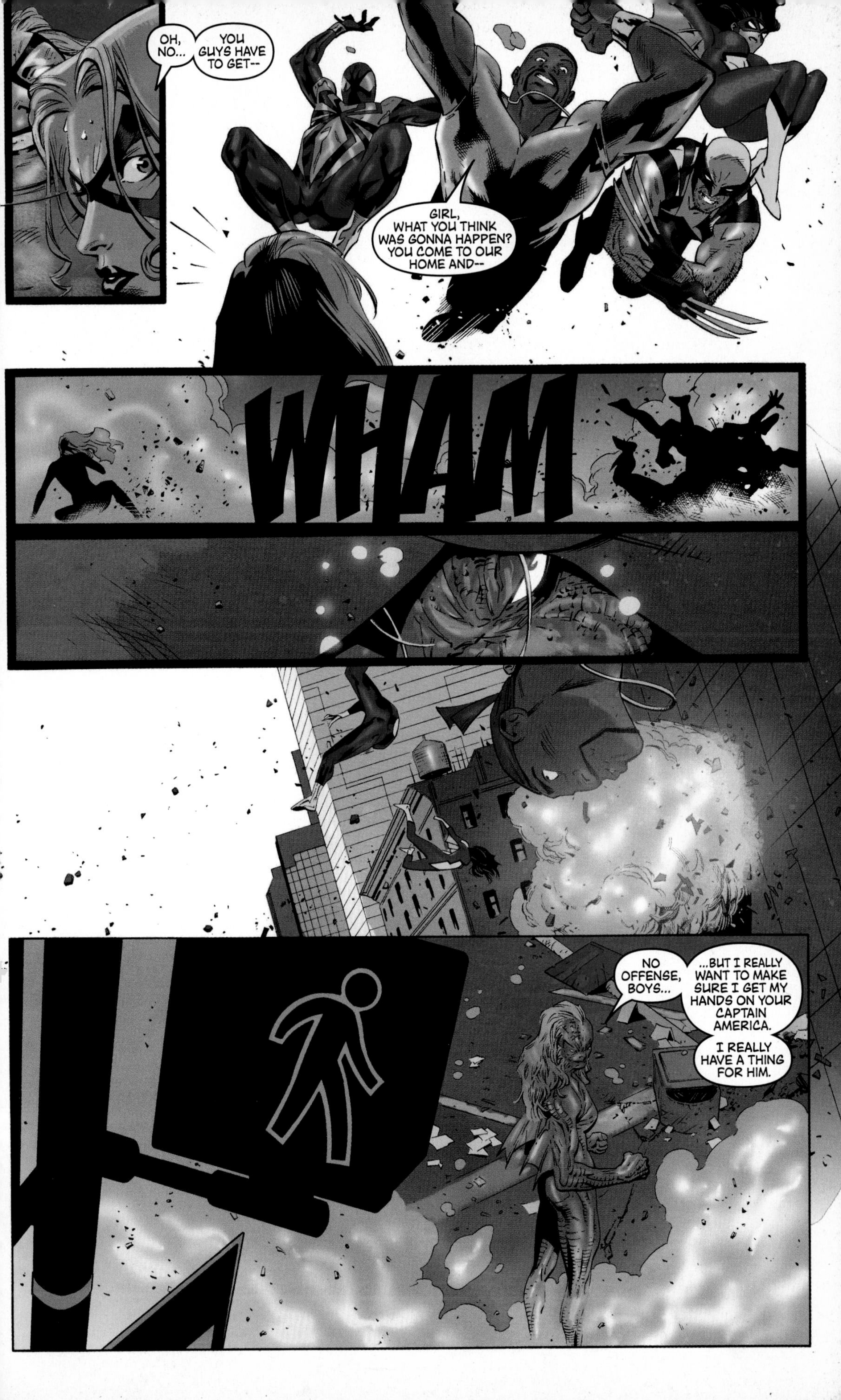
OH, NO...
YOU GUYS HAVE TO GET--
GIRL, WHAT YOU THINK WAS GONNA HAPPEN? YOU COME TO OUR HOME AND--
WHAM
NO OFFENSE, BOYS...
...BUT I REALLY WANT TO MAKE SURE I GET MY HANDS ON YOUR CAPTAIN AMERICA.
I REALLY HAVE A THING FOR HIM.

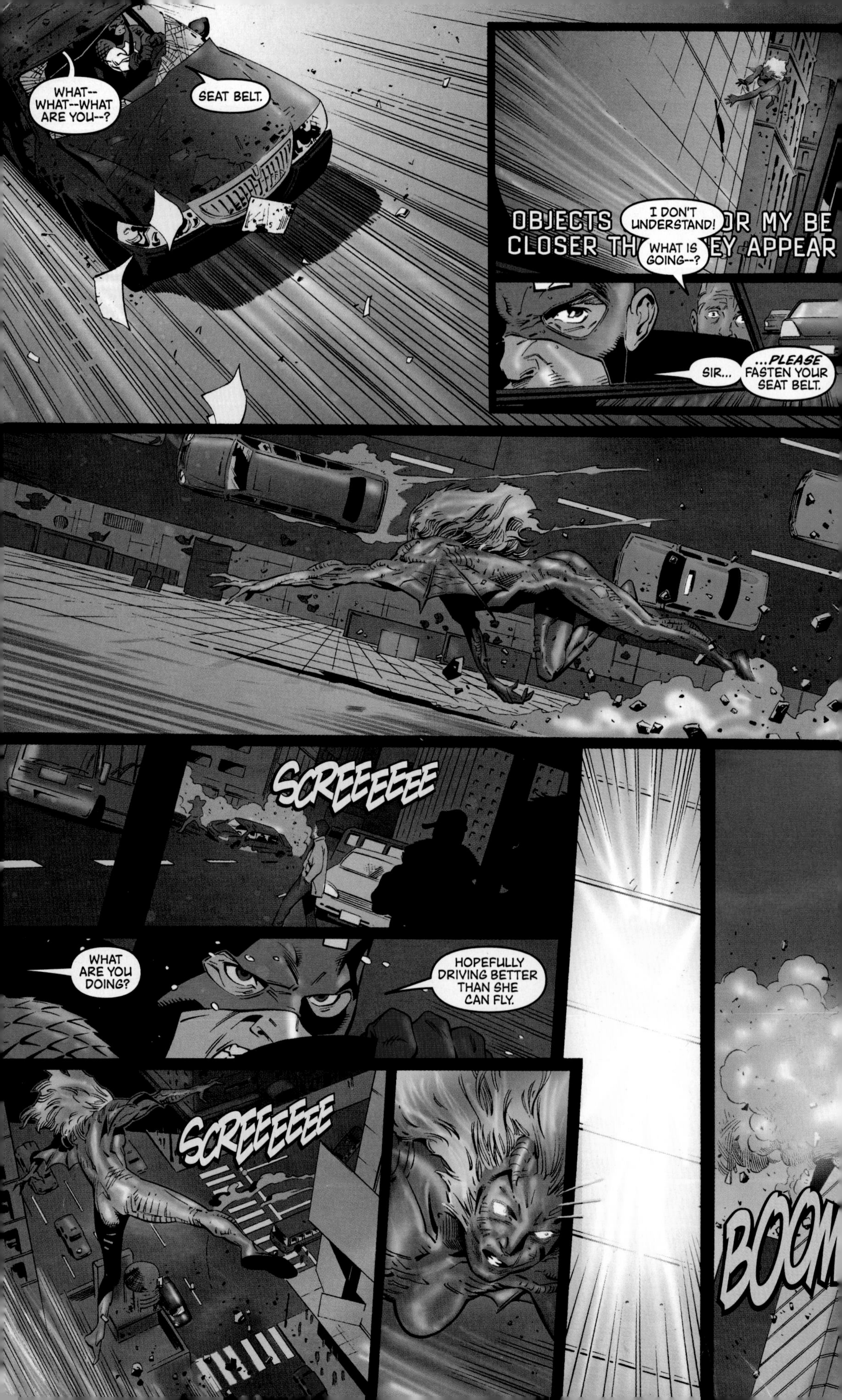
WHAT--
WHAT--WHAT
ARE YOU--?
SEAT BELT.
OBJECTS IN MIRROR MAY BE
CLOSER THAN THEY APPEAR
I DON'T UNDERSTAND!
WHAT IS GOING--?
SIR...
...PLEASE FASTEN YOUR SEAT BELT.
SCREEEEEE
WHAT ARE YOU DOING?
HOPEFULLY DRIVING BETTER THAN SHE CAN FLY.
SCREEEEEEE
BOOM

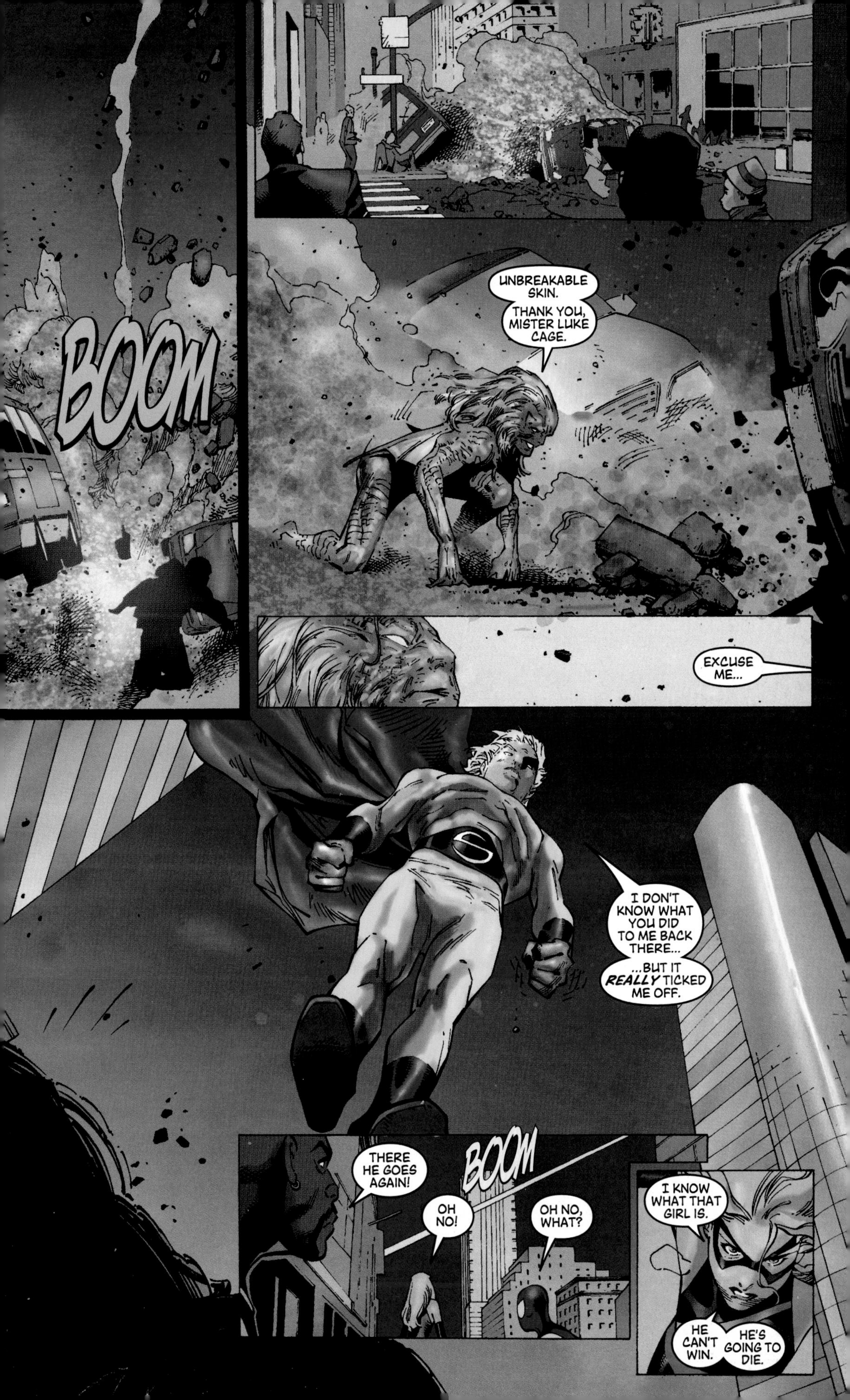
BOOM
UNBREAKABLE SKIN.
THANK YOU, MISTER LUKE CAGE.
EXCUSE ME...
I DON'T KNOW WHAT YOU DID TO ME BACK THERE...
...BUT IT REALLY TICKED ME OFF.
BOOM
THERE HE GOES AGAIN!
OH NO!
OH NO, WHAT?
I KNOW WHAT THAT GIRL IS.
HE CAN'T WIN.
HE'S GOING TO DIE.

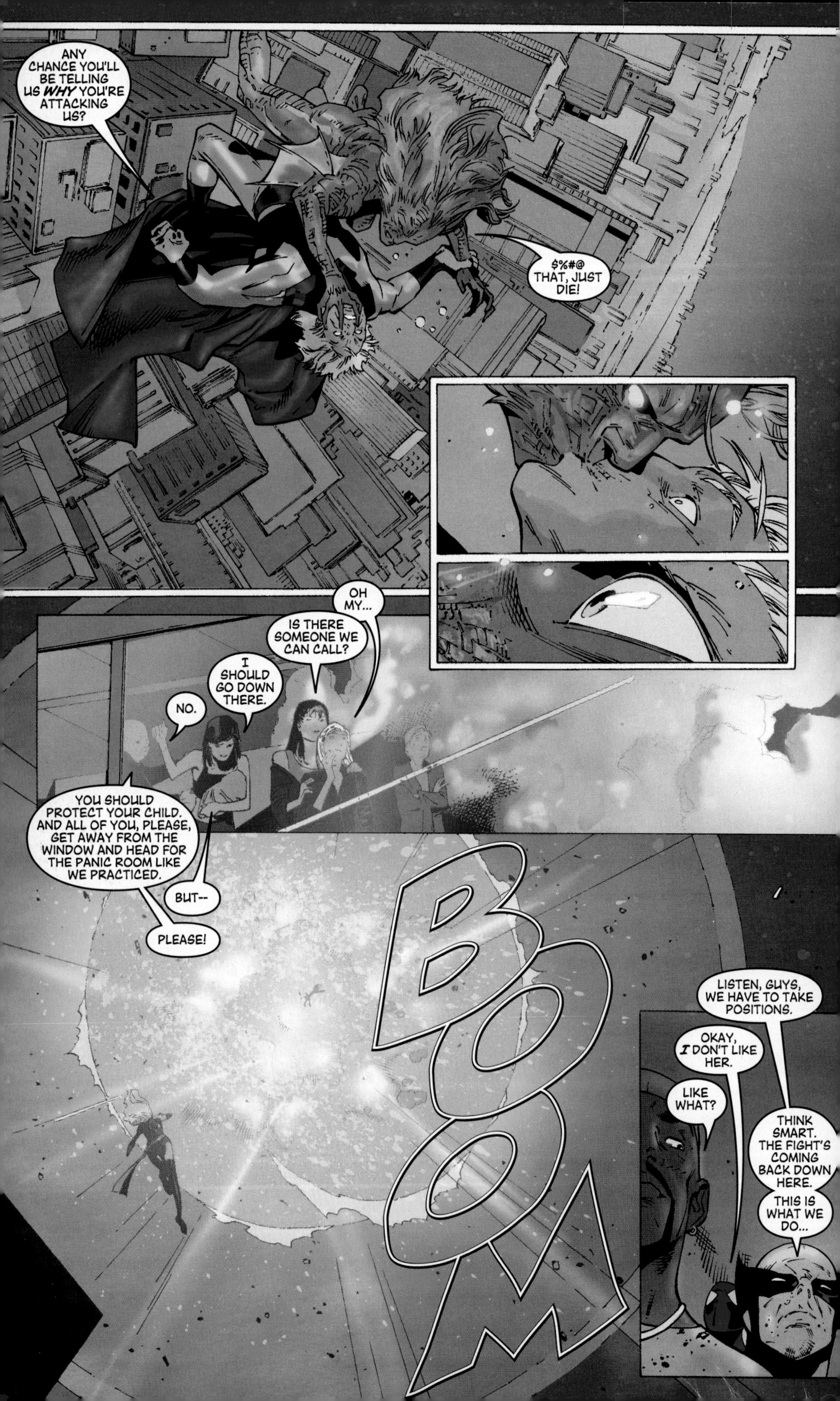
ANY CHANCE YOU'LL BE TELLING US *WHY* YOU'RE ATTACKING US?
$%#@ THAT, JUST DIE!
OH MY...
IS THERE SOMEONE WE CAN CALL?
I SHOULD GO DOWN THERE.
NO.
YOU SHOULD PROTECT YOUR CHILD. AND ALL OF YOU, PLEASE, GET AWAY FROM THE WINDOW AND HEAD FOR THE PANIC ROOM LIKE WE PRACTICED.
BUT--
PLEASE!
BOOM
LISTEN, GUYS, WE HAVE TO TAKE POSITIONS.
OKAY, *I* DON'T LIKE HER.
LIKE WHAT?
THINK SMART. THE FIGHT'S COMING BACK DOWN HERE.
THIS IS WHAT WE DO...

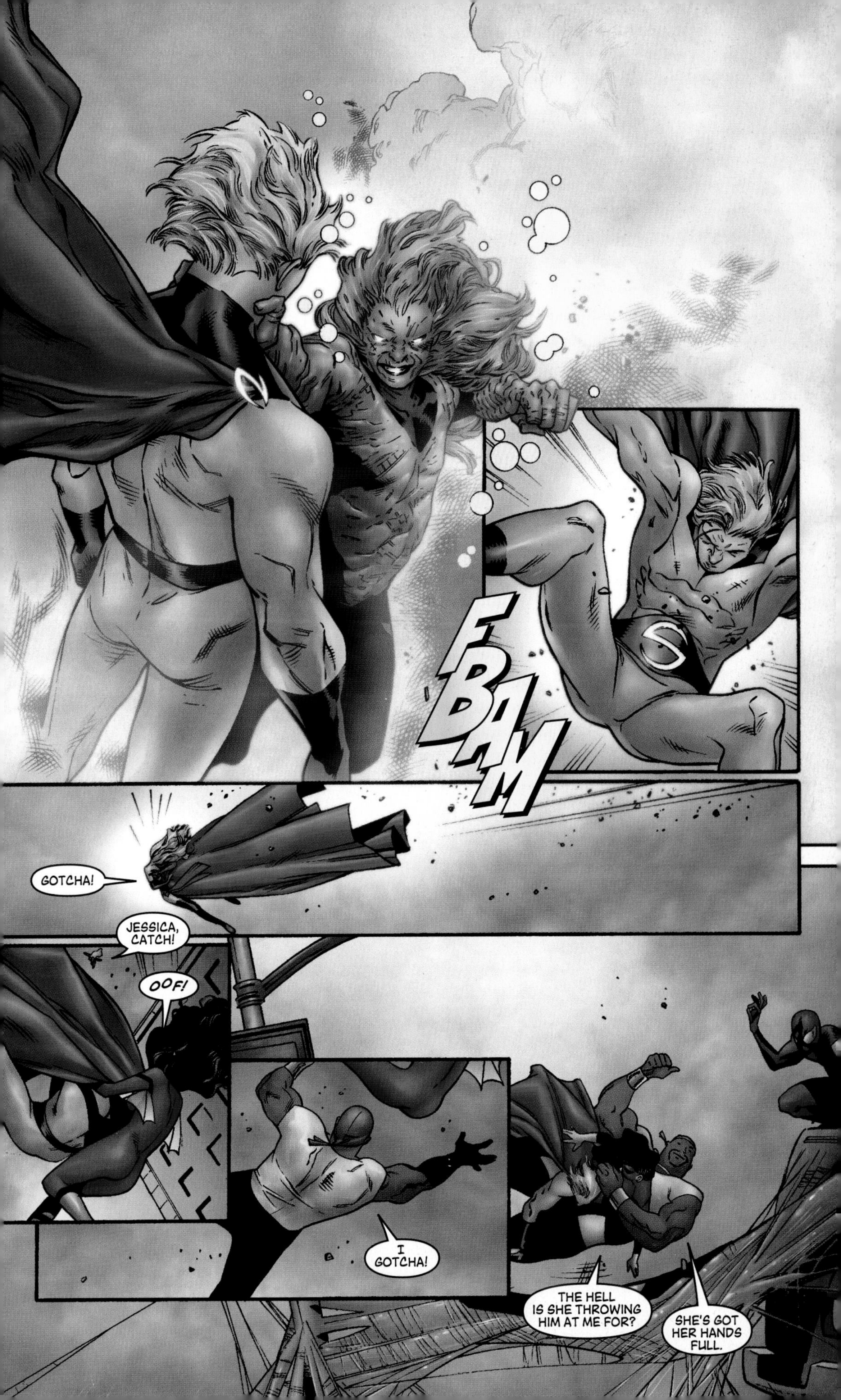
FBAM
GOTCHA!
JESSICA, CATCH!
OOF!
I GOTCHA!
THE HELL IS SHE THROWING HIM AT ME FOR?
SHE'S GOT HER HANDS FULL.

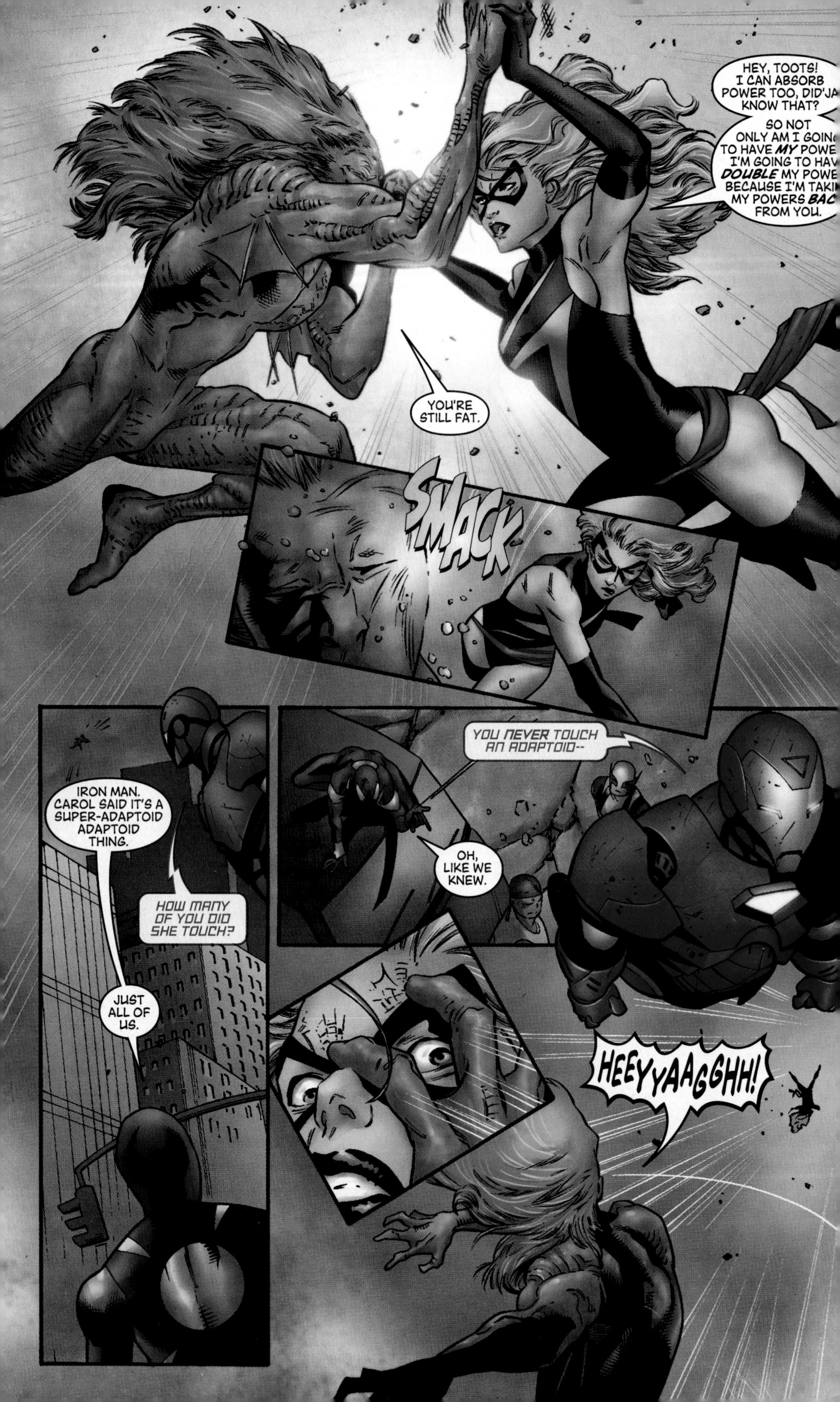
HEY, TOOTS! I CAN ABSORB POWER TOO, DID'JA KNOW THAT?
SO NOT ONLY AM I GOING TO HAVE MY POWE I'M GOING TO HAV DOUBLE MY POWE BECAUSE I'M TAKI MY POWERS BAC FROM YOU.
YOU'RE STILL FAT.
SMACK
IRON MAN. CAROL SAID IT'S A SUPER-ADAPTOID ADAPTOID THING.
HOW MANY OF YOU DID SHE TOUCH?
JUST ALL OF US.
YOU NEVER TOUCH AN ADAPTOID--
OH, LIKE WE KNEW.
HEEYYAAGGHH!

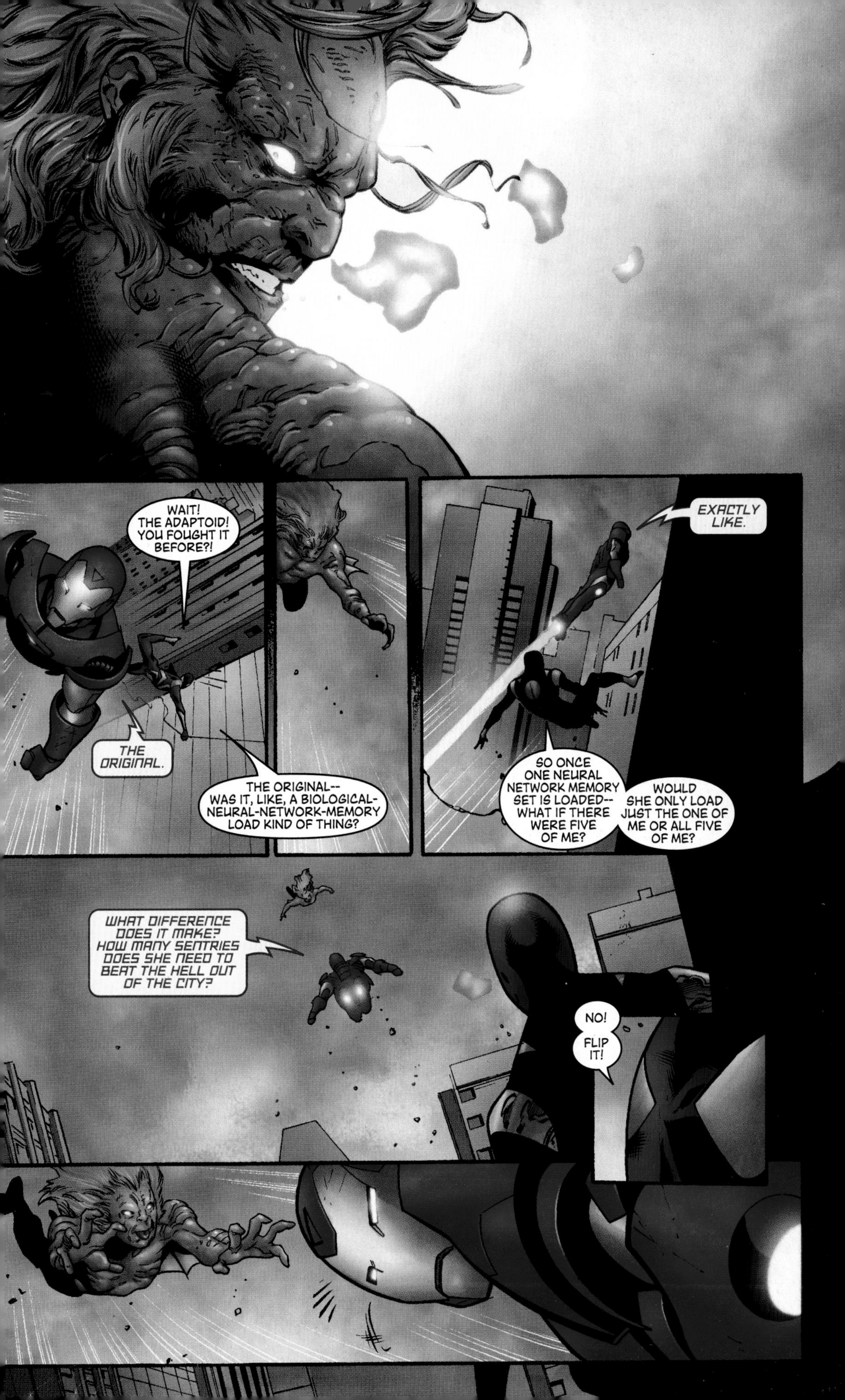
WAIT! THE ADAPTOID! YOU FOUGHT IT BEFORE?!
THE ORIGINAL.
THE ORIGINAL-- WAS IT, LIKE, A BIOLOGICAL-NEURAL-NETWORK-MEMORY LOAD KIND OF THING?
EXACTLY LIKE.
SO ONCE ONE NEURAL NETWORK MEMORY SET IS LOADED-- WHAT IF THERE WERE FIVE OF ME?
WOULD SHE ONLY LOAD JUST THE ONE OF ME OR ALL FIVE OF ME?
WHAT DIFFERENCE DOES IT MAKE? HOW MANY SENTRIES DOES SHE NEED TO BEAT THE HELL OUT OF THE CITY?
NO!
FLIP IT!

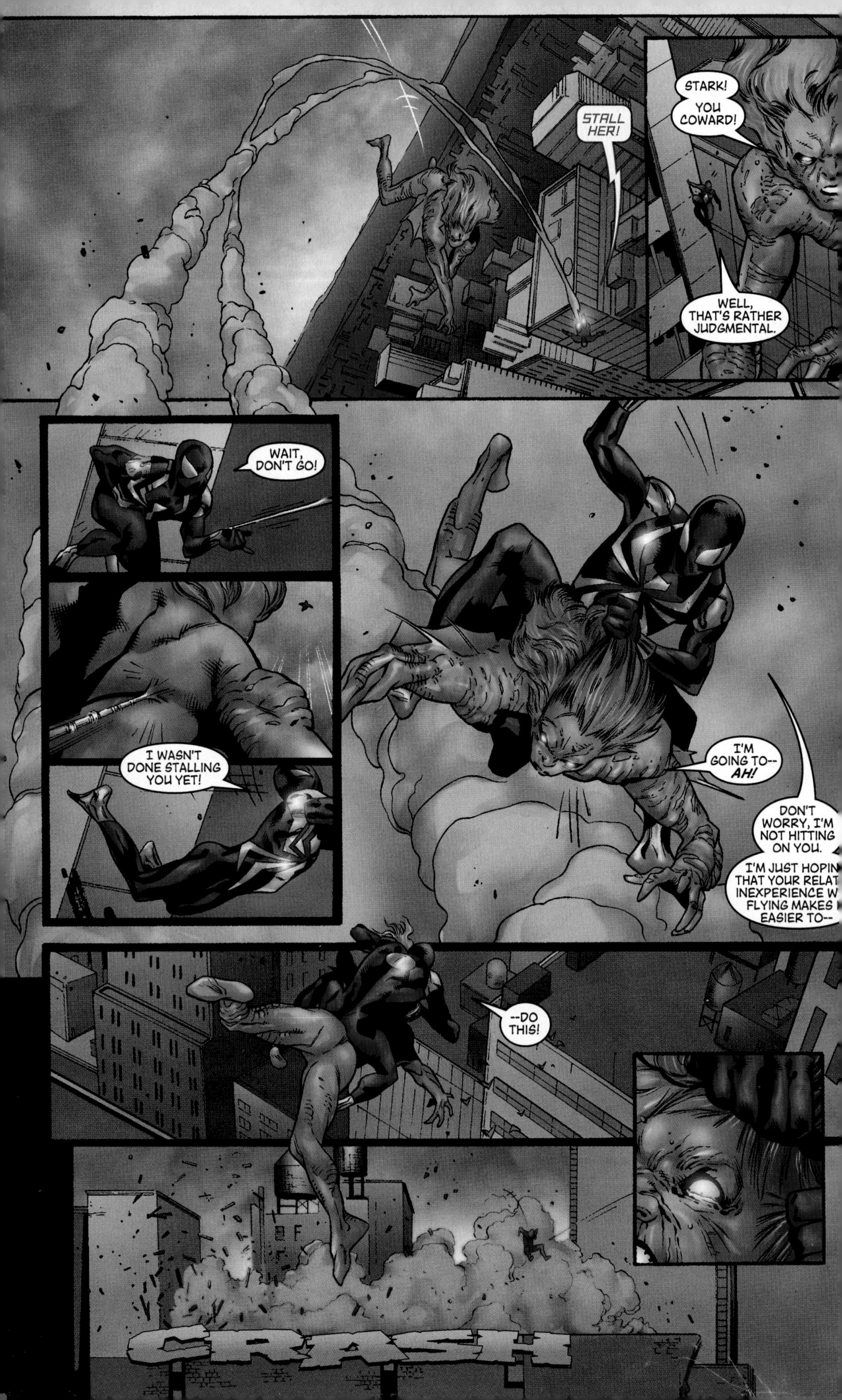

STALL HER!
STARK! YOU COWARD!
WELL, THAT'S RATHER JUDGMENTAL.
WAIT, DON'T GO!
I WASN'T DONE STALLING YOU YET!
I'M GOING TO-- AH!
DON'T WORRY, I'M NOT HITTING ON YOU.
I'M JUST HOPIN THAT YOUR RELAT INEXPERIENCE W FLYING MAKES EASIER TO--
--DO THIS!
CRASH

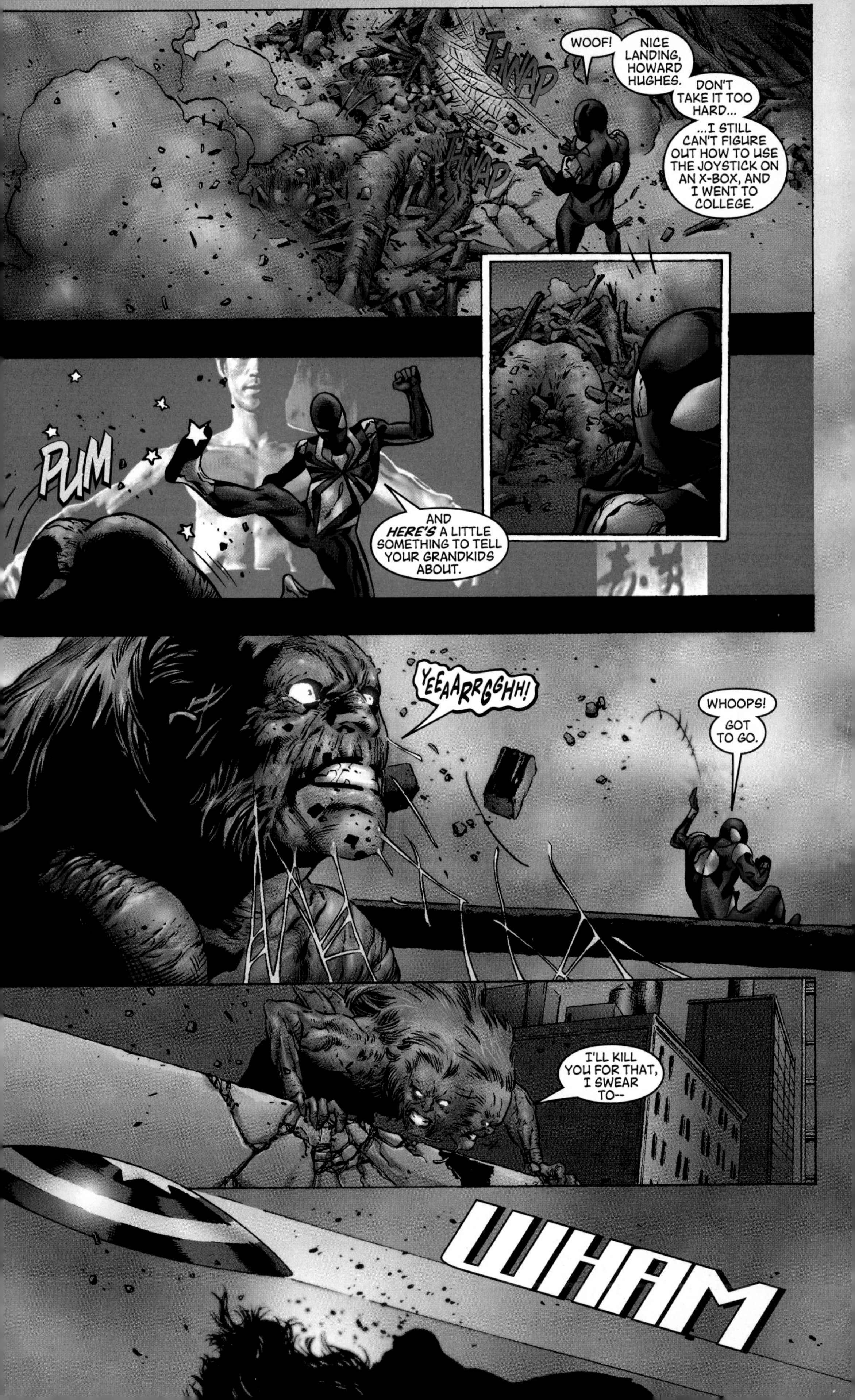
THWAP
THWAP
WOOF!
NICE LANDING, HOWARD HUGHES.
DON'T TAKE IT TOO HARD...
...I STILL CAN'T FIGURE OUT HOW TO USE THE JOYSTICK ON AN X-BOX, AND I WENT TO COLLEGE.
PUM
AND *HERE'S* A LITTLE SOMETHING TO TELL YOUR GRANDKIDS ABOUT.
YEEAARRGGHH!
WHOOPS! GOT TO GO.
I'LL KILL YOU FOR THAT, I SWEAR TO--
WHAM

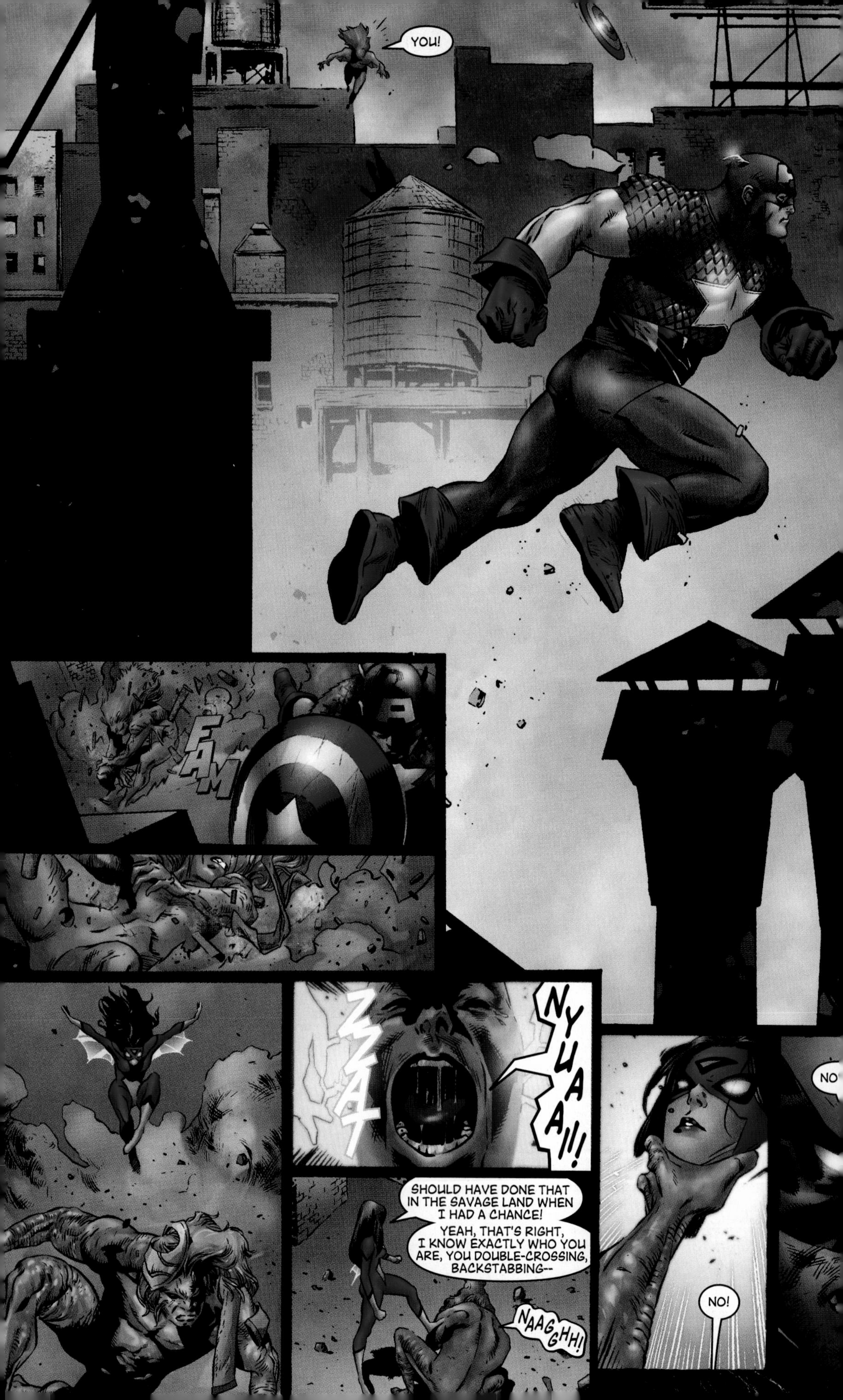
YOU!
FAM
ZZAT
NYUAAA!!!
SHOULD HAVE DONE THAT IN THE SAVAGE LAND WHEN I HAD A CHANCE!
YEAH, THAT'S RIGHT, I KNOW EXACTLY WHO YOU ARE, YOU DOUBLE-CROSSING, BACKSTABBING--
NAAGGHH!
NO
NO!

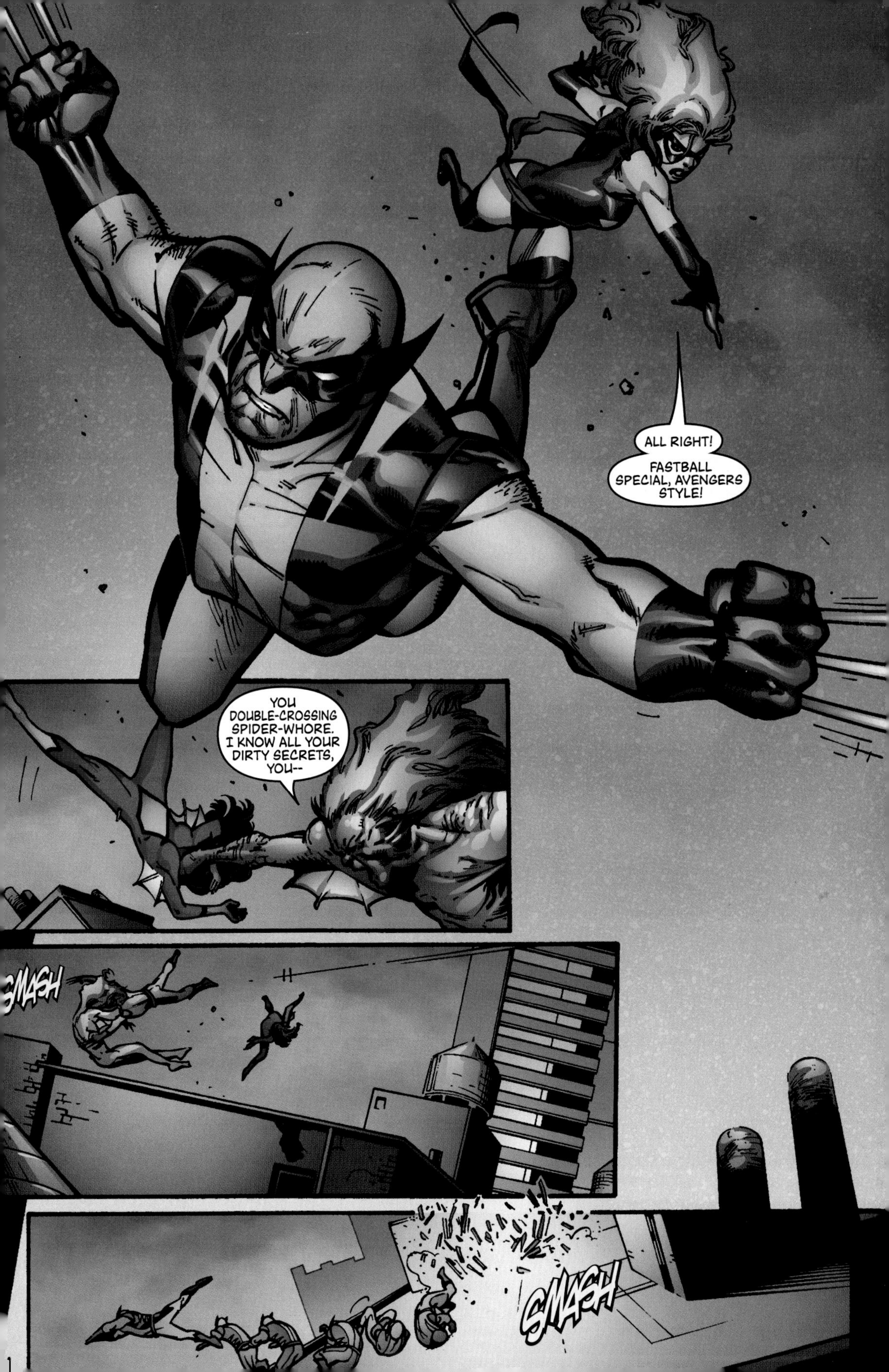
ALL RIGHT! FASTBALL SPECIAL, AVENGERS STYLE!
YOU DOUBLE-CROSSING SPIDER-WHORE. I KNOW ALL YOUR DIRTY SECRETS, YOU--
SMASH
SMASH

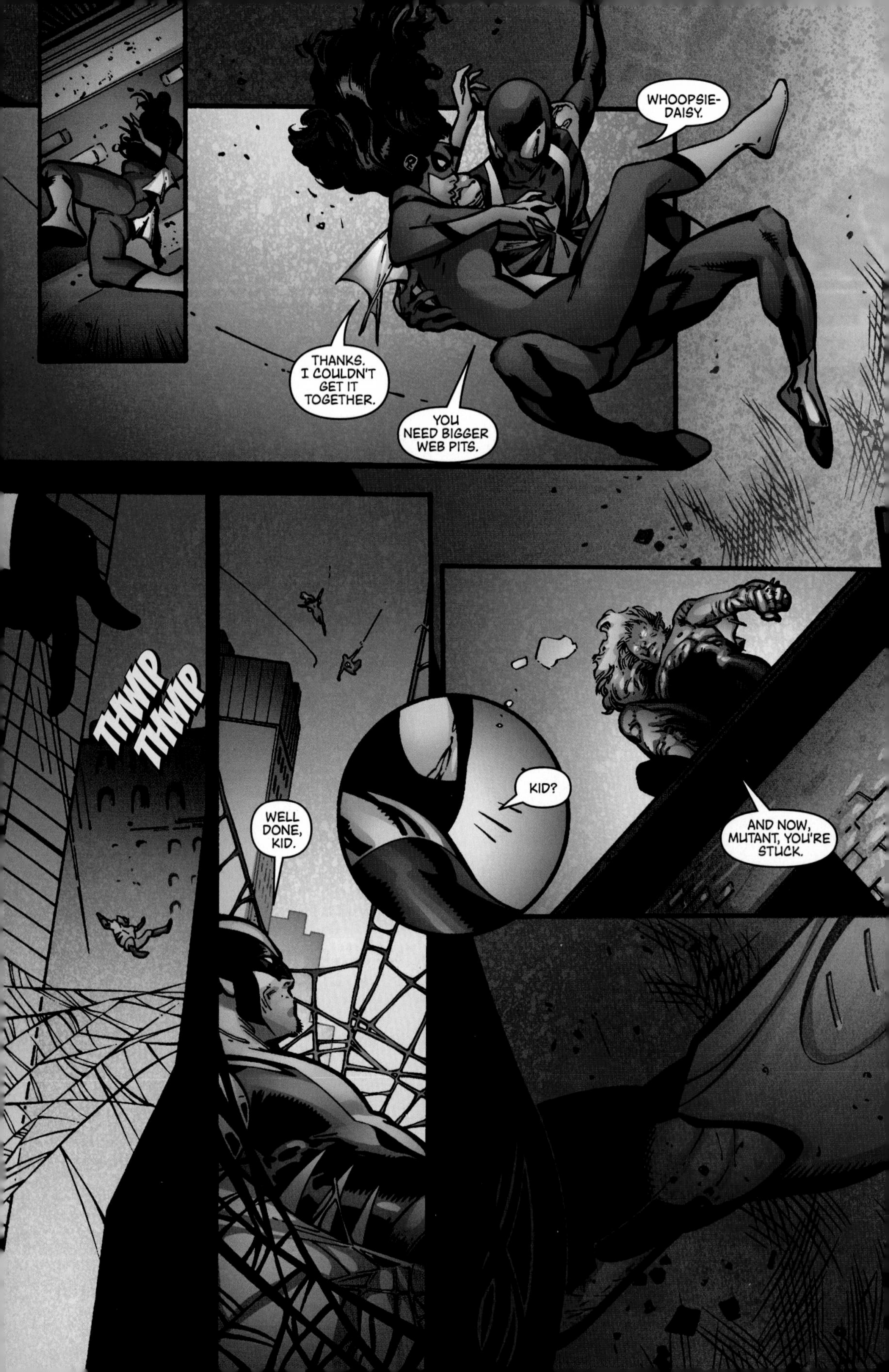
WHOOPSIE-DAISY.
THANKS. I COULDN'T GET IT TOGETHER.
YOU NEED BIGGER WEB PITS.
THWIP THWIP
WELL DONE, KID.
KID?
AND NOW, MUTANT, YOU'RE STUCK.

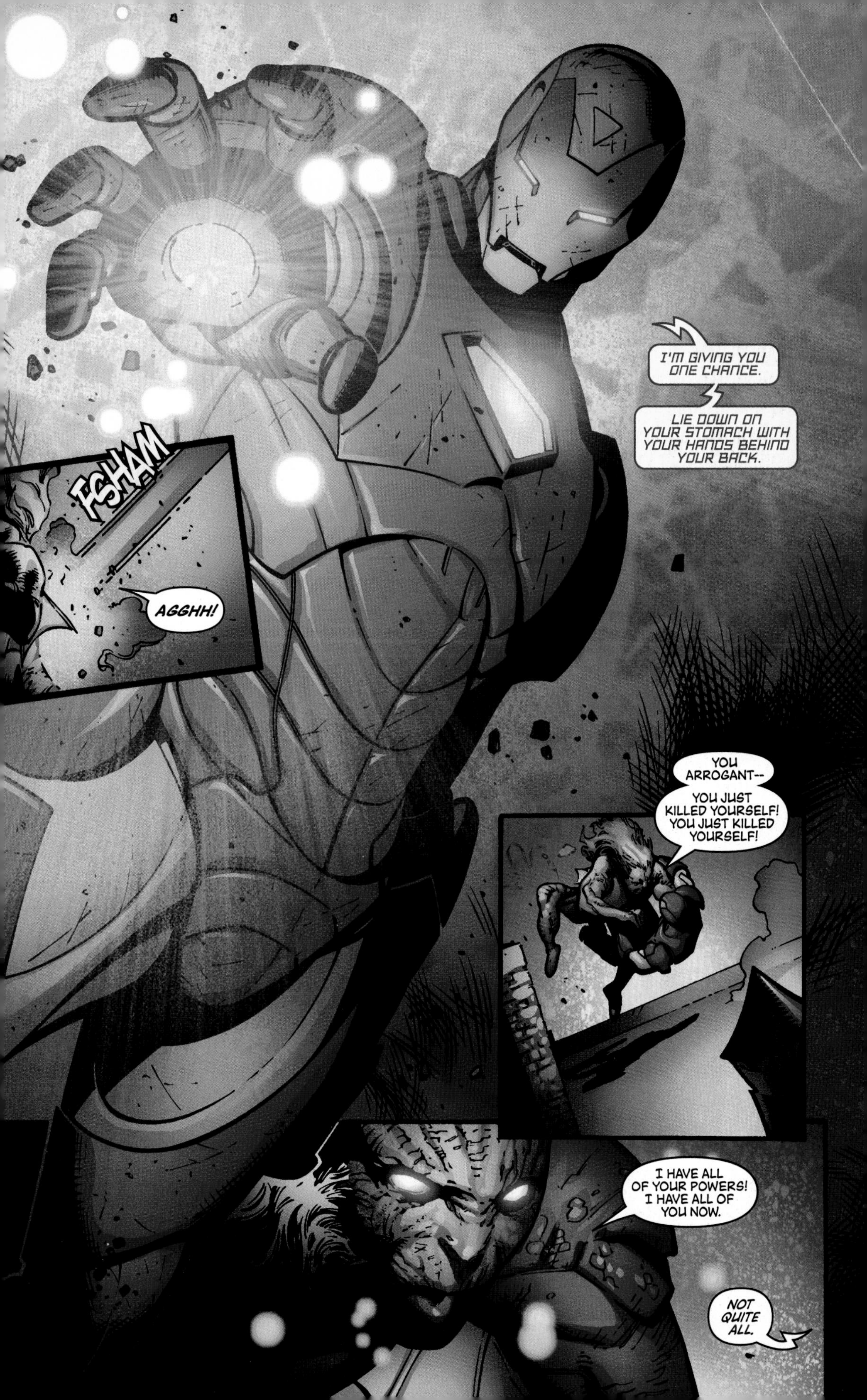
I'M GIVING YOU ONE CHANCE.
LIE DOWN ON YOUR STOMACH WITH YOUR HANDS BEHIND YOUR BACK.
FSHAM
AGGHH!
YOU ARROGANT--
YOU JUST KILLED YOURSELF! YOU JUST KILLED YOURSELF!
I HAVE ALL OF YOUR POWERS! I HAVE ALL OF YOU NOW.
NOT QUITE ALL.

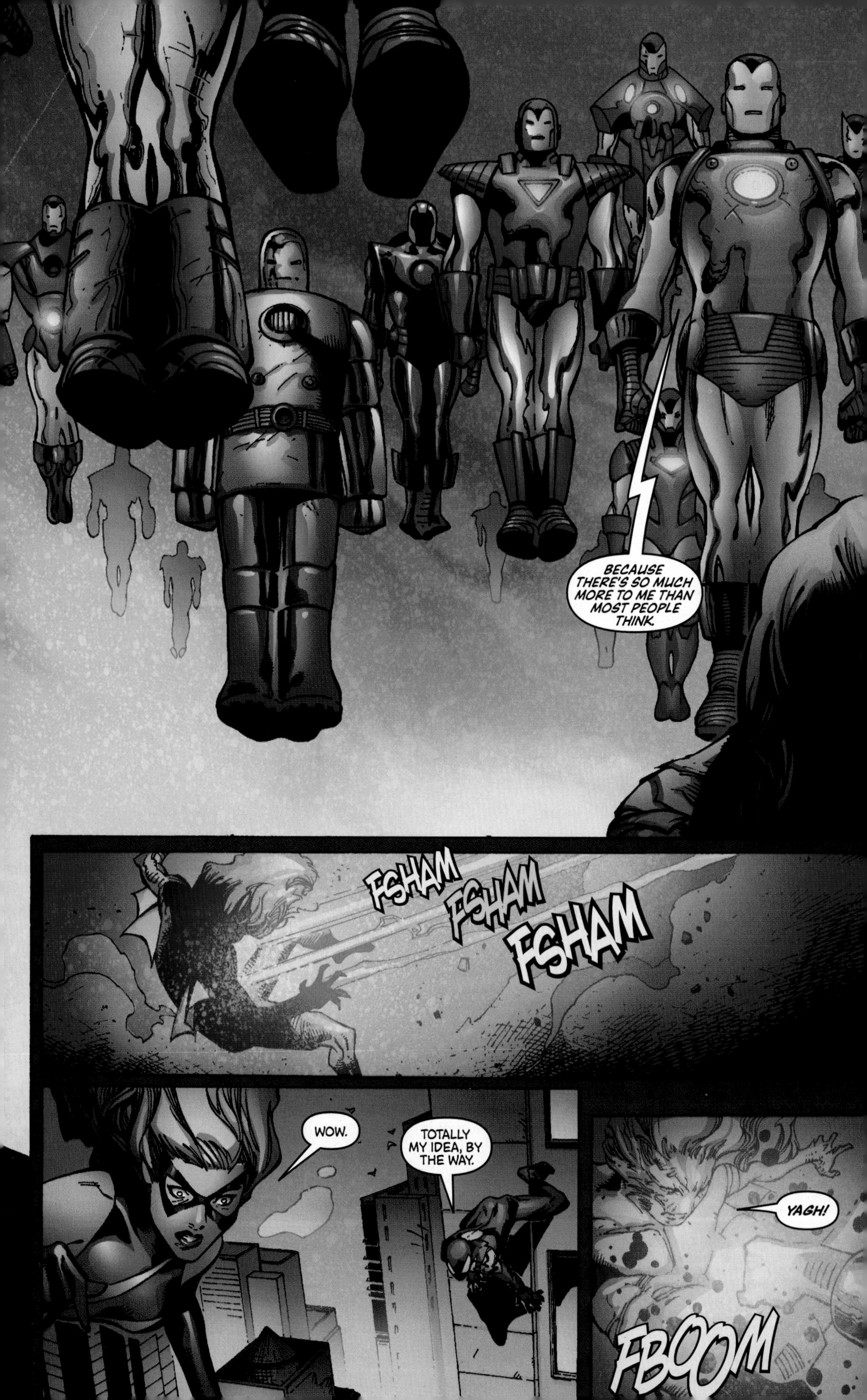
BECAUSE THERE'S SO MUCH MORE TO ME THAN MOST PEOPLE THINK.
FSHAM
FSHAM
FSHAM
WOW.
TOTALLY MY IDEA, BY THE WAY.
YAGH!
FBOOM

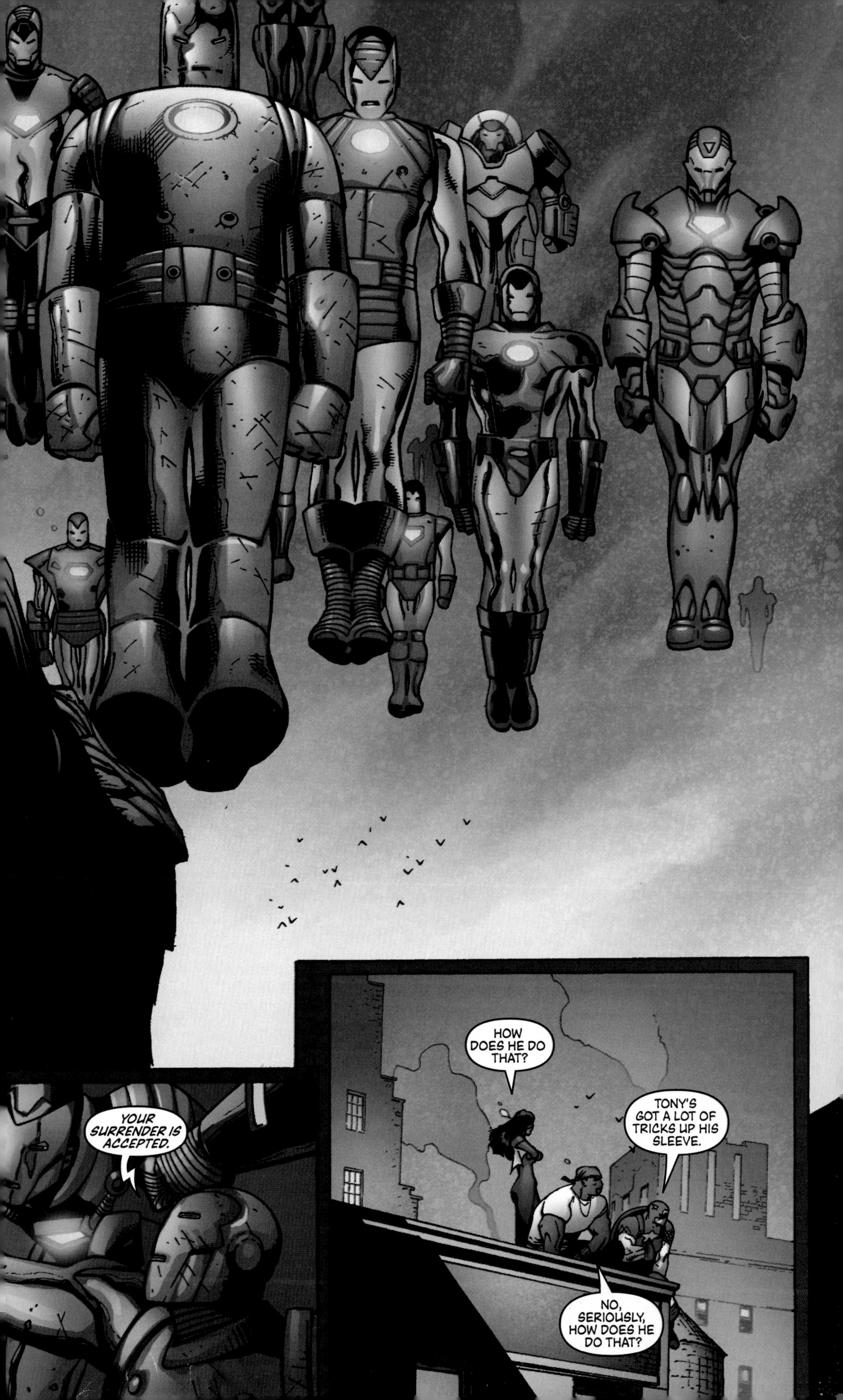
YOUR SURRENDER IS ACCEPTED.
HOW DOES HE DO THAT?
TONY'S GOT A LOT OF TRICKS UP HIS SLEEVE.
NO, SERIOUSLY, HOW DOES HE DO THAT?

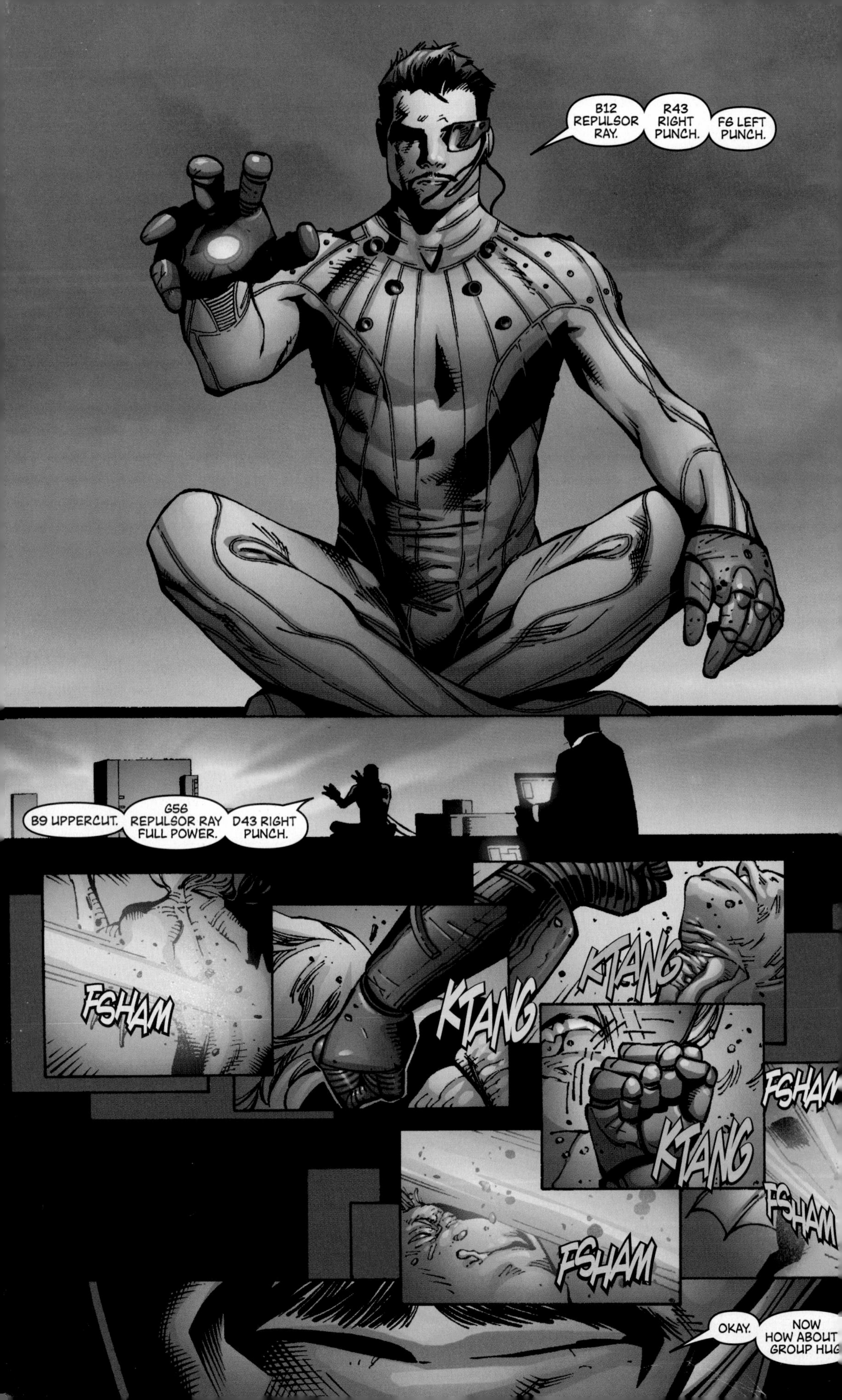
B12 REPULSOR RAY.
R43 RIGHT PUNCH.
F6 LEFT PUNCH.
B9 UPPERCUT.
G56 REPULSOR RAY FULL POWER.
D43 RIGHT PUNCH.
FSHAM
KTANG
KTANG
KTANG
FSHAM
FSHAM
FSHAM
OKAY.
NOW HOW ABOUT GROUP HUG

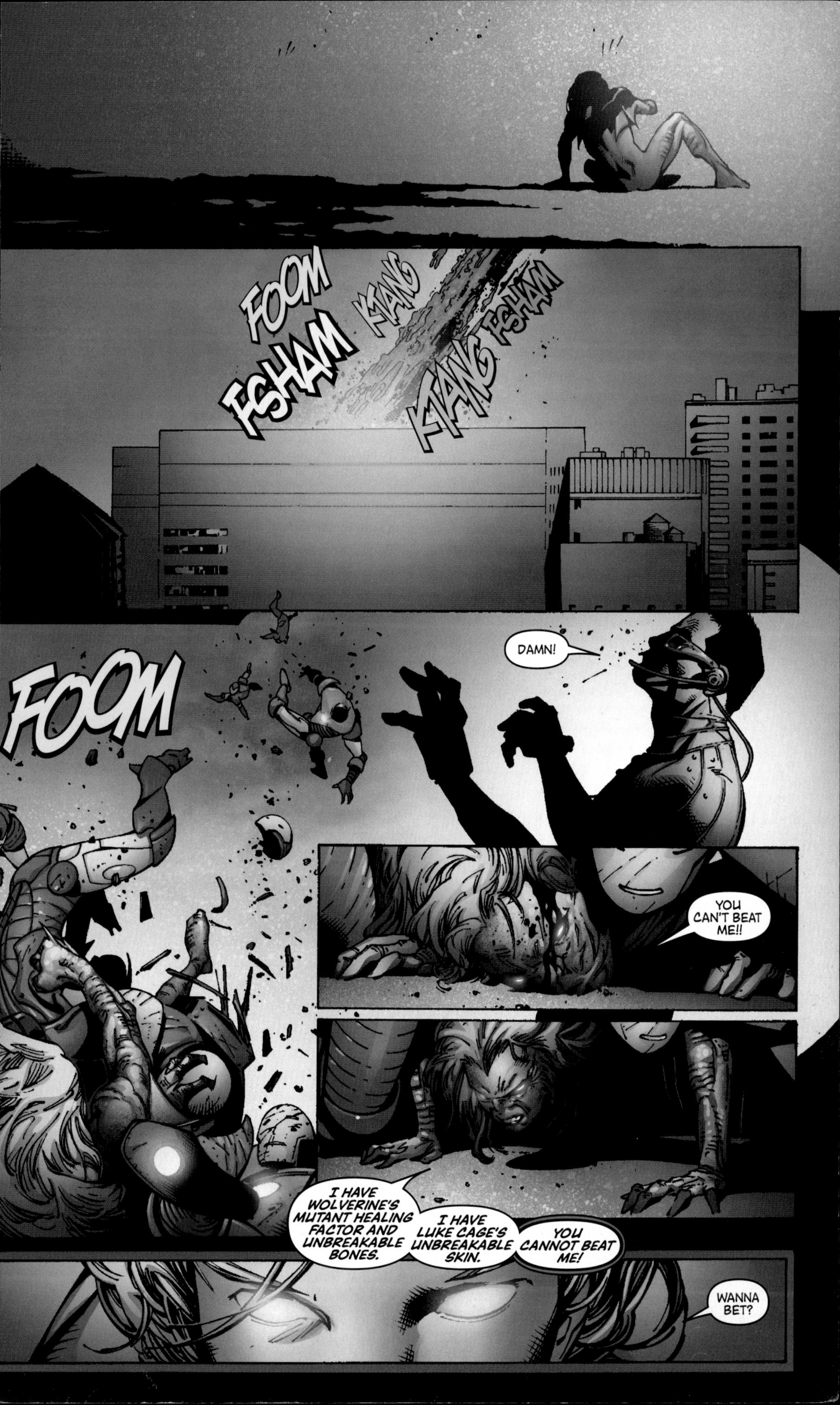

FOOM
FSHAM
KTANG
KTANG
FSHAM
FOOM
DAMN!
YOU CAN'T BEAT ME!!
I HAVE WOLVERINE'S MUTANT HEALING FACTOR AND UNBREAKABLE BONES.
I HAVE LUKE CAGE'S UNBREAKABLE SKIN.
YOU CANNOT BEAT ME!
WANNA BET?

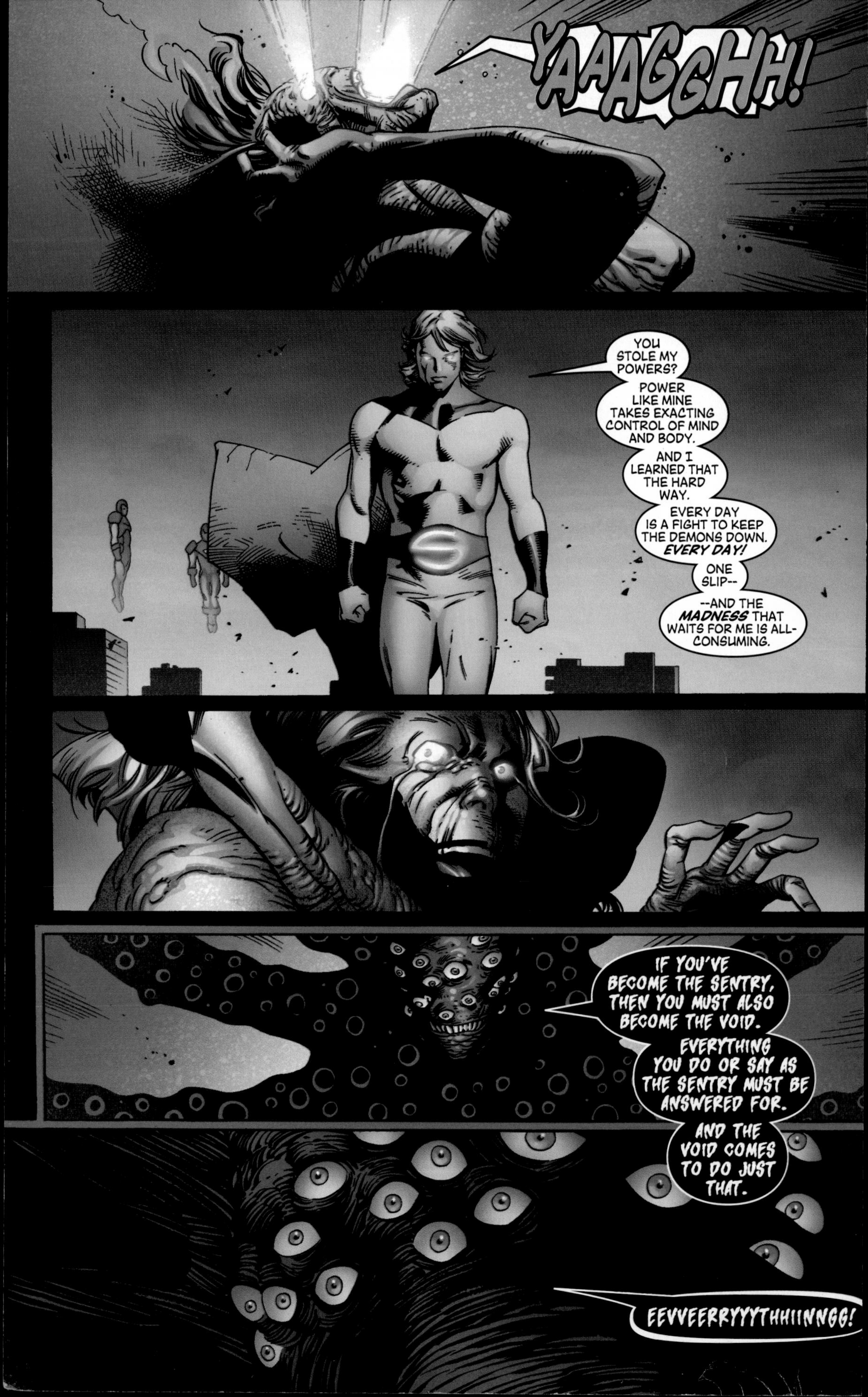
YAAAGGHH!
YOU STOLE MY POWERS?
POWER LIKE MINE TAKES EXACTING CONTROL OF MIND AND BODY.
AND I LEARNED THAT THE HARD WAY.
EVERY DAY IS A FIGHT TO KEEP THE DEMONS DOWN. EVERY DAY!
ONE SLIP--
--AND THE MADNESS THAT WAITS FOR ME IS ALL-CONSUMING.
IF YOU'VE BECOME THE SENTRY, THEN YOU MUST ALSO BECOME THE VOID.
EVERYTHING YOU DO OR SAY AS THE SENTRY MUST BE ANSWERED FOR.
AND THE VOID COMES TO DO JUST THAT.
EEVVEERRYYYTHHIINNGG!

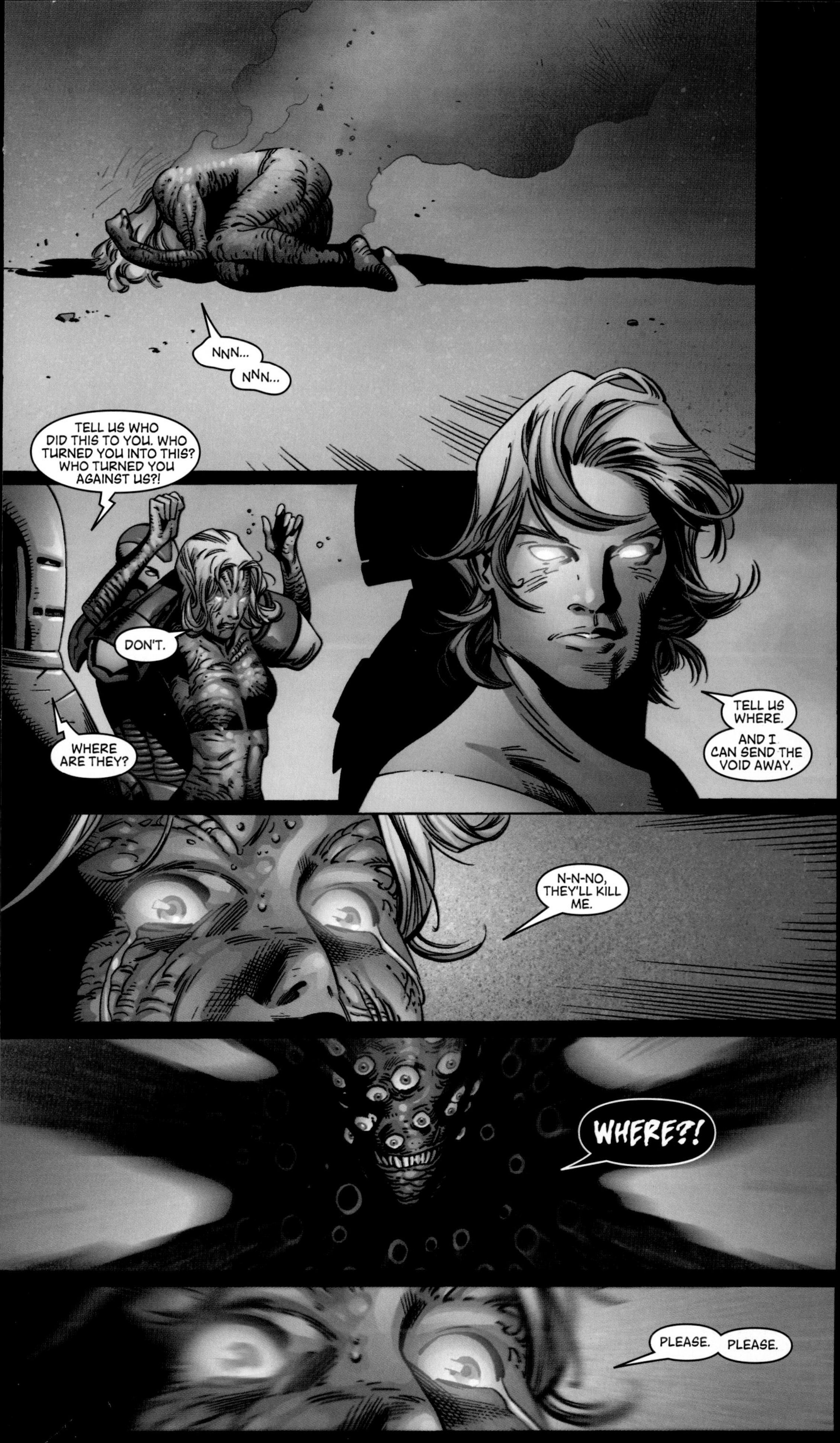
NNN...
NNN...
TELL US WHO DID THIS TO YOU. WHO TURNED YOU INTO THIS? WHO TURNED YOU AGAINST US?!
DON'T.
WHERE ARE THEY?
TELL US WHERE.
AND I CAN SEND THE VOID AWAY.
N-N-NO, THEY'LL KILL ME.
WHERE?!
PLEASE.
PLEASE.

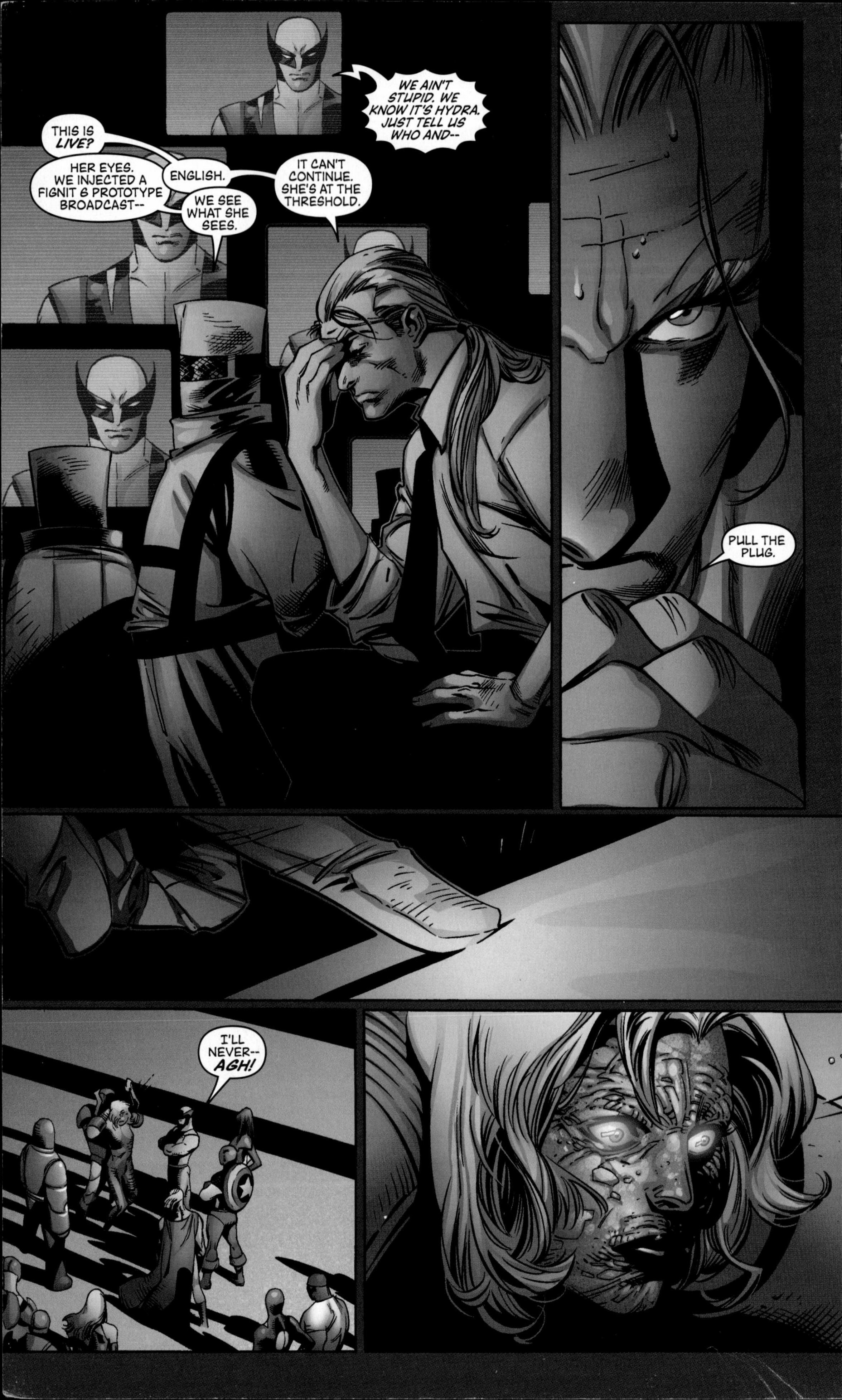
WE AIN'T STUPID. WE KNOW IT'S HYDRA. JUST TELL US WHO AND--
THIS IS LIVE?
HER EYES. WE INJECTED A FIGNIT 6 PROTOTYPE BROADCAST--
ENGLISH.
WE SEE WHAT SHE SEES.
IT CAN'T CONTINUE. SHE'S AT THE THRESHOLD.
PULL THE PLUG.
I'LL NEVER-- AGH!

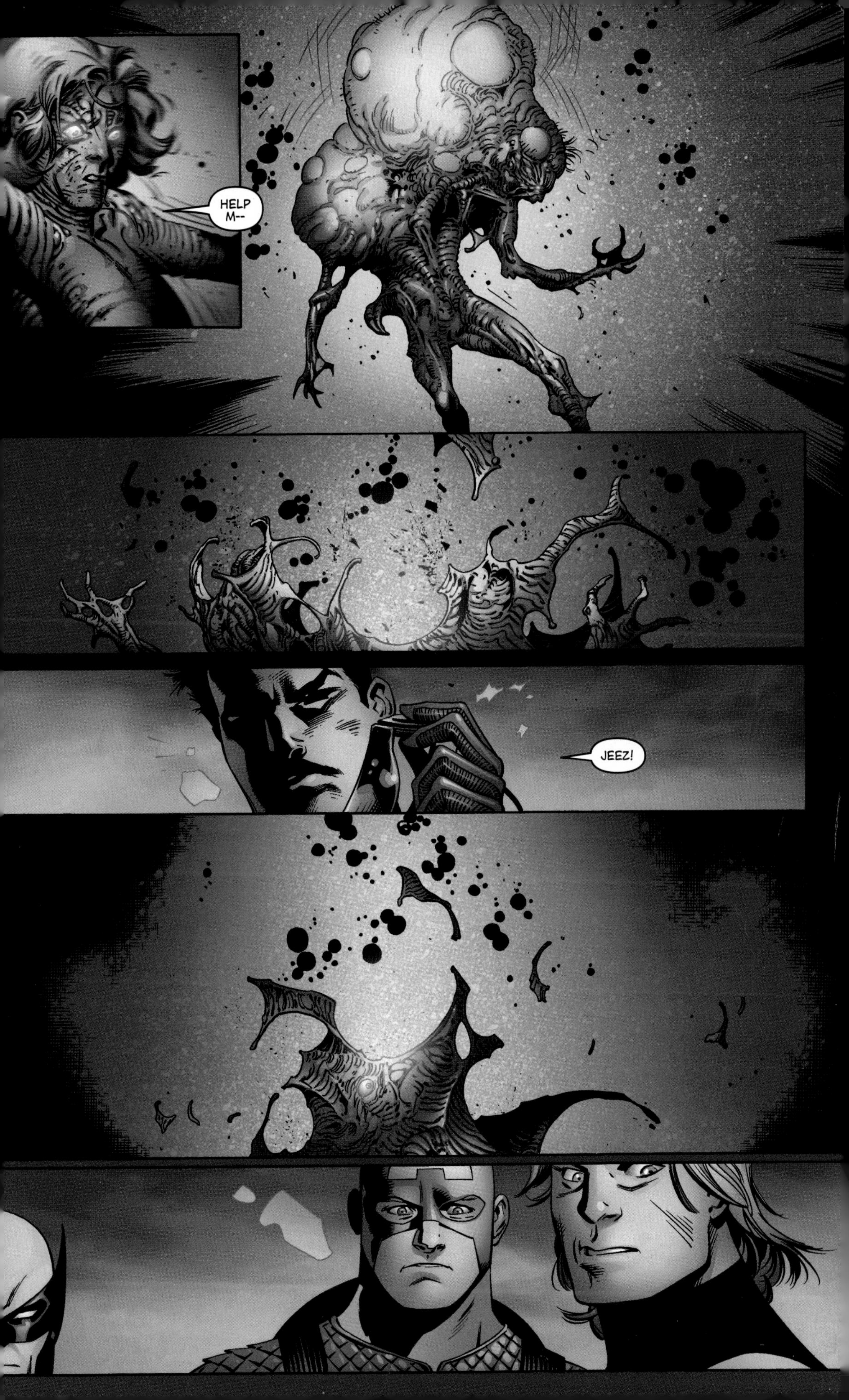
HELP
M--
JEEZ!

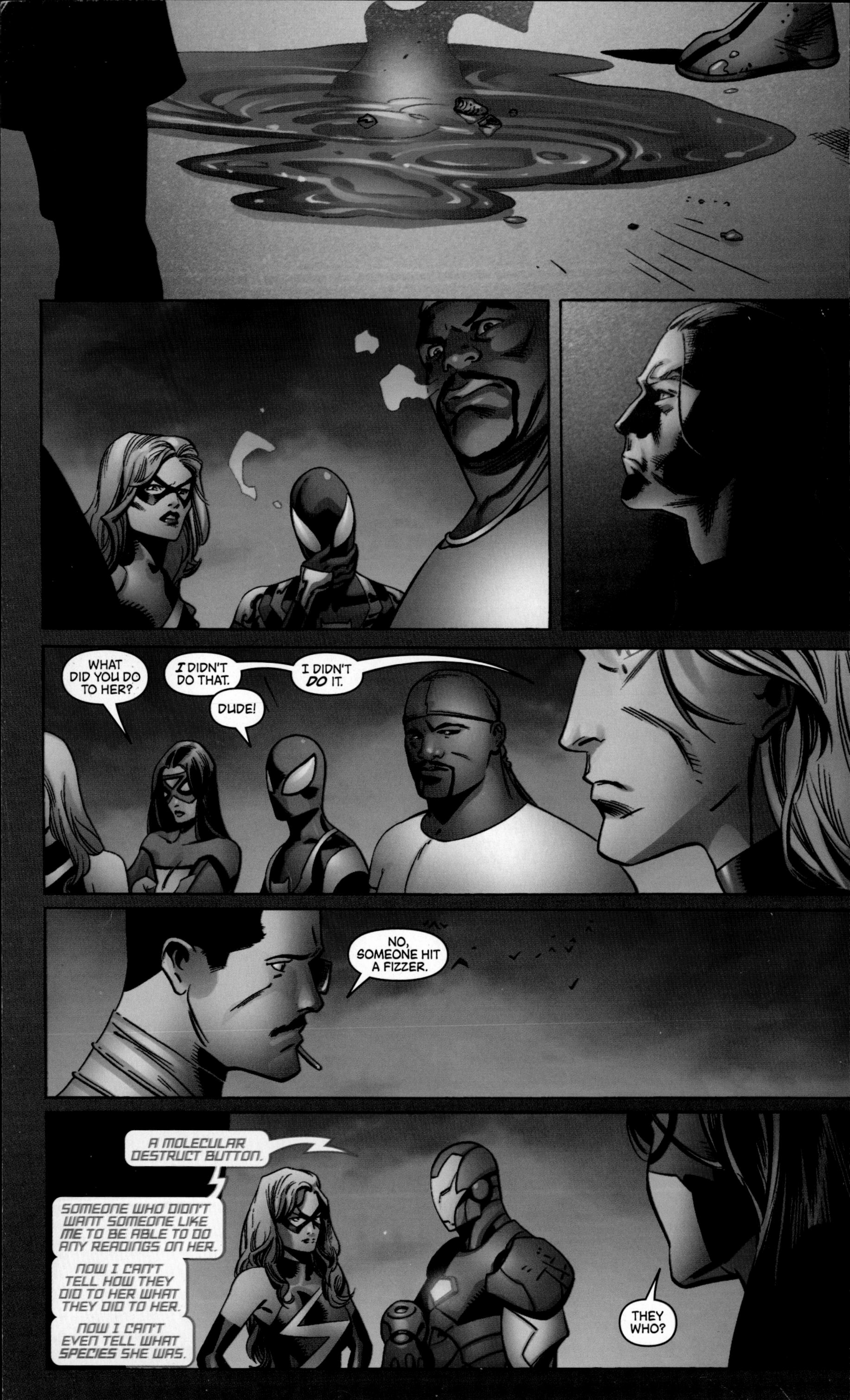
WHAT DID YOU DO TO HER?
I DIDN'T DO THAT.
I DIDN'T DO IT.
DUDE!
NO, SOMEONE HIT A FIZZER.
A MOLECULAR DESTRUCT BUTTON.
SOMEONE WHO DIDN'T WANT SOMEONE LIKE ME TO BE ABLE TO DO ANY READINGS ON HER.
NOW I CAN'T TELL HOW THEY DID TO HER WHAT THEY DID TO HER.
NOW I CAN'T EVEN TELL WHAT SPECIES SHE WAS.
THEY WHO?

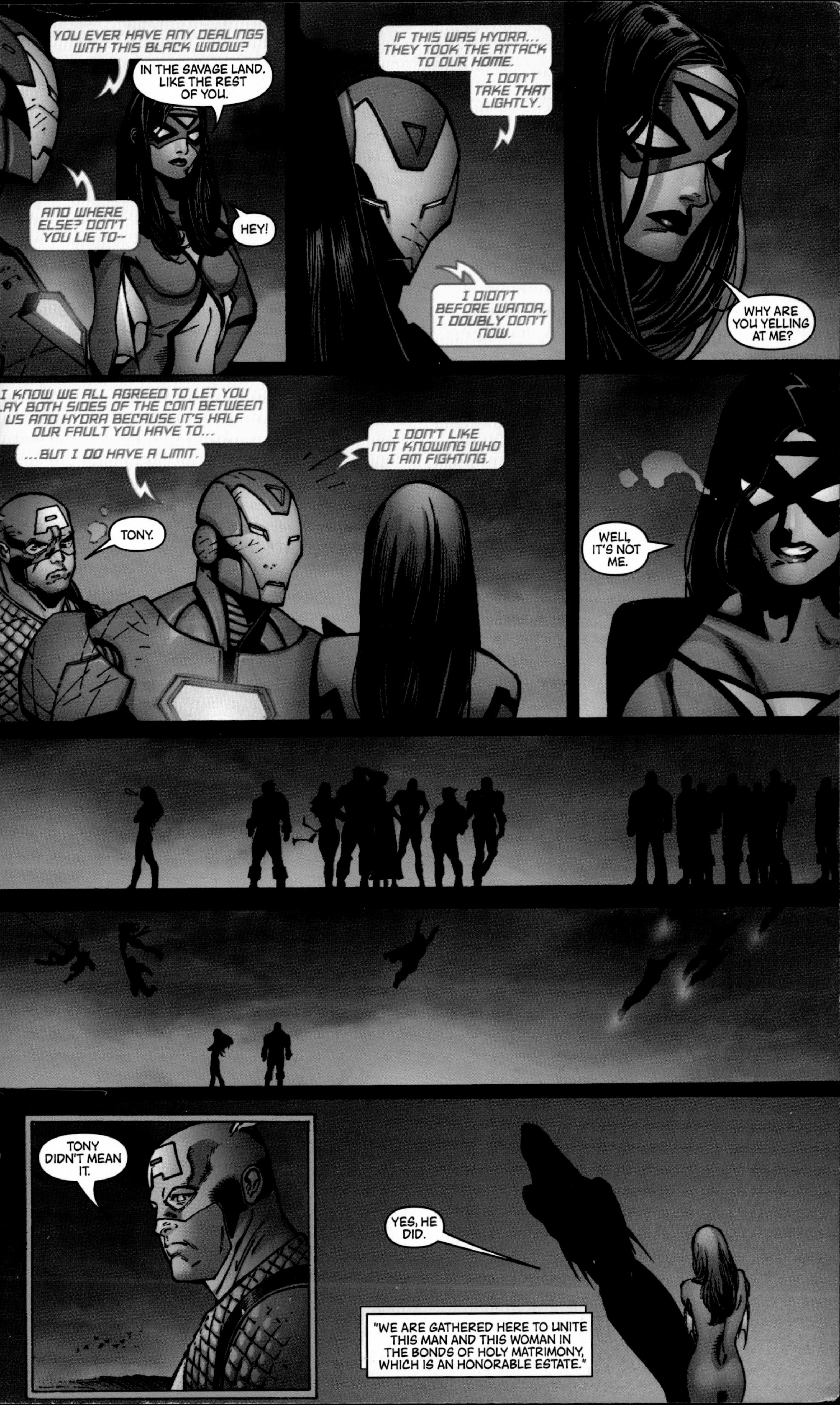

YOU EVER HAVE ANY DEALINGS WITH THIS BLACK WIDOW?
IN THE SAVAGE LAND. LIKE THE REST OF YOU.
AND WHERE ELSE? DON'T YOU LIE TO--
HEY!
IF THIS WAS HYDRA... THEY TOOK THE ATTACK TO OUR HOME.
I DON'T TAKE THAT LIGHTLY.
I DIDN'T BEFORE WANDA, I DOUBLY DON'T NOW.
WHY ARE YOU YELLING AT ME?
I KNOW WE ALL AGREED TO LET YOU
LAY BOTH SIDES OF THE COIN BETWEEN US AND HYDRA BECAUSE IT'S HALF OUR FAULT YOU HAVE TO...
...BUT I DO HAVE A LIMIT.
I DON'T LIKE NOT KNOWING WHO I AM FIGHTING.
TONY.
WELL, IT'S NOT ME.
TONY DIDN'T MEAN IT.
YES, HE DID.
"WE ARE GATHERED HERE TO UNITE THIS MAN AND THIS WOMAN IN THE BONDS OF HOLY MATRIMONY, WHICH IS AN HONORABLE ESTATE."

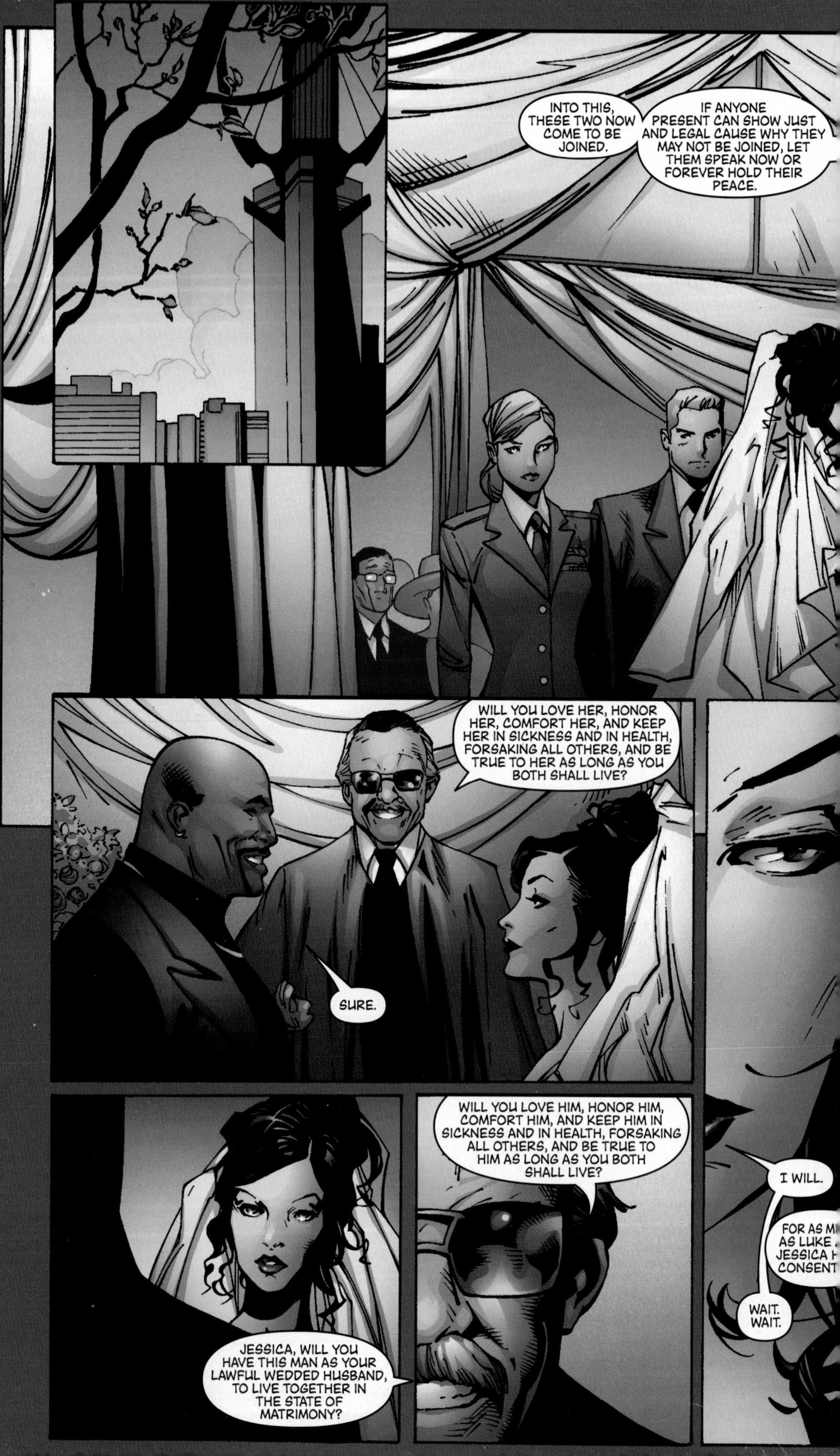
INTO THIS, THESE TWO NOW COME TO BE JOINED.
IF ANYONE PRESENT CAN SHOW JUST AND LEGAL CAUSE WHY THEY MAY NOT BE JOINED, LET THEM SPEAK NOW OR FOREVER HOLD THEIR PEACE.
WILL YOU LOVE HER, HONOR HER, COMFORT HER, AND KEEP HER IN SICKNESS AND IN HEALTH, FORSAKING ALL OTHERS, AND BE TRUE TO HER AS LONG AS YOU BOTH SHALL LIVE?
SURE.
JESSICA, WILL YOU HAVE THIS MAN AS YOUR LAWFUL WEDDED HUSBAND, TO LIVE TOGETHER IN THE STATE OF MATRIMONY?
WILL YOU LOVE HIM, HONOR HIM, COMFORT HIM, AND KEEP HIM IN SICKNESS AND IN HEALTH, FORSAKING ALL OTHERS, AND BE TRUE TO HIM AS LONG AS YOU BOTH SHALL LIVE?
I WILL.
FOR AS
WAIT. WAIT.

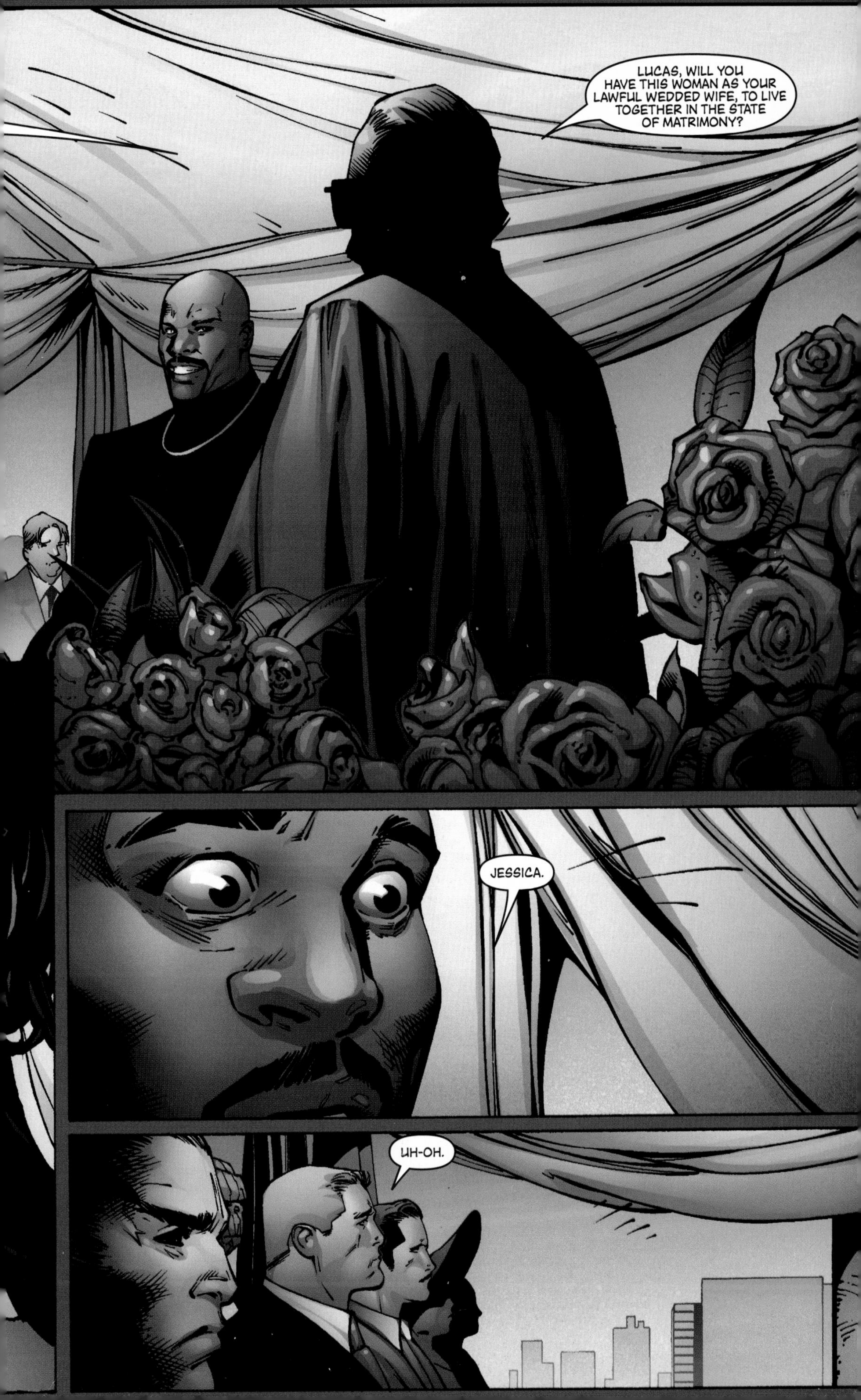
LUCAS, WILL YOU HAVE THIS WOMAN AS YOUR LAWFUL WEDDED WIFE, TO LIVE TOGETHER IN THE STATE OF MATRIMONY?
JESSICA.
UH-OH.

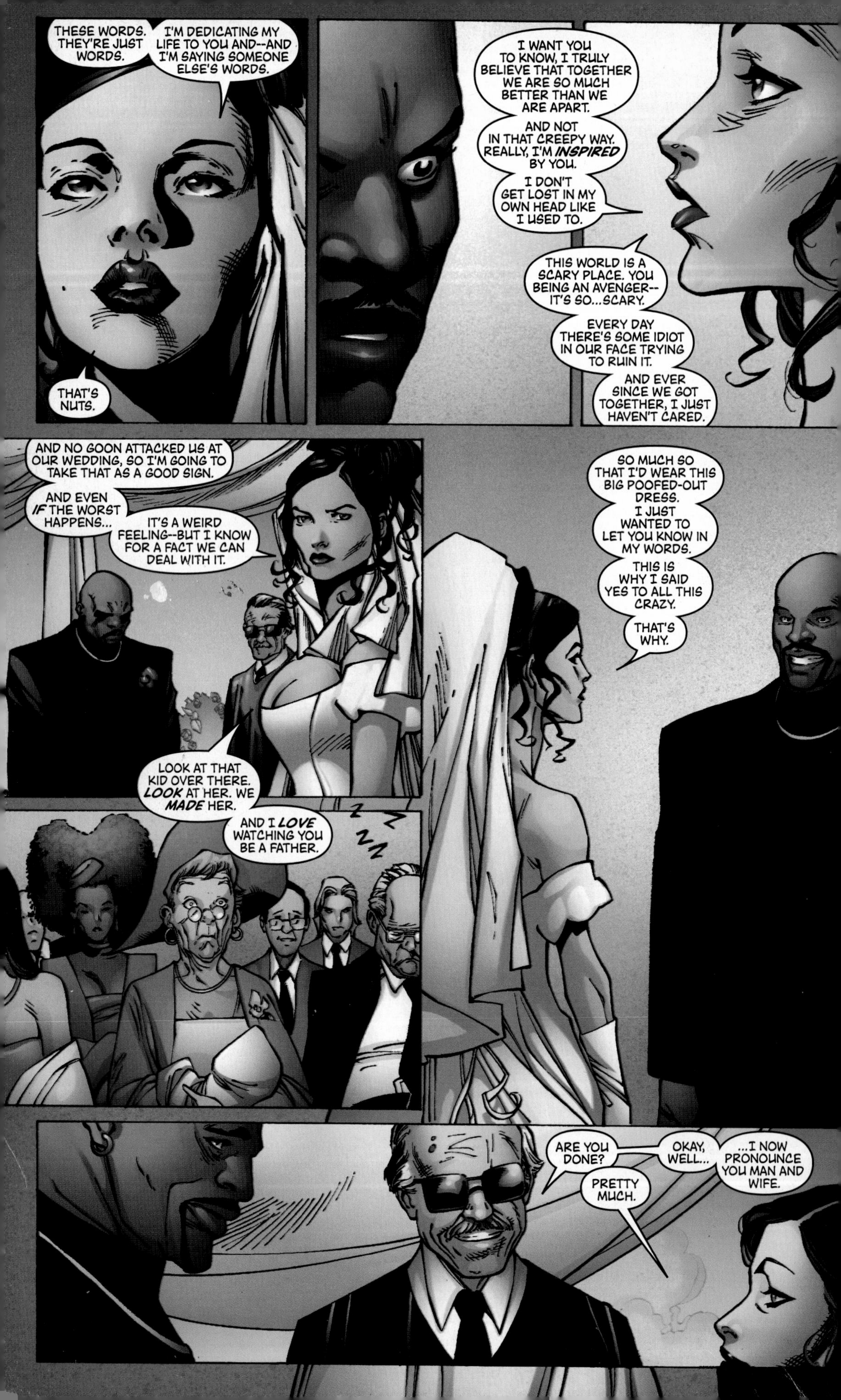
THESE WORDS. THEY'RE JUST WORDS.
I'M DEDICATING MY LIFE TO YOU AND--AND I'M SAYING SOMEONE ELSE'S WORDS.
THAT'S NUTS.
I WANT YOU TO KNOW, I TRULY BELIEVE THAT TOGETHER WE ARE SO MUCH BETTER THAN WE ARE APART.
AND NOT IN THAT CREEPY WAY. REALLY, I'M INSPIRED BY YOU.
I DON'T GET LOST IN MY OWN HEAD LIKE I USED TO.
THIS WORLD IS A SCARY PLACE. YOU BEING AN AVENGER-- IT'S SO...SCARY.
EVERY DAY THERE'S SOME IDIOT IN OUR FACE TRYING TO RUIN IT.
AND EVER SINCE WE GOT TOGETHER, I JUST HAVEN'T CARED.
AND NO GOON ATTACKED US AT OUR WEDDING, SO I'M GOING TO TAKE THAT AS A GOOD SIGN.
AND EVEN IF THE WORST HAPPENS...
IT'S A WEIRD FEELING--BUT I KNOW FOR A FACT WE CAN DEAL WITH IT.
LOOK AT THAT KID OVER THERE. LOOK AT HER. WE MADE HER.
AND I LOVE WATCHING YOU BE A FATHER.
Z Z Z
SO MUCH SO THAT I'D WEAR THIS BIG POOFED-OUT DRESS.
I JUST WANTED TO LET YOU KNOW IN MY WORDS.
THIS IS WHY I SAID YES TO ALL THIS CRAZY.
THAT'S WHY.
ARE YOU DONE?
PRETTY MUCH.
OKAY, WELL...
...I NOW PRONOUNCE YOU MAN AND WIFE.

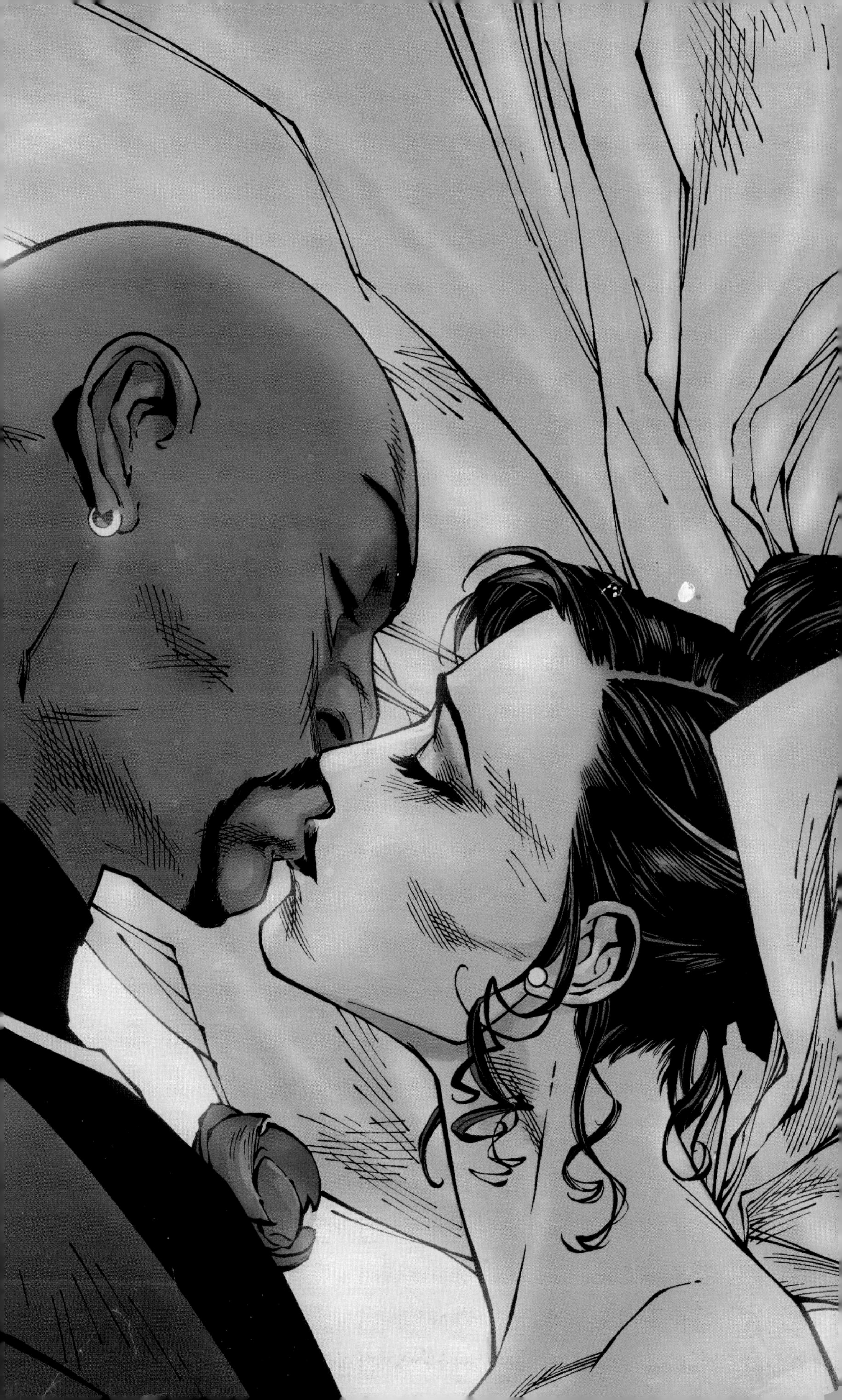

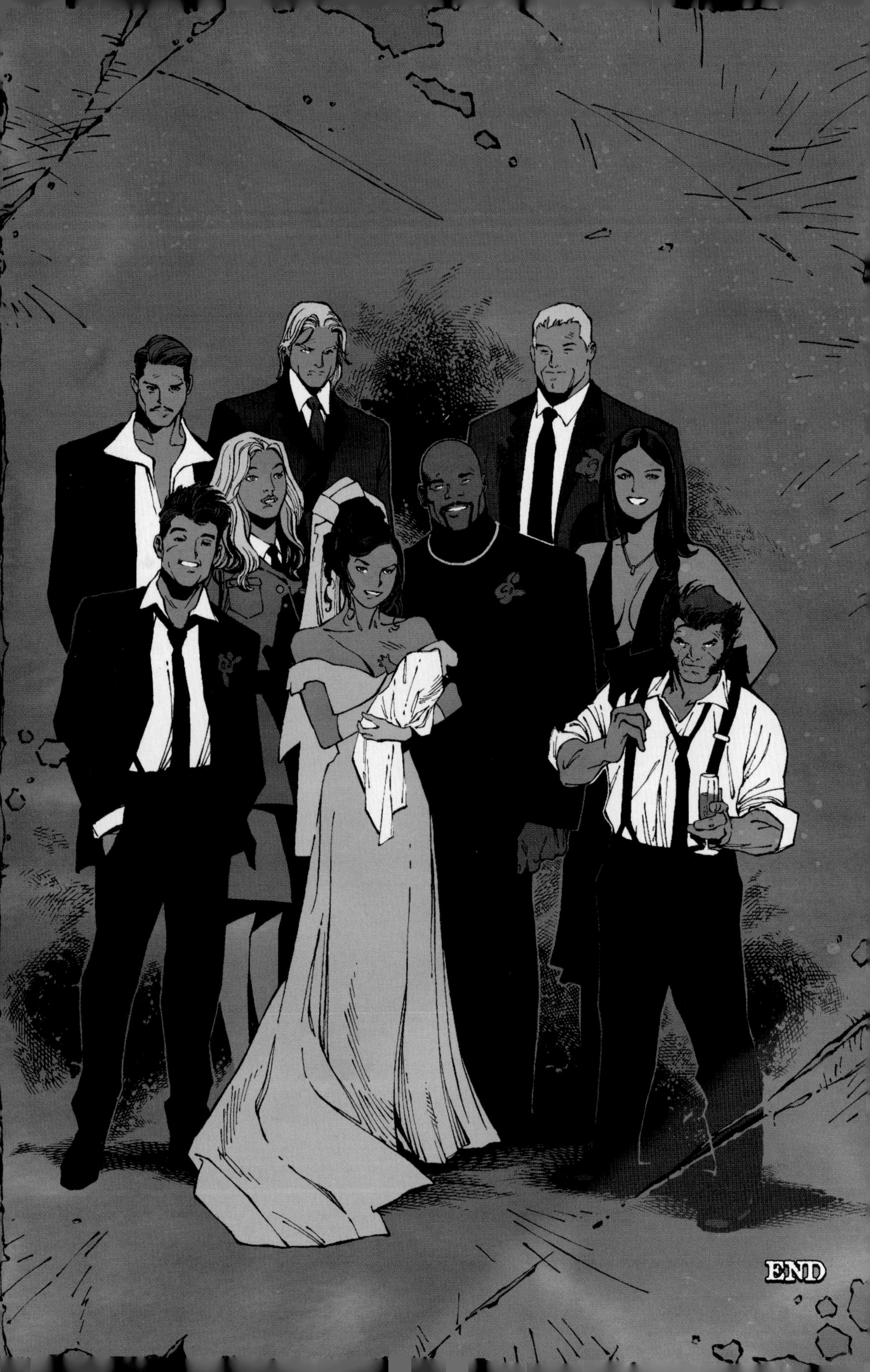
END

GOODBYE, PULSE!!

Sniff!

I just wrote one of these for DAREDEVIL. I hate writing these. I'm saying goodbye to writing a comic series I completely love writing. Characters I love more than some actual people I know. But, sadly, this is the end of THE PULSE.

WHY??? WHY DO I KEEP DOING THIS TO JESSICA JONES??!!

It's over, is why.

I said what I had to say and we're leaving on a high note, I think. Sadly, the timing of this sucked. We finally got the band back together. Finally we got the entire ALIAS art team back together. Finally Gaydos' schedule and this book's schedule aligned; finally Matt Hollingsworth came back to comics just to paint this book. And now the story is over. The book is done.

Truth is I thought the book would continue after we had left and originally, you might have heard, it was going to, but this is the last issue. Paul Jenkins was supposed to take over this book, but instead will be producing a comic called CIVIL WAR: FRONT LINE that will launch out of the staggering CIVIL WAR event that is coming your way in May. It's the right move for Marvel but sadly, it puts this book on indefinite hiatus. Other books on indefinite hiatus: ROM, SPACEKNIGHTS, US1, and SECRET DEFENDERS. So don't hold your breath :).

But thankfully, we do not leave you empty-handed. You want more Jessica and Luke, look no further than the pages of the NEW AVENGERS ANNUAL that is being drawn even as we speak by my HOUSE OF M pal Olivier Coipel. Will they get married? Will any super-villains crash the wedding? Will we show the honeymoon?

Also, Marvel is in the final stages of production on THE ALIAS OMNIBUS -- every single issue of Jessica Jones' life before THE PULSE in one gorgeous hardcover. It's something I am insanely proud of, and I hope you check it out. Fair warning—it's a Max book and a little raunchy. But if you liked this issue you'll love the Omnibus!

There are so many people to thank. First off, cover artist Mike Mayhew who really delivered some gorgeous, unique, exciting cover work. Three of these covers are my all-time favorite covers I've ever had on any of my comics.

Matt Hollingsworth came back to comics to color this last story and I am eternally grateful.

Michael Gaydos has been with Jessica since day one and this book was not the same without him. Mike is an amazing collaborator and I am just blessed to know him. Mike and I are not done together. Stay tuned.

A very special thank you to Mark Bagley, Brent Anderson and Michael Lark, who really made this unique book a special place for Marvel fans. Andy Schmidt loves this book more than even me and you can tell from his work on it. Thank you, Andy, for all your hard work. Editorial doesn't get the credit it deserves on so many levels. I want you people of the Earth to know, it is not easy to be an editor, it takes a special kind of person.

And of course, you my friends, thank you for making this book successful. Thank you for all your letters and emails about Jessica. Your support for Jessica was seen by Hollywood. In fact, we were this close to getting a Jessica Jones show on TV, maybe one day we still will. That was a crazy experience I'll share with you at a con if you see me.

Though I am leaving this book and it's leaving the shelves, I am not abandoning Jessica, Luke, or the little Cage baby Promise.

Meanwhile, stop by my Web site Jinxworld.com. The message board is crackling and we'd love to hear from you--unless you're a disgruntled D-Man fan. Then we really don't want to hear from you at all.

See you over at Avengers Tower.

BENDIS

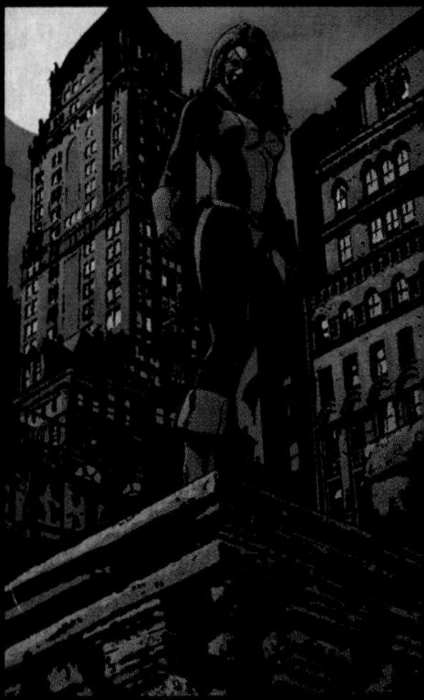